I Am White

Eagle Woman Flies with Raven

Rita Makkannaw

With
Carina Gerken Christiansen

Order this book online at www.trafford.com
or email orders@trafford.com

Most Trafford titles are also available at major online book retailers.

Printed in the United States of America.

ISBN: 978-1-4269-5151-0 (sc)
ISBN: 978-1-4269-5152-7 (hc)
ISBN: 978-1-4269-5153-4 (e)

Library of Congress Control Number: 2010918395

Trafford rev. 10/27/2011

 www.trafford.com

North America & International
toll-free: 1 888 232 4444 (USA & Canada)
phone: 250 383 6864 ♦ fax: 812 355 4082

Dedication

I dedicate this book to my late husband Raven,
the love of my life, who taught me two most important
lessons

Be Who I Am

Love really does exist

Rita Makkannaw

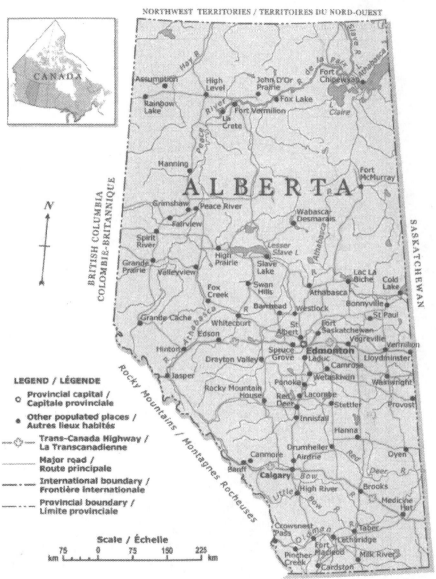

NORTHWEST TERRITORIES / TERRITOIRES DU NORD-OUEST

BRITISH COLUMBIA
COLOMBIE-BRITANNIQUE

SASKATCHEWAN

ALBERTA

Assumption
High Level
John D'Or Prairie
Fort Chipewyan
Rainbow Lake
Fox Lake
L. Claire
Fort Vermilion
La Crète
Manning
Fort McMurray
Grimshaw Peace River
Wabasca-Desmarais
Fairview
Spirit River
Lesser Slave L.
Grande Prairie
High Prairie
Slave Lake
Valleyview
Lac La Biche
Cold Lake
Fox Creek
Swan Hills
Athabasca
Grande Cache
Barrhead
Westlock
Bonnyville
Whitecourt
St Paul
Edson
St Albert
Fort Saskatchewan
Vegreville
Vermilion
Hinton
Spruce Grove
Edmonton
Jasper
Drayton Valley
Leduc
Lloydminster
Camrose
Ponoka
Wetaskiwin
Rocky Mountain House
Wainwright
Red Deer
Lacombe
Stettler
Provost
Innisfail
Hanna
Canmore
Drumheller
Airdrie
Oyen
Banff
Calgary
Bow
Brooks
High River
Medicine Hat
Crowsnest Pass
Taber
Pincher Creek
Fort Macleod
Lethbridge
Milk River
Cardston

Rocky Mountains / Montagnes Rocheuses

N

LEGEND / LÉGENDE

○ Provincial capital /
  Capitale provinciale

● Other populated places /
  Autres lieux habités

◇ Trans–Canada Highway /
  La Transcanadienne

  Major road /
  Route principale

  International boundary /
  Frontière internationale

  Provincial boundary /
  Limite provinciale

Scale / Échelle
75   0   75   150   225
km   km

USA / É-U d'A

Appreciation

I would like to thank the following for their support and most valuable input in the creation of this book.

First and foremost, to Carina Christiansen, without whom this book never would have been written. She continually told me that I needed to share how I overcame so many challenges as others could learn from my experiences.

She also encouraged me to share about the beautiful love Raven and I shared as we faced a world hostile to the cross-cultural union.

She and I share the belief that the Canadian public has a right to know about the history of our country, and how that history affects people today. Without her encouragement and never-tiring support, I know I would have dropped it, thinking I could not convey the messages I was attempting to share.

To Henry Laboucan who shared many stories which resulted in clarity about many issues.

I would also like to thank my dear friend Jan Redsted, who designed the cover for the book. I acknowledge how much thought and prayers went into the design. From the bottom of my heart, I appreciate him and his most important contribution.

To my wonderful proof reader and editor Jan Simmonds who has worked so quickly and efficiently. I do so appreciate her input, and I learned a lot about punctuation in the process.

To Erik Schou Hammerum who helped put the final touches to make this book even better than before.

And last, but most important, to the Elders with whom I sat and learned so much. I cannot begin to express the depth of my gratitude, and the honour I feel at having the privilege of serving them tea at my kitchen table. The sharing of their stories, their laughter and their tears has meant more to me than words can possibly express.

Hai hai, Ish nish, thank you from the bottom of my heart.

Contents

Prologue

After losing the love of my life—my late husband Raven—and my home, I wandered to the land of my birth where I felt I could find the peace to heal my broken self. During the healing process I realized how extraordinary much of my life had been. I have lived through many challenges and have bounced back to live a good life. I did not become aware of the spiritual guidance I had each time until after I met Raven who was a beautiful North American Native man with much knowledge and wisdom about spirituality and humanity. How privileged I feel now to have learned so much from his people, some of the wisest people of this world! My heart was often sad because of the misunderstandings which I experienced time and time again between my birth people and my adopted people. Helping to shed light on these misunderstandings became such a strong driving force in me that I made the decision to share. Knowledge and understanding of differences can most often lead to harmony and peace.

My apprehension also stems from the fact that too many non-Native people have come into the Native Community for a week, a month or more and have then taken the right to write without permission and without understanding.

I not only have permission but have in fact been requested to share the universal knowledge of spirituality.

"You are to help others understand about spirituality and *who* they are," they would say. "It is not your place to teach the sacred ceremonies that belong to our people, but the universal knowledge of the spirit you are to share. With the true understanding of self come peace and harmony, even within the struggles we all face." Although the teachings are simple, they are also at the same time very profound.

The written word has many limitations and yet so much power. It is the limitations with which I struggle the most. Even though the Cree people had a written language long before the Europeans came to Canada, they never used it to tell their stories. They were always passed orally. The heart of the stories passed down from one generation to the next since 'time immemorial,' as Raven used to say, cannot possibly be captured in the written word.

"The heart of the people does not fit on a flat piece of paper," one old woman once said. "When you write our stories, when you put them to paper, you bastardize them." Then I struggled with how to bring the teachings without the stories as is the Native way. Now I have decided that telling my own story and my teachings will, perhaps, shed some light on the reality of life the way I was taught. As for the stories, they have to be sought from the story keepers.

My story and my life are from today, from this modern world in which we live. The teachings of the old knowledge are from time immemorial. This is a story of love between two people of different traditions and the challenges faced because of the cultural differences. It is a story of how we can live a life connected with the Creator, with nature, with family, with co-workers and, most important, with ourselves, especially in this fast-paced world. It is a story of the difficulties faced by the first people to live on the North American Continent.

Raven and I together devoted our lives to bring understanding and harmony to this, the modern world in which we live. The old teachings are as relevant today as they were for hundreds of generations past. Human nature has not changed. Only the way we live our lives has changed. Our toys have changed. Our cultural teachings have changed, but human nature has not. We still cry the same, we laugh the same, we love the same. We still feel sadness and happiness and all the other emotions that are a part of who we are.

Raven never liked the term "Native Culture." He would explain that the word *culture* refers to *something that is cultivated.* The old ways are not cultivated. They are natural to all people. Therefore he would use the term of *traditional knowledge*, referring to knowledge that goes back to creation time. The old teachings of all the great teachers who have walked this earth are the same. Some great teachers are walking this earth right now. We only need to learn from the teachings and incorporate them into our lives for peace and harmony.

I know peace and harmony in the world will not happen in my lifetime, but all Native people do their work knowing it will have the greatest impact in the seventh generation. Every step we take toward understanding ourselves and others is a giant leap for the generations to come.

Chapter 1

From Dream to Nightmare

It was a beautiful fall day in 1961 and I was on my way home from school. I was shaking my head to make my long ponytail swing back and forth on my back, as I climbed up the trail of the Notikewin River bank, which was a short-cut to our little wooden house located on the north side of the village of Manning.

I turned for a final look at the river, before it would be out of sight. I felt the beauty of that autumn day with the crisp clear air after the first killer frost a few nights earlier. The water looked bright blue as it reflected the cloudless sky. The yellow leaves of the poplar trees lining the river bank were beginning to fall. They were silently flowing through the air down to the water where they floated and bobbed in the slow-moving current.

As I stood there enjoying the crisp fall air I recalled how in April 1954 my father moved to Canada and Mom followed with the six of us in tow the following December. I was third in the family. There were promises of land for ten dollars for a quarter section, one half mile by one half mile. We started our new life in Grande Prairie, in northern Alberta. We were poor, could not speak the language, and not at all prepared for the cold Canadian winters. Dad found an old log house for us to live in. It was so cold that frost would collect around the edges of the floor and the electrical outlets would frost up. It was nothing short of a miracle that the place did not burn to the ground.

I thought about how, on the coldest days, I had walked to school behind my older brother and sister with tears freezing on my cheeks. We had only our thin corduroy coats Mom made for us and gum boots which were not at all appropriate for the cold Canadian climate.

The only sound we would hear, on those coldest days, as we walked to school in the darkness was the crunch of the dry white snow under our feet as no one even tried to start their vehicles when the thermometer dipped down to -40 degrees centigrade or Fahrenheit (it's the same). When we finally arrived, the school would be closed due to the cold. Closures were always announced on the radio, but we did not have a radio. We could not have understood it anyway even if we did.

I remembered my mother's old saying that God looks after the dumb, the drunk and the blind. Someone certainly had looked after us as no one got sick, or frostbite and I do not remember ever being really unhappy. We would all sit in a row on the kitchen counter and sing the old songs like *Der er et Yndigt Land*, *I Danmark er Jeg Født*, and *Vi Sejler op ad Åen*, which are all about our fatherland. When we got tired of that, we would play active games to stay warm. We were children and we needed to move. We survived and we were happy and healthy.

I remembered how on May 14th, 1955, my 10th birthday, we packed all our belongings in Karl Christiansen's truck and drove four hours north to the village of Manning, where my father opened his own blacksmith shop. We rented a little thirty-six square meter house close to the shop. There were eight of us squeezed in. I hated the crowdedness and spent as little time in the house as possible. I would visit friends' houses or go exploring or swimming in the river which ran through the town. We were poor, but so were most others.

We got the land we had dreamed about in Denmark, but that turned out to be another nightmare as it was all forest and we had to clear it and ready it for crops, or we would lose it. How I hated the farm and the way my father made us work out there every weekend throughout the summers from dawn until dusk.

We had come a long way, though, in the seven years we had lived in Canada. We had built our own home, had acquired modern blue jeans and warm jackets and boots. We had overcome many challenges, including the language barrier and were well established in our little community.

How I loved the fall and the sound of my feet shuffling through the crisp fallen leaves. At the age of sixteen, I was generally satisfied with life. I loved school too. It had taken time though. When we first came I was teased at school because I dressed funny and did not speak the language. I never seemed to fit in with the rest of my classmates, but I loved to learn and to read.

I was pretty much a loner in school, but that was not bad as I had many older friends and a good social life outside of school. We used to hang out together downtown in the two restaurants or just do some cruising, as we used to say. That was just driving up one street and down the other. There were only two streets downtown both lined with small shops and a movie theater where we all went on most Saturday nights. That does not sound like much, but we had fun together. We always sang the latest songs on the hit parade. There was only one radio station: CKYL out of Peace River. When a good song came on the radio we would stop the cars and get out and dance in the gravel streets. Everyone always had funny jokes to tell. Life was simple, but good.

Nothing could have prepared me for what was to happen next. My life was to be turned upside down in just a few minutes. As I approached our little wooden house, which we had built just a few years earlier, I saw my father sitting by the kitchen table as he always did, but when I entered the house, he was not there. His half-eaten meal was still on the table. I thought it was strange as I had just seen him and now he was gone. I went directly through the kitchen and the living room and opened the door to the small bedroom I shared with my younger sister Karin, just as I had done hundreds of times before. As I opened the door, there stood my father in the middle of my bedroom with his pants around his ankles, fully exposed from the waist down. I quietly closed the door and slowly backed up, through the living room, and the kitchen and into my brothers' bedroom.

My head was pounding, my knees were weak, I could not think. My father had never before been in my bedroom. What was he doing there? Why would he take his pants off and wait for me in my bedroom? I could think of only one reason. He was going to try to have sex with me.

In those years no male person would even be seen in underwear in front of us girls. Not even my brothers. It simply wasn't done. Now there he stood naked from the waist down in my bedroom, exposing himself.

I stood in the middle of the floor, holding my breath for as long as I could. I was terrified that he might hear the sound of my breathing and find me. After what seemed like an eternity, I heard my father's footsteps in the kitchen. I was as quiet as could be, but my heart was pounding so loudly I was afraid he would hear it. All I could think of was to escape, but I would have to go through the kitchen where he was. I prayed silently that he would just leave. No such luck. I could hear his heavy footsteps coming toward the boys' room and I realized he was too close to the doorway and I could not escape. As he entered, he came up to me and put his arms around me.

That was the only time in my life my father touched me. I instantly became nauseated. I could not stand his shop smell on me. I started breathing through my mouth to ease the smell. My stomach was turning, my head was spinning and I thought I was going to throw up. His blacksmith's arms were so strong I knew I could never defend myself against him. I had to figure out a way to escape from his powerful grip.

"I am sorry you had to see that," he said.

"I have to go to the bathroom," I said and quickly pushed him away. To my relief he released me and I ran outside and hid behind the house. Then I started heaving. My stomach was empty. Then came the yellow bile and it was so bitter.

The bitterness helped me keep my sanity. What was he thinking? Why would he show himself to me in that way? It made me sick to think about what his intentions might be. I was terrified. I had to get out of there. It took all my energy just to think of the next move. I was afraid to start walking across the open field behind our house as he would see me for sure.

After what seemed like an eternity, I heard the door open and close behind him. I snuck down to the end of the house and saw him walk toward the shop. As soon as he was out of sight I snuck back into the house and grabbed the forty dollars Mom was keeping safe for me. I ran as fast as I could, out the door and across the newly plowed field. It was only when I reached the safety of the trees on the other side that I stopped. I broke out in tears and my brain slowly began to function again.

Through the pain, the fear and the tears, all I could think about was to get to our friends Bob and Betty who lived fifteen kilometers south-east of Manning. At least there I would be safe.

In a state of shock and with my head pounding, I headed east. All I thought about was putting one foot in front of the other. As I looked down at my feet, they at least looked real. They were solid. They were the same as before. I just kept looking at them in wonder as they projected me forward. After about an hour of half walking and half running, with tears rolling down my face, I looked up for the first time. I was travelling across a ploughed field and about twenty-five meters away was a row of trees.

Suddenly out of the trees stepped the biggest black bear I had ever seen. He stood up on his hind legs and just looked at me. My heart moved up into my throat as I stood there face to face with that bear. I hardly dared to breathe. Slowly, I began backing up. My knees were weak as I took one step at a time backwards. The bear looked as if it were frozen. It never moved. We just watched one another as I started to walk slowly backwards. I was in a state of terror. Finally I reached a field of high grass behind me. The bear went back on all fours, but continued watching me.

Exhaustion overcame me and I collapsed to the ground. I just laid there on my back looking up at the sky. As I lay there, a gigantic eagle started circling above my head. How beautiful, I thought, if only I could be so free. How wonderful it would be to fly like the eagle. As I watched it circle, I suddenly felt the deepest loneliness of having no grandparents, no aunts or uncles or cousins. At that moment I realized that I was on my own and had to take care of myself. The eagle kept circling and as I watched it I wondered if it would take care of me.

Suddenly I knew I had to make a plan, but for now I was too tired to think. Soon I went to sleep and started dreaming. I dreamt the bear came and stood over me. As it gently put its paws around me and held me, I felt a total peace take over my mind, heart and body. Suddenly the bear disappeared and I awoke. The eagle was also gone. I had no idea how long I had slept as I had no watch. I slowly got up and continued the walk to Bob and Betty's. I did not think much. I just felt empty as I continued on my journey. In the emptiness was relief. I did not have to think about anything. I just once again put one foot in front of the other until I arrived at my refuge and safety.

I arrived in late afternoon and as I entered they were ever so surprised to see me.

"What are you doing here?" asked Betty

"I ran away." I said and could say no more.

I ran out of the house and behind the building that had previously been a store. There I sank to the ground and began once more to sob. Soon Bob came out and just sat with me saying nothing for a long time. He just let me cry until I stopped. Then he asked what had happened. I told him. He told me not to worry, that I could stay with them as long as I wanted. I started to sob once more, this time out of relief. I was safe.

That night Bob and Betty went into Manning to pick up my clothes. They just whispered to Mom that I was with them and safe. Betty assured my mother that it was okay for me to stay there. Mom packed what I needed. They told me that my father had acted as if nothing had happened. He just talked as usual.

I could not go to school from Bob and Betty's as it was too far and I had no transportation. A week later I went to town with Betty and did go and see Mom at her work. She asked me what had happened. I told her that Dad just lost it and I became very afraid. She said she had seen that side of him before, and to take whatever time I needed to figure out what I wanted to do with my life. She assured me that I could always come home any time. That thought just frightened me no end. I knew I could not stay there again.

After about a month at Bob and Betty's, I realized that I could no longer just stay with them either. I had to get my life in order and sitting out in the country was not moving me ahead in any way. I was not going to school and without transportation I could not work. I decided I had to get to Edmonton, which was six hundred kilometers away, but was the nearest city. At least there I could find work and it was far away from Manning. First I needed money and city clothes. All I had was two pairs of blue jeans and three tops.

With my goal of escape clearly in my mind, I set out to do whatever it took to achieve it. The only way I could get money to escape was to work, and the only way I could work was to temporarily move back home. I had to make a plan.

I got a job in a local restaurant as I could at least wait on tables, and with the tips I would have instant cash. I took evening and night shifts so I could go back to school. That way I was never home during the day when my father would have the opportunity to be alone with me. It worked, but I knew this arrangement could not continue for long. It was too stressful to face my father and I was not getting enough sleep.

Finally, just after Christmas, I decided it was time to catch a ride to Edmonton. I had purchased clothes which would suffice for work and

I had forty dollars in my pocket. I thought I could rent a room for about twenty-five dollars and that would give me enough to eat until I got my first paycheck. I had an address for Helge and Karen-Margrete Ahlefelt, who had visited us a couple of years before. They had told me that I could come and visit any time.

It was January and bitterly cold. Every day I went out early in the morning and went from store to store until closing time. I could not find work, but I could not go back home. Karen-Margrete advised me to take a job as a live-in nanny. That way I would have a roof over my head and three square meals a day. That seemed a good solution at the time.

Little was I to know that once again I would learn a major life lesson. My employer was a well known lawyer in Edmonton. Living with them revealed to me the amazing knowledge that you did not have to be very smart to become well-educated. He certainly knew law. He knew all about football. She knew all about bowling and fashion, but when it came to world affairs, my poor immigrant parents knew more than they and their friends. I then concluded that I too could get an education if the opportunity ever arose. Being a nanny was not exactly what I had in mind when moving to Edmonton.

Jack Thompson, whom I had met about a year before moving, came to Edmonton one day. I really liked him and it was great to have someone to go out with on my one day off a week.

Ironically it was my father who introduced me to him when he caught a ride home to Manning from Peace River at Christmas. My father liked his aquavit, a Danish liquor, Jack liked his lemon gin. They mixed the two liquors together, both thinking the other's was a mix. When they arrived home they were both very drunk. I did not recognize that in Jack as he was just funny. Jack and I went to the local Boxing-day dance together on December 26th. We had continued to see each now and again since.

Chapter 2

Marriage and Children

One day Jack came to Edmonton. He was mate on a Canadian Coastguard boat and worked every summer on the Mackenzie River. They set out buoys and targets, which are wooden structures set on the banks of the river. The boat captains would aim for them in order to navigate through deep-enough water. Jack was always up north through the summer shipping season. Now he was on stand-by time. He drove a turquoise 1957 Chevy Biscayne, which was the hot car of the day. He was good-looking and as he was fifteen years older seemed very mature to me. I was impressed.

We would go out together on my one day off a week. It was good to have him there. At least he was steady, had good employment and I loved being with him. We would drive all over the country and then go for hamburgers for supper. That was a novelty for me as there were no hamburger joints up north.

One day he told me there was something he had to tell me. "I have a six-year-old daughter and her mother is Native," he said. "I am not seeing the mother."

"Where is your daughter?" I asked.

"She stays with her grandparents. She is okay there. I got a letter in the mail saying I was the father. When my mother found out, she told me she would sooner that I go to jail than marry an Indian. My sister had married a Métis man and she was not pleased. She told me to see a certain lawyer and he took care of it. The paternity suit was dropped. I do not know what he did, but I never heard anything again."

I thought that if we got married we might have an instant family which would include a child to take care of. I actually liked the idea, but Jack said he would not take her away from her grandfather. They were inseparable.

One day Jack rented a motel room and took me there. I was so nervous, as I had never been alone in a room with a man before. After we had eaten our fill of smoked oysters and crackers, we ended up in bed. He was so gentle and kind, but in a hurry. I knew nothing about sex. Before I knew it, it was over and I wondered what was good about that. What a shock!

A month later I knew I was pregnant. I was only 17. When I told him, he made me go to a doctor to confirm it. Sure enough, I was. It was the first of April and he would be going north soon. I told him he did not have to marry me, that I could just continue to stay where I was and I would make out. I was not sure if he wanted me or not. I knew I wanted him, but never wanted to make him feel I had trapped him. He agreed we should get married, so it had to be right away as he would be leaving and I wanted to go north with him. That afternoon we went shopping for an engagement ring. Then I called my Mom and told her to get ready for a wedding since we had decided to get married before he left for the north, so I could accompany him.

My poor mother. I gave her only ten days to prepare. She rented a hall, hired a caterer and a band even before we came home. Invitations were by phone. We had no out-of-town relations or friends so it was not too difficult. We arrived home five days before the wedding. Mom and I went to Peace River and purchased a wedding dress. My sister Karin and Jack's brother Larry stood up for us so everything went very smoothly. My father would not allow me to have a dance without being able to serve liquor. In those days the law was that no one under the age of 21,except family members, could be present where liquor was served. That meant my friends could not come. I was really sad about that, but could not stand up to him at that time.

Jack just told me it was not important so leave it alone. He also refused to go to a church. We solved that by being married at my parents' place with only family present. I was really happy about getting married to him, so accepted the situation and made the best of it. I was just seventeen, he was thirty-two.

I knew he loved children and I wanted a good father for mine. He didn't drink much and was never disorderly. He was a sharp dresser and always drove a nice car. I was looking forward to a good life with him. I was excited about being a mother too. Life was good on this my wedding day.

Little could I know that within just a few hours my life would once again come crashing down.

The wedding ceremony, the supper and the dance went well. I did miss my friends, but had accepted that they could not come. The night came to a close and off we went to a nearby motel. I was so nervous. Jack said nothing and took off his clothes and jumped into bed. I turned my back when he undressed as I did not think I should watch. I went and got my suitcase and decided to go and change in the bathroom.

"Turn the lights out!" he said. "I do not want anyone to know we are here."

When I came out and crawled into bed beside him, he said, "I do not believe in kissing and hugging and all that stuff. You will have to put out whenever I want you because a man has to have what a man has to have. If you do not, I will be forced to go somewhere else and it will be your fault. You would not want that, would you?"

"No," I said quietly, not knowing what else to say.

He then jumped on top of me and took me. The whole process lasted less than thirty seconds. He got off, turned over and went to sleep. I was a mess in every way. I hated the feel of the wetness between my legs and quietly got out of bed and went and washed up. "There," I thought, "that's one thing taken care of. How do I take care of the let-down feeling in my heart and the pit of my stomach?"

The pain was almost unbearable. I had dreams of a loving relationship with my husband, children, a home filled with love and laughter. I realized then that he wanted sex and that was it. He really did not care about me. I knew he liked the idea of being married, as he had often said he longed to have a wife. I wondered if I should have seen it coming, but I could not see how I could have. He had hugged and kissed until that night. As I got back into bed I lay awake for a long time trying to figure out what to do now. I knew he did not love me, but could I live without love? I knew he would be a good father and I was ever so aware of the child I was carrying and that I wanted him or her to have the best. I knew he was a good provider. I knew he was safe. Of those things I was sure.

In those years divorce was very rare and to think of leaving for such frivolous reasons without even giving our marriage a chance was just not an option. I came to the conclusion that if I would just be the best mother and wife then he would eventually love me. He would not be able to help it. Now I had a plan of how I could live despite feeling I was deceived and raped by my new husband. It was nearly daybreak when I dozed off.

Soon I was awakened by him and he took me again. I just let him, as I knew it was a part of *the plan.*

On April 14, 1963, we turned on the radio and heard how the river at Hay River, the town in the Northwest Territories that we were supposed to move to, was blocked by an ice jam and the whole town where we were to live was flooded. When we enquired, we learned that we would not be able to get housing, so I would not be able to go north with him after all.

I did not want to live in Manning. I was afraid of what might happen with my father. Besides, since I was pregnant, I would sooner be away where no one would be watching to see how soon my stomach would grow big.

I told Jack that I wanted to live in Edmonton and he was happy to oblige as then he did not have to drive from Manning to catch a plane for the north. We found the most awful basement suite ever, in a private home. Everything from couch to chairs to floors was various shades of red. The windows were so small they hardly let any light in and were certainly not big enough for escape in case of fire.

The home was located in Jasper Place which was not a part of Edmonton at that time. That made it cheaper. Jack told me that since the landlord was a cop I would be safe and he would not have to worry about me.

He decided to put his car in storage as he did not want me driving it. I was just grateful to be near buses so I could easily get around. He would not allow me to purchase a television either. We did not have it up north and I never thought much about it at the time. As soon as we were settled, Ethel, who I thought was my friend, came to stay. Ethel was a girl who I knew from school. She had a crush on my older brother and they were seriously dating. Jack invited her to come, but I was not pleased as we only had a few precious weeks together, and I so wanted to prove how good a wife I would be to him. I really felt she was intruding, but Jack insisted it was a great idea.

She and Jack really gave me a hard time. They would laugh at everything I did. When I cooked a meal, they would sit and play with the food and laugh together. I was heartbroken.

Nothing was good except my pregnancy. Jack reluctantly put my name on his bank account as there was no other way in those days to get funds to me. I did not have a bank account. He told me I could only buy food and pay rent. I was not to buy anything until he was there. I did think that was reasonable, as after all it was his money. Soon the day came for Jack to leave. I was expecting to go to the airport, but he would not hear of it. He said it was too embarrassing to say good-bye in public. I was devastated. Ethel told me she wanted to go back to

Manning, so she left too and I was alone. I thought she would stay for a while, but after the way she treated me I was not sorry to see her go.

That summer I spent mostly exploring. I would walk two kilometers to the city bus stop and hop the first bus going anywhere and ride it until it came back to my bus stop. I spent time making baby clothes and lived a very quiet and lonely life without friends and without family. I missed Jack terribly. He did write a few times; I would read and reread his letters over and over. I kept hoping that he would have a change of heart after being away. Life went on one day after the other. I loved being pregnant. It was that little life that kept me going.

One day in October Jack suddenly appeared at the door. He had not let me know he was coming. I was so happy to see him that it really did not matter. I was eight months pregnant by that time and knew I could not bring a new baby to that horrible place we were living in. He agreed to find something better. We found a cute attic suite where we had trees and hundreds of birds outside the window. I was getting close to giving birth and I was happy. The first thing Jack did was go and buy a television. That was the first time I really began to see who he was and it was not pretty. He was so selfish and I was beginning to wonder how I could ever make a life with him. My hope was still pinned on the expectation that he would be a good father and in time he would care for me when he saw how good I was.

On December the 5th, 1963, my waters broke and Jack drove me to the hospital. After I was admitted and settled, he informed me that there was a hockey game on TV, so as nothing would happen for hours yet he might as well go home. He left and never came back. Margo was born shortly after six the next morning. Although I had specifically told them I wanted to be conscious for her birth, they had put me under at the last moment against my will. That was the hospital rule in 1963. It was also normal procedure that babies were fed by bottle by the nurses for the first twenty-four hours. No one brought my daughter to me. I had not yet seen her.

By that time I was beside myself. No husband, and of course my imagination was taking over and I was beginning to wonder if my baby was dead or badly deformed. Why were they keeping her from me? We were not allowed out of bed, so I could not go and find her. All newborns were kept behind closed curtains anyway. Jack finally returned at regular visiting hours in the afternoon. At least *he* could go and see her when they opened the curtains for viewing. When he saw how many people were at the window he refused to go down there. He protested that everyone was just silly the way they were "ooing and awing" so he was not going to go anywhere near there. He would not even see her! I was devastated. I thought if he could at least see her I would know she was okay. He absolutely refused.

When late that afternoon the doctor came in, he found me crying uncontrollably; then, when he learned that the nurses had not brought my daughter to me, he was furious and made them go and get her immediately. When I finally held my daughter, she was so perfect. I could not believe it. The love was totally encompassing. There was not one part of me that was not love. As I held her I just knew life would be okay. Giving her back to the nurses was one of the hardest things I ever did, but I had no choice. One week later, without Jack having even seen her, he came and took us home.

After putting my beautiful daughter on the bed, I went to hang up my coat. When I turned back, Jack was holding her so tenderly, totally engrossed in his little girl. I was ecstatic. Perhaps it was going to be okay!

He certainly stuck to his word though about not kissing me or hugging. and sex continued to last less than thirty seconds. I developed severe pain in my ovary area, but the doctors could find nothing wrong. They just told me it must be in my head. No, I thought, it is in my ovaries, but if my head created it, my head would take it away. Through visualization and relaxation I finally learned to control it and eventually could actually make it go away.

Jack was a great father and that meant the world to me, so I really felt the rest was worth the sacrifice. After all, he did not drink too much, we always had food in the house, he never beat me and he was the wonderful father I had thought he would be.

Sixteen months later Rocky was born. His father was not there for his birth either, but by that time we had moved back to Manning, so I had family around me.

Jack was always respectful in public and it was obvious he loved his children. Everyone, including my family, thought he was the greatest and they never failed to tell me how lucky I was to have such a good man. The few times I wanted to say something, I was so sure it would sound too trivial—so I said nothing.

As a result of two close births I developed varicose veins and decided to have them stripped. The surgical procedure did not turn off whatever triggered the pain to go on, so I had as much pain years after as I had the day after the operation. I learned to live with excruciating pain. No one even to this day has any idea why. The chronic pain I suffered was to influence my life in more ways than I could imagine.

After the birth of the children, Jack did not want to go away again. He took odd jobs here and there.

Despite all my efforts our relationship did not improve.

One day he got a phone call from Bev, his daughter. Her uncle, who kept Jack informed on her development, did whatever he could to get them connected. I asked if he didn't want to see her.

"If she is not okay where she is, I would like her to come and stay with us." I offered.

"I will not take her away from her grandparents," he said firmly. "I do not want to talk about it anymore." I really felt bad as I thought our children had a right to know they had a sister, but she was his child, not mine, and I had to accept that it had to be his decision.

In 1965, close to Christmas, there was a knock on the door. I answered and there stood his daughter Bev. She was ten years old, rather small in stature and she had long black hair. Her eyes were pure black and she was so beautiful, she took my breath away. I asked her to come in, but she remained in the porch, and I called Jack. I saw her give her father a big hug. My heart went out to that little girl and I know Jack's did too. She left little gifts for Margo and Rocky. Once again I asked Jack if we couldn't keep her. "Bev's mother is Native and with my mother's attitude I cannot. I will not hurt my mother, so it is impossible," he answered.

That year I went out and bought her the most beautiful outfit I could find. It was just something I needed to do. "She will come to us when she is a teenager," I thought. I came to the realization that I could do nothing but accept that Jack would not have his part-Native daughter in his life.

She did not come during her teen years and I knew virtually nothing about what her life was like. Through the years she would call occasionally, Jack never shared what their conversation was about, only that she had called.

Chapter 3

Independence

As time went by Jack became more and more angry whenever I spent any money for anything but rent, utilities or food. He would not talk to me for days and always threatened to take my name off the bank account. I had taken over all the running of the household and I began to fight back by telling him I would stop paying any more bills, or buy anything including food if he did. He would become responsible for everything. The threats continued, but he never did carry them out.

I knew I had to get out from under his financial control, but did not want to go to work and leave the children with babysitters. I struggled trying to figure out what to do until one day a woman told me she could not get to Peace River to buy a sewing machine. Hers was not working and I volunteered to fix it for her. Mom had taught us all well. Then it suddenly dawned on me that if I could get a franchise for Singer sewing machines, I could work from home and do presentations at the community halls that dotted the country. I could also take machines to people's homes. In other words, a home based business. Something unheard of, back in 1966.

One fine spring day I made the three-hour drive to Grande Prairie where the regional Singer store was. When I approached the owner with the idea he was not keen on it. He told me that women did not sell sewing machines. I was shocked. After much discussion, and me continually coming back to the question "Why not?", he finally told me that if I could go down to the basement, find a certain model machine and carry it back up, he would allow me to try. He had nothing to lose as I volunteered to work on commission only. This business gave me money for clothes and personal needs. I did not do as well as I had hoped, but I was satisfied. After about eight months, head office pulled the machines as they did not think I was selling enough. That was the end of that.

In the meantime, the government set up a nursing orderly course and Jack decided to take it. There was a large demand, so getting a job would be easy. Off we went to Edmonton so he could take the course. The Government paid two hundred and forty dollars a month for a family of four. Every cent had to be carefully managed as I did not want to go to work. I told everyone who came in from the north that they had to bring wild meat if they wanted to stay with us. We purchased vegetables directly from the farmers. I sewed all our clothes and we even parked our vehicle and purchased one bus pass which we could take turns using. We made it without going into debt or me going to work.

Then it was back to Manning where he was promised a job.

One day after five years of marriage to Jack, five years of many tears and broken dreams, I knew I had to make a decision whether to stay with him or not. I weighed the consequences of staying versus the consequences of leaving. I decided to stay. He was a good father and I could not separate him from the children. Then and there I decided I would make a good life for myself. I had to become independent within the marriage. I would not continue to live in this misery. Getting my high school diploma was the first step.

In 1971 my son and I both started school, I in grade twelve, he in grade one. The only way I could get my diploma was to go back with the young people, which was unheard of in those years. I learned lots as in just eight years there had been an enormous shift in the cultural values of the young people. Drugs had come on the scene for the first time. Getting drunk and laid was the norm. Unbelievable that such a drastic change could occur in such a short time! On the positive side there was much more openness and the students were not the blind followers many of my generation were. Those young people were good to me and accepted me as one of them.

My first job after graduation was in a bank. A new bank manager, Mr. Tingley, had come to town and moved in just a few doors down. He was very excited when we met and he found out I needed a job, as he was short one cashier. I, too, was excited at the prospect of having good employment because there were not many jobs available in our small town and I was still carrying the stigma of being an outsider. No one seemed to forget that we were only poor immigrants and by that time my father was drinking more and more, so it was not good to be a Jorgensen in Manning. Of course the new bank manager knew nothing about local dynamics. He only saw me for who I was. My co-workers happened to be the very people who had given us such a hard time in grade school when we first came to Canada. The very first day I knew I was in trouble when Mr. Tingley asked Judy, one of the cashiers, to do the training. She refused to show me anything and would not answer any questions. By the end of the day I was sick to my stomach and my head was pounding. As I walked slowly home along the gravel road I tried to figure out a plan, but could find no solution.

The next day Mr. Tingley asked how it was going. I had to tell him what was going on. He did tell Judy to do a proper job, but she taught me only the very minimum. When I was not sure of what to do for a customer, I was forced to ask for guidance. She would roll her eyes in front of them and snicker as if I was not too bright. My stomach would turn over each time it happened. I was so unhappy—I could not do my job properly under the circumstances. One day she went to Mr. Tingley and told him I was a slow learner and she felt I could not handle the job. The other cashier, Gloria, backed her up as they were best friends. He called me into his office and asked for my side. I told him what was happening but by the look on his face, I knew he was beginning to question whether they were right. When he started watching us more closely, he did see what was going on. Things went better for a short time, but then they changed their tactics and started teaching me to do things that were outright wrong. When I came to the realization that nothing in my place of employment was going to change, I quit.

My next move was working part-time evenings in the diagnostics department of the hospital. That created an interest in becoming a lab/x-ray technician. My mother, who was the lab/x-ray technician in Manning, was planning to move to Whitecourt. I made arrangements with the administrator for her job if I got qualified. He agreed. I did not have a contract, in those days it was not considered necessary. A person's word was trusted.

In 1973 I took my daughter Margo, then ten years old, with me back to Edmonton to lab/x-ray school. Rocky remained in Manning with his father.

The first morning of school, the head of the program came into the classroom, proceeded to the blackboard and wrote in big letters GOD. Then he turned to us and said, "That is me: George Oliver Debonair. I am God. I will decide whether you sit in that seat or not." He pushed us to the limit. He tortured us at every opportunity. It did bring us closer as a group. We were forced to wear the skirts of our uniforms below our knees in a time when mini-skirts were the style. We made a pact that we would perform one last act of defiance and shorten our skirts for graduation. It was such fun to see the look on his face when we walked into the auditorium. We knew we got the last laugh, as he could not deny us our diplomas.

The next year he overstepped his limit when he told one of the students she could not take time out to go to the doctor. She went anyway and he kicked her out. She laid an official complaint against him. After an investigation, he was dismissed. The girl was reinstated. In the end there was justice.

When I returned to Manning, I told Jack he had to take over the cooking when I was working full time. He did. Every day people told me how wonderful he was that he let me go to school and even did the cooking for me. I was "so lucky to be married to such a wonderful man!" I could say nothing. No one understood as I told no one about his disrespect for me, about him taking me whenever he wanted, about how I let him. I made the best of my life with work and the children. That part was all very good. I stopped expecting anything from Jack. No expectations, no disappointments.

In 1975 Jack was tired of his work at the hospital as a nursing orderly and wanted out. My mother was leaving Whitecourt Hospital so I applied for and got the position of Lab/x-ray technician there. The deal I made with Jack was that we would both quit work in Manning on Friday and I would start work in Whitecourt on Monday. He was to take care of everything regarding the household. That worked great except that he decided that the easy life was better than working.

Come summer he did speak to someone who had their own carpet cleaning machine and was making really good money. We purchased a machine and one day Jack went to Manning for a week cleaning carpets. He came back with a big roll of money. That was great, but he refused to advertise or do anything to get jobs around Whitecourt, so of course he got no work, and if I got him a job from the staff at the hospital, he would tell me that I was pushing him to work, and he was just too busy doing all the work at home for that.

In Whitecourt I was to get another most important teaching. For the first time in my life I really learned how to laugh.

I was very serious about almost everything in life at that time, raising my children, being a good citizen, wife and employee. Marjory Adams was our lab assistant. She came in part time and was a great support to all the technicians. Her greatest gift however was her sense of humour. Everything that was said she would turn into something funny. She teased everyone and had nicknames for us all. The lab became "the zoo." The head tech at the time became a long drawn-out "Dr. Sloooaaaaan," Marj was "Hippo," I was "Tomcat," Dr. McKay was "Giraffe," Cher got "Bear." There was "Tookalook" who got her name when she went to a party where she walked in on a guy in the bathroom. Marj never missed an opportunity. One day "Tiger John" also joined our zoo.

Marj looked after all the ordering of supplies for the lab. One day after receiving the wrong size lids for our specimen jars for the third time, she calmly went to the phone, called our supplier and asked if they had ever heard of miracle lids. She told them that no human could possibly make that same mistake three times in a row, so the lids must be changing size in transit. We all got a good laugh and the right size lids in the next shipment.

One day we were told that the administrator was bringing in a new person, with a degree, to be head of the lab. He had hired him over the phone sight unseen. He could hardly understand his English. Not only was he right out of university, but *he* was a man.

With the diversity required in a small hospital diagnostics department we were not looking forward to the change. We were not pleased. Not even a little bit. It was hard enough to cope with the workload with each of us doing the work of one and one half technicians. We did not need another burden. We did decide to at least give him a chance as we knew it would not be easy to work with us either.

On his first day of work, in walked John. He was Chinese and very young: I could not see how he could possibly fit into our busy little department and our crazy humour which is what kept us afloat under the stress of the workload and responsibility we had. The first thing he said after introductions was that he knew nothing about running a lab such as ours as he had just finished university, so if it was okay with us he just wanted to spend some time learning. One for John. What a relief! He did just that and took guidance and advice from all of us. He took over slowly and was not afraid of tackling any job, even washing up if necessary. He turned out to be fun to work with and his great sense of humour fit right in with ours.

One problem he had was understanding the slang expressions of the English language. So often people used to laugh at him and he would not know why. We set out to teach him and had great fun doing it. One expression we never corrected him on was a favourite: when one of us was down at lunch and he answered the phone, he would just say, "She is out to lunch," not knowing it meant "She is a little crazy." We all had many good laughs about that. He came in with four big strikes against him, but because we all agreed to give him a chance, which was something we had to talk ourselves into, he turned out to be the best in every way. I will always be grateful to the zoo and all the people in it. We were all free to be ourselves and we could laugh and cry and work ever so hard, but there was always respect for one another.

The administrator came one day and told us the Minister of Health, Neil Crawford, would be making a visit to the hospital and he wanted to see the lab and x-ray department. He warned me that I was to behave when the minister came. I promised I would, but I had other plans. We were still doing wet developing of x-ray films which means being away from the patients for up to five minutes every time we had to go to the darkroom, which was small and without ventilation. The acid fumes were unbearably strong. The big day arrived and of course we were very busy. After introductions the minister asked how things were. I told him there was something I wanted to show him. I led him into the developing room and closed the door. I explained how not only did we have to leave the patient, but we also had to breathe the toxic fumes into our lungs. I held him in there conversing until he started coughing and sputtering. Then I opened the door and explained about how daylight processing allowed us to keep an eye on the patients while loading the films for processing. It would also put an end to us breathing the toxic fumes and so there would be less sick time to pay. Daylight processors would pay for themselves in no time. It was not long before we were approved for the new equipment. Many other hospitals were also approved around that time. I like to think it was because the minister learned something that day.

Working in the zoo was such a special time. We were able to be totally ourselves under sometimes extreme circumstances. There is so much responsibility for the staff of small rural hospitals. There is no backup, there are no specialists—no one but each other and we were a team, through thick and thin, through good and bad. Such was life at Whitecourt General Hospital.

One day I discovered a large lump in my breast. My mother had uterine cancer and my grandmother had died of breast cancer, so I panicked. Dr. McKay removed the lump the next day. Thank God, it was not malignant! Soon after, another lump appeared: it too, was removed, and fortunately, it was not malignant either. Dr. McKay told me that after going under anesthesia four times within just a few months, I could not continue to tolerate the anesthesia and I should consider having my breasts removed because I had such a high risk of cancer with my family history. He made an appointment for me to see a plastic surgeon and arrangements were made for the surgery.

I would have stayed in Whitecourt, as I loved my job and my co-workers, but the schools were not good. Margo had entered junior high. One day she came to me and was very upset because all her friends were using drugs, even at school. I went to the principal and he confirmed it. I told as many people as would listen that I thought something should be done. Not one parent would support me as they did not believe what I was saying. Margo started to get harassed at school. Many things went missing from our place and one night we had a visitor who owned a TR 6 sports car. Someone had put spikes against every wheel. Luckily she noticed and called the police. They refused to respond. The next day they came and warned Margo that they were keeping an eye on her. Her big crime was writing her and her boyfriend's initials on a fence with chalk. None of the other girls who had written on the same fence got a warning, only Margo. That was the first time I questioned that our police force was perhaps not so perfect.

She was entering her teen years and I did not want her harassed at school or by the police. Life was difficult enough without that. Besides, they had a very low average of young people graduating from the only high school in Whitecourt. I knew I had to get the children to better schools.

By this time Jack had stopped making any decisions whatsoever, but always laid the blame on me for everything such as my using too much money or not keeping the house in order. He was so perfect in every way. If I said anything to defend myself he would just squint his eyes, give me the most evil look and say in a low voice that I had better keep my mouth shut or else. I stopped caring about that, too. I realized then that I had to bring in the money and make all the major family decisions myself. I made a decision to move to better schools for the kids. He was not working anyway and obviously had no intention to start now.

Bev, his daughter, continued to phone off and on, and every time she did I asked the same question about her coming to stay with us. He just said that everything was so good here, so why would we need to take a chance and mess things up. "Margo and Rocky have a right to know they have a sister," I said, but he would not allow me to tell them and he would not do it himself.

Chapter 4

Red Deer

Schools in Red Deer had a good reputation and in 1978 I applied for a job as lab x-ray technician at Michener Center, an institution for 1600 mentally retarded people. These mentally retarded residents of that institution were to become very important teachers of my life. They were to teach me how to see spirit.

Many were non-verbal and had the mentality of a baby or very young child in an adult body. The smell of urine and the noise on the wards when I made my rounds in the mornings was horrendous. Most people were extremely deformed. There was one young girl of about eighteen years, who was half the normal size; she had no movement of her arms, and was confined to a wheelchair as her spindly little legs could not carry her. Her face was literally shaped like a triangle and her chin was the same length as the rest of her face, which came down in a very sharp point. She was also non-verbal, but seemed to be a happy child and the long-time staff said, "Isn't she cute?" My only thought was, "No she is not. There is nothing cute about her. She is deformed and ugly," but I did not say anything. I didn't get it. As time went by I got over the shock of seeing so much deformity and misery in one place; I too one day looked at this same girl when she came to the laboratory for blood tests and suddenly found myself thinking, "She really is cute." Was I surprised! I got it. I could not believe it.

After that I started to see the spirit of the residents. I marveled at the fact that many had achieved all we on the outside were striving for: true happiness. Yes! While there were many who never got to that point, there were also many that did. Some, when they were taken outdoors, could sit under a tree and look at the leaves, the birds and the sky for hours and be in complete harmony with what was around them. Is that not the epitome of life? To achieve total harmony in all that is around us? I learned to see spirit in that place, to get beyond the physical and into the reality of who those people were.

In May 1979 I had both breasts removed. I had to go to Edmonton to the larger hospital for the surgery. I really thought I was prepared for the loss of my breasts. I also thought I was prepared for Jack dropping me off at the front door as he had said he would do, but when I entered that hospital, my heart sank. I never felt so alone in my life. I called the few family and friends in Edmonton, but everyone was too busy to come. The day after surgery they moved many patients to another floor in the hospital. One nurse came in and I asked her how long I would have to remain in the hospital.

"I know nothing about you plastics patients," was her reply. Plastics patients? It felt like she had hit me in the stomach. How could she call me *plastic* just because a plastic surgeon performed the surgery? Obviously she did not care either.

I was told that the cancer society would send a representative to talk to me about the prosthesis that was available after breast removals. She did show up a couple of days after surgery but when she discovered that I did not have cancer she turned on her heels and left. I just shook my head and wondered why she could not understand that losing my breasts was devastating, cancer or no cancer. "I guess I am not sick enough for anyone to care," I thought. Any way I looked at it, no one cared about me. I had never before experienced such loneliness.

That evening I went to the waiting room to just be around people as I was afraid I would lose my composure if I stayed by myself. There were three other patients in the room and they were laughing together. It was good to hear that laughter. Soon the woman in the group came over and told me they were going to the cafeteria for coffee and I had to come with them. I meekly followed them as I could not bear being alone. I did so enjoy their laughter. Soon I too was laughing. Total strangers were my angels when I needed them most. They saved my sanity that day.

When I arrived back in my room I thought long and hard about that day. It had gone from the worst loneliness I had ever known to a most wonderful time with complete strangers. I thought about how much people's words and attitudes affected me at a time when I was so vulnerable. I knew I had much to learn from the experience of that day.

That evening I coined the phrase *'elevator relationships.'* They are relationships that generally only last as long as a ride in an elevator, but are so uplifting. They occur in lineups at a grocery store, a brief meeting at a bus stop or while waiting at a traffic light.

They can make or break a day. They can send some people into or out of a depression. They are so important.

At Michener Centre I saw the best of humanity and also the worst. Some staff were kind and caring and truly gave love to the residents while others were extremely abusive. Many times I x-rayed broken limbs and when I asked the poor victim what happened they would get the "look" from the staff and just say, "I don't know," or "I don't remember."

There were so many sad stories of sterilizations. The Centre still kept laboratory slides of tissues which were removed from the residents. They used them for scientific studies.

My boss Gail still defended the sterilization program which had been stopped some years prior to my coming to work there. When I talked to her about exposing what was going on, she said, "Your best bet is to keep quiet if you do not want to be hurt or worse. If your family is important to you, you better keep your mouth shut."

I decided to do that for the time being, but was always looking for a way I could expose what was happening. Every once in a while an article would hit the papers and I would be thrilled, but soon it would die down and things would return to the hell it was before. I never spent time on the wards so never saw anything directly and without that I could do nothing.

Jack continued in his same old pattern, but he affected me less and less. I carried on with my life and had all the love I needed from my children. We had such fun together. He continued to be a good father and his greatest joy was Rocky's hockey. Margo and Rocky did well in school and made good friends. Because of that I decided not to make any major changes at that time.

One afternoon in 1982, after not hearing from her for many years, Jack's daughter Bev phoned and gave him an ultimatum: either we had to get together or he had to tell her he would never see her again. She had to know where she stood with him. "Don't you think it is about time?" I asked. "She is your daughter and Margo and Rocky have a right to know they have a sister." He decided to see her and we made arrangements to go to Grande Prairie where she lived.

We called the kids together and Jack had to tell them. It was probably the hardest thing he ever did in his life and I was not about to bail him out. Not this time. This was his responsibility and for once he had to stand up to it. When he finally got brave enough and he told them they had a sister, they both turned to me. "Don't look at me!" I said.

Both at the same time turned to their father and said, "You?" They were both obviously surprised. His whole life was about image and he had certainly gone out of his way to portray me as the 'bad guy' and himself as being 'perfect.' At that moment I realized how successful he had been. Never, until that moment, had Margo or Rocky even thought that he could do anything immoral. They were stunned. It was also unbelievable to find out that they had a sister.

"Mom, what did you think when I used to get mad at you because you would not have any more children and I wanted a sister so bad?" asked Margo.

"So many times I told your father to tell you, but he would not, and it was not my place to say anything, it was his."

"I understand that, Mom," she said.

I was relieved. At least they were not blaming me for the secrecy.

She sent pictures and we discovered for the first time that she was married and had three children, Theresa, Evelyn and Richard. We did go to see them that Easter. They lived in a modest three bedroom bungalow in a middle-income part of town. I had never seen Jack so nervous before. He went in first and Bev gave him a hug and thanked him for coming. Then he introduced Margo and Rocky. All were a little nervous, and they just looked at each other and said nothing. They were all smiling, so I knew it would be okay.

I was bringing up the rear and when Bev and I finally came face to face, she gave me a polite little hug and asked, "Do you mind if the kids call you grandma?"

"No," I said. "I am married to their grandfather, so I guess I am their grandmother." I hadn't thought about it until that moment. I was thirty-seven years old and the grandmother of three, the oldest ten years old. That was an adjustment, let me tell you!

Her home was spotless, she was wearing makeup and wore a very nice sweater and black dress slacks. Her kids were perfectly dressed and very well behaved. This was good. I thought.

I was up before anyone else the next day and as I was sitting at the table having coffee, Evelyn, the second oldest, came and climbed up on my lap and said nothing. I just held her for a long time until she was ready to move again. Richard, the youngest, came up to me and looked at me with his big blue eyes. "Grandma," he said with great emotion, "I just love you every day."

That day those three children wound their way right into my heart and from that day forward they were my grandchildren. Just before we were ready to leave Bev asked if she could talk to me. "All these years I hated you because I thought my dad wouldn't see me because of you. I just knew I would hate you when we met, but I don't," she said tearfully.

"It is always easy to hate those you do not know." I assured her. "You have had a hard life, and perhaps it was good for you to have a scapegoat. When we have someone you can safely lay blame on, we do not have to lay blame on those we love. It did not hurt me. I did not know."

Bev and I became very close that day and have remained close for all these years. I have always admired her courage through all the challenges she faced. It has been a gift to finally have my step-daughter and her children in my life.

Chapter 5

Seeking Gold

The way the residents at Michener Center were treated was too much. The abuse, which I could not prove, was so hard on me as I could do nothing. The government also came in with a new policy of "normalization." In my opinion it was disastrous.

They were sending residents into the community to live—residents who did not have the ability to make decisions necessary to cope with everyday life. One day when I was in town, I met one Judy, a beautiful young girl of about 19 years of age, with epilepsy: I had become quite attached to her at the center. She looked awful. She was thin and her color was an ashen grey. She told me she and her boyfriend, who was also a former resident, were hungry. They had not eaten for three days.

"Are you not getting money for groceries?" I asked.

She told me she had a support worker who brought them money every month. They would buy lots of groceries but it never seemed to last until she came again. My fears were confirmed that day. These people could not cope without proper support.

I took her to the grocery store and bought them enough food to last until they once again got their grocery money. The image of that beautiful, sweet young woman, who had the mentality of about four to five years, has haunted me all these years. That was the final straw for me. I could not be involved with an institution that was that heartless.

Early in the spring of 1982, my best friend Joan told us about some friends who were mining for gold on Boulder Creek in northern British Columbia. She said they had invited her and Wayne to join them at the claim for the summer. A gold-seeking summer sounded too good to pass up. Joan got permission for us to go too.

Margo and Rocky were eighteen and nineteen and were done high school. Both worked and had their own income. They were living at home, so I decided they could take care of things and learn some valuable lessons.

Everyone told me I was crazy to give up a very good paying government job at a time of high unemployment and cutbacks, but I could not work there anymore.

Jack had visions of striking it rich, let me tell you! I had visions of getting away to a clean place, away from all the misery, the smells of the institution and just renew my life. We joined a gold panning club and learned the tricks of gold. My one claim to fame was in 1982, when I won the Alberta novice gold panning championship. The same year I won the regional log-sawing contest as well. I was on a roll, but it ended real soon. That was it. I was never to win any other contest again.

So Jack and I packed up and headed off to the gold fields at Atlin, up in the far north-west corner of British Columbia. We had our little sluice box and shovels, and determination.

It was a long tedious drive as there was mostly forest and not too much else to look at except for the odd little town where we could gas up and purchase supplies. Jack said very little. All along the way I would see eagles flying overhead. The first time I shared that with him he just grunted, so I did not bother any more. After a four-day drive we arrived.

However, our friends were not there so we could not set up. We were not sure where the boundaries of their claim were, and we did not dare set up on someone else's claim. That would have been trouble for sure. After a few hours, with no one showing up, Jack started to lose it. He paced back and forth repeating, "We are losing time. We are losing money!" I wondered if this was gold fever. By noon the next day everyone had appeared: there we were, all perched on a ledge on the side of a mountain. There were Mary and Walter in their little trailer, Joan and Wayne in their truck and Jack and I in our little camper.

One day Roy arrived to work the claim. He was 82 years old. He'd had a heart attack the year before, but he had a dream which had been with him since he was a young lad in Scotland. Like us, he also came to strike it rich. Roy was the most spoiled man I had ever met, but was in better shape than any of us. He could out-walk us all. He never failed to point that out and he never failed to get one of us women to butter his toast either. That was Roy!

One thing about miners, they are all liars about the gold they find. Everyone knows everyone is lying and they all love the game. It is part of the culture of gold miners.

We all worked hard, Mary and Walter with their big equipment and us with our little sluice boxes. At the start we used the pan to hunt for gold by testing out the sand and gravel. At the end we used the pan to separate the last of the gravel from the gold. The sluice boxes were designed with a layer of indoor/outdoor carpet at the bottom, followed by a very fine mesh screen and finally a sheet of expanded metal, which was designed to stop any big nuggets from getting away. We hooked up a water pump and spent the day shoveling the sand and gravel into the sluice boxes, and washing it with water. The gold, being the heaviest, would fall to the bottom, catch in the meshing and be washed out at the end of every day. That is when the gold pan would be used to do the final separation of gold and sand. Whether the operation was tiny like ours, or huge like so many on the creek, it was all the same concept. It has been done that way since the discovery of gold and it continues to be done to this very day.

The eagles stayed with us all summer. Sometimes I would point them out, but mostly no one else saw them so I gave up sharing. I thought maybe there was something wrong with me.

Suddenly one day the roar of a big helicopter interrupted the stillness. Before it landed Walter told us to disappear until it left. I went to our camper and peeked out under the curtains. An armed guard came out followed by men with briefcases. They disappeared into Walter's trailer and stayed for about a half hour. Then as quickly as they had come they disappeared. Afterwards Walter told us they were gold buyers who came once a year. Anyone who came near them or the helicopter risked getting shot.

In August I worked a three-week cover off for the lab/x-ray technician in Cassiar, a small asbestos-mining town about four hundred kilometers west across the mountains. It was the smallest hospital I had ever seen, only six beds. Years later I went back and to my surprise the town had disappeared. There was nothing left. Every store, the swimming pool, the ice arena, every home was gone. Not a trace was left. I have often wondered about why they would do that. Was there an environmental threat? Did they want to keep people out or was it just a cleanup as the town was no longer viable with the mine closing? Someone knows, not me.

One day in mid-September the water pump on the sluice box broke down and it was getting very cold at night, so we decided to go back home. We never struck it rich, but it was a clean place and I did renew.

We had heard no news from the outside world for six months. That was the first time I began seriously questioning the reporting of our media. The Middle East was in conflict and some of the good guys had become the bad guys and vice versa. The one-sided slants of the reports became very obvious. My suspicions were confirmed when the church brought a group of young people from war-torn areas to our town and I asked each to comment on the Canadian media coverage of their country. All said, we get only one perspective, one side of the conflict in their countries.

Chapter 6

Spiritual Awakening

After trying for some months to secure employment, I finally got a job in Breton as the department head of diagnostics. It was a great job. For the first time I had the opportunity to run a department and make a substantial difference.

In 1986 we took a trip to Vancouver to visit Jean and Jim, who had been our closest friends in Manning and were now living at Maple Ridge. They had another friend, David, doing some renovations on their house. David was an old friend of theirs whom they had known for many years from their days in northern Alberta. He was a little heavyset, not very tall and wore old jeans and a checkered shirt. I would have guessed him to be in his early fifties.

Jean told me he was a very interesting fellow. He had left the north at an early age and got into property development in Vancouver at a time when the housing markets were down. When they took a sharp upward turn in the sixties he became very wealthy. He was sharp and had a nose for good investments in property. He had everything: beautiful home, fast cars, a beautiful wife and many friends.

Then one day he was in a terrible motor vehicle accident. He almost lost his life. He spent many months recuperating and when he finally was able to get back on his feet, everything was gone. Property prices had plunged. His partner had not looked after his interests and he was bankrupt.

Something else had happened to him as well. While he was lying in the hospital close to death his spirit would journey out of his body. That was the first time he became aware of the spirit as a separate entity from the physical. He then began questioning the connection between the spiritual and the physical healing of the body. That opened up a whole new world which he had never entered before. He began his search for knowledge about *who* we are as spiritual beings. Although broke, he would sneak into many medical conferences, pretending to be a doctor, and became very knowledgeable about the latest developments in the medical field. He had no money, but he had a hunger to learn about everything that made us tick physically and spiritually. In his search he met with Native people and learned much about healing and spirituality from them.

One day Jean got a very bad headache and she asked David, "Can you take the pain out of my head?"

"I can try," was his reply. As he began to gently massage her head, working his hands through her hair, I was dumbfounded at what I saw coming out of her head.

Something resembling a clear bubble was wrapping itself around his fingers and then he just blew it away and it disappeared into thin air! I knew it was her pain. With all the pain I had suffered for so many years this was the first time I had seen or even heard anything like it. Would it be possible for me to finally get some relief from the agony I had suffered so many years? I remained silent for a long time. It was too mysterious.

Finally as we were eating supper I asked him how he took the pain.

He said, "Easy!"

I asked if he could help with all types of pain. He just shrugged his shoulders. "Pain is something you can learn to live with," I said.

Then he turned to me and said, "No one has to live with pain."

"I do," I replied and then proceeded to tell him that whatever had triggered pain to start when I had surgery on my legs never bothered to shut off, so I had as much pain fourteen years later as I did the day of the surgery.

"Do you want to be rid of it?" he asked.

That was the most bizarre question anyone had asked me and I told him so. He agreed to see if he could help.

That evening we went out in the field behind the house. He began to do a relaxation exercise with me, but I put a stop to it.

"You are not hypnotizing me!" I said.

He assured me that I would have full control at all times and I could stop the process any time I wanted to. I decided to go along with it. I did so want relief from the constant pain in my legs.

He continued through the relaxation exercise and then began to ask my legs questions relating to the cause of the pain. There was no reaction until he asked if my legs were angry. Then they suddenly began to tingle—just a little at first, but soon the sensation became stronger and stronger until it was almost unbearable.

"Yes!" I said.

He asked the same questions again with the same result.

"Okay," he said. "Maybe, God willing, I can help." He started to pray and move his hands gently down my legs, barely touching them. It felt like he was pulling an elastic band from my legs with his hands. Each time he would get to the feet it would feel like it would release from his hands and snap back into my legs, but each time there would be a little relief.

When he finished working on my legs, and told me to stand up, I could not. My head felt like it weighed a ton. I could not lift it. He put one hand on my forehead and one behind my neck. Waves of energy started flowing through me. It was overwhelming. David told me that a visitor would come that night and would bring me a question.

I went to bed early as I could not bear to be around people. Something had happened to me and I needed to be alone with it, whatever it was. As I entered that beautiful space between the two worlds of awake and asleep, I saw a big bald eagle sitting on the end of my bed. It was solid and it was real. I just looked at it and it looked at me. I felt so frustrated because I so desperately wanted to communicate, but could not. The next thing I knew was Jack getting into bed. I had no idea what time it was, but the eagle was gone. I went right back to sleep.

The next morning as I entered the house, I met David in the front hall. He asked if anyone had come. I told him about the eagle. He became very emotional and tears started rolling down his face. I was confused.

David tried to explain: "You are entering a new life and many new things will happen. You have been chosen and one day you will teach others." I did not like what I heard. I did not want to be chosen for anything. I did not really believe him, I had no reason to. Besides I had developed a good solid life for myself. I had become accustomed to Jack's ways and actually enjoyed the fact that I was free to make decisions.

On our drive home from Vancouver I started to see things I had never seen before. I saw the life in everything around me—the rocks, the trees, the flowers, the water, everything had life. I knew this was something very special; I was so touched by what I saw that tears started falling, but my head kept interfering and I worried if this was schizophrenia. At one point there was a river alongside the road. I knew I had to walk in that water, and I asked Jack to pull over. He did, without a word, to my surprise. I got out of the car and as I was walking toward the river, I could see and feel life in every rock. As I stepped into the river, the water too was alive. I felt an energy flow coming from the water around my ankles.

A whole new world of spiritual awakening was opening up and I could not understand any of it.

I was overwhelmed by the beauty I saw and the power I felt in all nature, everywhere I looked, everywhere I walked. When I went for a walk in the woods, I turned in wonder at what I saw and felt. It was as if every cell in my body came alive and was interacting with everything around me. It was as if I were no longer solid, but a mass of energy that interacted with all the other energy around me. That aura of beautiful energy remained for four days. I was never to be the same again. In those few days I learned so much which I was afraid to put words to. When I stopped to think about what was happening I would wonder again about schizophrenia, but that did not make any sense either as I felt so good, so special. There were so many questions, without any answers.

I had thought I knew a lot. I was an avid reader and kept up with the news regularly, had a great career, and was very active in community, politics and family. Here I was, seeing and feeling things I could not explain nor did I have any resources to turn to. Suddenly I felt I knew nothing. I needed to begin a new journey of discovery. My whole life was a question mark. The pain in my legs, although present, was only half as severe as before. My heart came to life in a way I had never felt before. I knew it was good, and knew I would begin a journey of discovery.

The first day I went back to work there was a calendar on my desk from Grant MacEwan College opened to a course on therapeutic touch. I picked it up and went straight to the administrator and told him I was going. I never thought about it, I had never heard about it before and did not know why I even wanted to go, but I did.

"Therapeutic touch?" he said, surprised. "That has nothing to do with your work."

"I know," I said. "I am not asking anything from you. I have lots of banked overtime and I will pay the fees myself."

"Do you have someone to work for you?" he asked

"Yes," I replied.

I will never forget that conversation because it was as if everything came automatically. I had always been a careful planner and would not have approached my boss without everything in place. I had not even read the full article when I went to him.

In the following weeks I went to the forest at every opportunity. I even spent my lunch breaks in a little ravine close to the hospital. It was extremely difficult to be at the hospital or at home, but I had to be at work and I had to be at home. I was totally confused. I could not understand what was happening to me. On one hand my heart was soaring with an overwhelming feeling of joy and enthusiasm for all the new feelings and sights that were coming, while on the other hand I was afraid of the unknown. Everything in nature was so beautiful. Everything was so alive, so vital, and yet so perplexing.

I was afraid of losing my grounding. I needed to continue working and functioning in the solidity of my life. So many things were going through my mind. I suddenly understood why some people up and left everything behind for 'enlightenments and personal developments.' That was not where I was about to go. All my life I had both feet firmly planted, as the saying goes, I was grounded. I was not about to go flying off on some far-out mission of discovery. *That* I knew.

The day came for the start of the therapeutic touch course. Everyone sat in a circle. The facilitator asked us to give our name, occupation and what we knew about therapeutic touch. As one by one the others shared about how they saw aura and how they felt the healing in their hands and how they saw colored energy between their hands and how they had touched people and they became better I was in awe of it all. Never had I heard of such things. Never had they come into my life. When it came to my turn, all I could say was "My name is Rita Thompson. I work as a lab/x-ray technician in the Breton hospital and I have no idea why I am here, but this is where I am supposed to be right now."

The facilitator nodded in understanding. I did not understand anything.

As it turned out, therapeutic touch was a technique of healing by moving a person's energy for balance, which in turn enhances healing and pain reduction.

The day I returned to work, a gentleman named Tony came in for an x-ray on his knees. He had been admitted to the hospital one year before for the first time. He was fifty-nine years old and a bachelor. All his life he had farmed close by. No one could figure out why he was ill. He went through every test possible, all of which registered normal, but he was very ill none the less. Pain would move from one part of his body to the next and there were times he could not even hold a cup to drink because he was shaking so much.

It was late in the afternoon and all was quiet in the department. I decided to call Dr. Pujara and explain to him about my new teachings and ask him if it was okay to try it on Tony. He told me to go ahead as long as I explained it to him and he agreed.

I did that and began working on him. I had been taught that each treatment would take about one half to one hour, but to keep working until I was satisfied the energy field was in balance and flowing. The half-hour came and went as did the hour and still there was no balance. I began to doubt myself and had to step back several times to once again re-establish the center we had been taught to stay in. After nearly two hours I finally felt I was done.

Tony stood up, took his crutches in his hand and walked out of the room as if there was nothing wrong. I just looked in amazement as he walked out the door. Dr. Pujara came up about an hour later and asked how it had gone. I asked him to check for himself. He came back with a big grin on his face and told me to continue tomorrow and the next day. I did work on him both days and it only took about a quarter of an hour to bring balance. Tony wanted to go home, but there was no doctor to discharge him on the weekend. He was not a happy camper. The next time I saw Tony was about a year later when he came in with battery acid in his eye. By that time I had worked more with the healing and was able to give him some relief from the pain. I continued to use the technique for many situations with remarkable success in most cases. Not all.

People began to come to our home for healing. Jack would often meet them at the door with a comment like "I don't believe in all this stuff." It definitely affected some people. It was getting more and more difficult to have him around. One day for the first time I suddenly knew we had to split. However, the law in Alberta was such that if he did not work and I did he would be able to sue me for support. I had no desire to support him at all, as he was not employed only because he was lazy. I spent much time trying to persuade him to go to work, to no avail. I even offered to open a convenience store as there was none in Breton and he thought it was a great idea until he found out that he would be working it. Then he would not hear of it again.

The healing work I was doing was in a way overwhelming for me. I saw the results, but understood nothing. I often asked myself who I was. What was happening to me? Sometimes it was a little frightening as I did not understand.

I saw many things I had never seen before. One evening Jack and I were driving home from a visit with friends. It was a pitch-black night with no stars or moon. Jack was being especially nasty that evening with all his sly remarks about how I knew nothing. Suddenly in front of the windshield appeared the silhouette of an eagle, which was at least two meters wide. The eagle passed through the windshield, perched on my shoulder and wrapped its wings around me. Tears began to flow down my cheeks. I had to keep my head turned to the window so Jack could not see them.

I began to see eagles flying everywhere I went. They would circle over my head as I walked to work. Several times they would swoop down in front of my car when I was driving. Once, as I sat by a lake, two eagles came and sat on the ground about five meters away. When it was time for me to leave, they simultaneously lifted off and flew together at my eye level in front of the car. As they flew they would look at each other, nod and then in unison they would shift flying paths to the right, the left or up, occasionally looking back at me. Suddenly they flew off into the sunset. I was sure that these eagles that appeared so often must have a message for me, but I still had no idea how to communicate with them.

I knew I needed help to understand, but what kind of help? I spoke to many people and told them only a little of what was happening, but none had the answers for which I was searching. Where could I find my answer? Who would understand? I desperately needed help to understand my connection to the eagle, the healing and all the new things that were entering my world. I had to continue my search.

Chapter 7

Lawrence Mackinaw of the Cree First Nation

In 1986 I was working at Breton General Hospital and at the same time practicing therapeutic touch. My heart, which I had not paid much attention to for so many years, was coming alive in a whole new way after the incident regarding the healing of my legs. I worked well with my brain, but now feelings and emotions long buried were awakened. The colors in nature were sharper and brighter than I had ever seen before. All my senses became substantially more acute. I was becoming more sensitive to other people's energy, good and bad.

A new world was opening up, a world I knew nothing about. I began searching for someone who understood this new space. I asked David, Jean's friend who worked on my legs, if he could connect me with someone in the area who understood the world as I was seeing it. He did give me the name of one fellow, John. I told him only that I was seeing many eagles and that I was doing healing. He told me a great story about how he had acquired his land. He had flown over it in a light plane and he knew immediately that he had to have that land. Later he found out that it had belonged to Gabriel Dumont, a very wise Métis leader. He said nothing about the healing or the eagles. I realized he did not have the understanding or was not willing to share about the transformation I was going through, the new knowledge I was acquiring. I was concerned that I would be seen as insane. I knew what was happening and I just wanted to understand what it meant.

I knew I was not hallucinating, I understood that it was something I knew nothing about. All I wanted was an explanation, a clarity.

The healing became much stronger as time went by and visions, although few, were becoming much more vivid. Previously I had confidence in most everything. Now I knew so little.

Karen, a dear friend, told me about Lawrence Mackinaw, a Cree man who lived in the vicinity and also did healing. I asked her to call me whenever he came to town and I would meet them wherever, whenever. I also got his phone number and tried to call, but I was told he was either too busy or not home. It is not easy to establish contact with most Natives in Canada.

One afternoon a Native man appeared in the doorway of the lab where I was working. He was well dressed in a multicoloured wool jacket, blue jeans and very expensive cowboy boots. He was rather small in stature. I knew immediately it was him. He walked over to the bench where the other technician was working. When he asked for me, my heart started pounding. Now I would get to talk to him. How long I had waited for this moment! How long I had waited for answers to so many questions!

She brought him over and introduced him as Lawrence Mackinaw. We shook hands. The energy coming from him was so soft and kind and at the same time so powerful. I had never experienced anything like it. We just looked at each other until he said, "Your heart! Your heart!" I said nothing. I could not speak. After what seemed like an eternity we finally found our voices and exchanged phone numbers.

It was to be nearly a year before we had an opportunity to talk. Many things happened in our lives that year. There were so many deaths for both of us. Three of my friends died suddenly, I lost my brother to cancer, my father was killed in an automobile accident and my mother was very ill. It was a terrible time. That year he too lost five people he was close to, including his father and brother.

One day the phone rang and it was Lawrence. We made arrangements to meet for supper at a restaurant in the neighborhood. As I shared about the healing, the visions and the feelings I was struggling with, he would just nod in understanding and say "Mmm hmm" and "Yes." "It is good," he would say. He just understood everything. I could not believe it. Not once did he question the authenticity of what I said. From Lawrence I learned that the visions and the healing were so normal, so ordinary. That was my biggest relief. I was not insane. I knew it was real, but to find out it was ordinary was such a relief.

He shared a little about himself: about how he had gone to residential school and was grateful as that was where he learned to read and write. He told me how he hated the name Mackinaw. He did not want to be called a Scottish overcoat. He also told how his grandmother used to help all the white women deliver their babies when the settlers first came to Alberta. She learned a little English from them and always told him that the white people were people too, and not so different from their own people. She taught him not to discriminate.

As I drove home, tears began to flow—tears of gratefulness and relief. I had rarely cried after my resolution to stop the tears some twenty years before.

We did meet again on occasion, and shared more. The visions, the eagles, the healing, and the connection I felt with nature, all normal. That felt so good but was at the same time disturbing in a strange sort of way. If it was normal then why had I never heard of such things before?

In the meantime, Jack was becoming more difficult; it became very clear that our marriage was finished. I just needed him to go to work, as I had no desire to pay spousal support just because he was too lazy to work. Finally one day the opportunity came: his brother asked him to come and cook for him in the gold fields! It was so perfect as he loved to cook and he loved the gold fields. My intention was to send him separation papers after he had put enough time in to collect unemployment insurance so he would get a good start on his own.

That was not to be, as he came back in June instead of October as planned. When he came to the house I asked him what he was doing back so early. He went eyeball to eyeball with me and hollered, "Can't I even come home anymore?"

I just said, "No. This is no longer your home."

I told him I was going to work and he had twenty-four hours to clear out everything he wanted. I told him to empty the house if he wanted to. I would not be back until the next day.

When I did come back he had not taken anything, but at least he was gone.

Lawrence called the next day and told me Annie, his wife, had kicked him out and she had scattered all his clothes on the ground outside their house. He was very upset about it as he felt she had no right to throw his clothes out that way. He was thinking of leaving anyway, but the way it happened really hurt him.

Lawrence and I started spending more time together. We talked about everything from soup to nuts, but mostly about human nature and spirituality. He said we were all born the same, but many white people had forgotten *who* they *were*. They had put money and possessions ahead of all else. Money had become their God. In the process they forgot about their hearts. My first reaction was to defend my people, but I wanted to understand what he really meant by that, so I decided to say nothing until I learned more. When I thought about my ex-husband with his attitude I knew he had a point. I started to pay more attention, and I realized he was right.

Something else was happening to me that was so confusing my mind. There was sadness in my heart for the breakup of my marriage to Jack. I would often feel depressed but could not understand why, as I was the one who had made the decision to split. I was, for the most, happy to be out of the marriage. I certainly had no regrets about my decision, so why the depression? I actually got the answer to that one from a talk show. A woman was describing exactly the same experience as mine.

She was the one who broke up her marriage. She was so happy to be free and yet there was sadness in her heart. One day she was told to let go of the dream. She, as I, had married for life. We had a dream. It was shattered. The marriage was finished, and thankfully so, but the dream had to be mourned. Once I realized that it was mourning, I knew how to handle it; I was able to allow myself to go through it until I could put my heart at rest.

One day Lawrence and I decided to go to the Rainmaker Rodeo in St. Albert. I was to meet him in Edmonton. On the way I saw three black ravens and one white one all hopping around on the road. I told him about it and he became very quiet and said nothing. We drove on to St. Albert. That was the first time we went out in public together. Everyone welcomed him and they all came to talk to him. That was when I learned how popular he was in the horse racing circuit.

That night I thought about what the reaction would be when I faced people the next day at work. I knew what my people would say about me going out with an Indian: it would not go over well. I was a little afraid of the fallout because I was on town council, and this would not be politically acceptable.

To my surprise a Native woman came knocking on the x-ray room door the next morning and asked, "What do you want with him? He is a respected member of our community."

I knew my people would disapprove, but was not expecting it from his. After all, I was a respected member of *my* community.

Soon after, when I was down for coffee at work, I got a call that Annie, his ex, was on her way and she intended to kill me with an ice pick. My physiotherapist friend Ann told me to hide in her department. As I sat there shaking, I realized this was not going to work. I asked her to go and tell the administrator I needed to talk to her.

"You better go and get the police," said the administrator. I ran the two blocks from the hospital to the police station. My heart was pounding so hard—I was so afraid. It felt like I was running in slow motion. I kept thinking, "What if Annie catches me before I get to the police?"

When I explained to the RCMP officer about the phone call, he called the hospital and confirmed that Annie had been there, but had left. I went back to work, but it was hard to concentrate. I was shaken. It took all my strength just to hold the pipettes still and keep my hands from trembling as I transferred the blood samples for analysis.

The RCMP officer called me at the end of the day and I was told Annie was with them. She wanted to talk to me and the officer suggested I come to the station. I told him I had nothing to say to her and he told me she would talk to me one way or the other and perhaps it would be safer if they were present. He had a really good point, so I went up there. She kept asking what I wanted with Lawrence. I just said that he was my friend. She kept warning me to stay away from him. I said nothing, but I knew that would not happen.

The police officer told me that I was just looking for trouble getting mixed up with Indians. Then he told me I had better stay away from Lawrence. I left feeling I would not have any support or protection from the police should there be more trouble involving the Mackinaw family. That was the second time I felt let down by them.

When I got home there was a sign on my door that said 'Sleep lightly white squaw as this is going to be your last night.' It was from Jack, my ex. I called Lawrence and he said he would come and stay with me. I told him not to come as things were bad enough; if they caught us together it would be too dangerous for both of us. I assured him I would be okay. He came anyway. That night we stayed together in his camper.

The next day I went to the hospital administrator and asked for a leave of absence. "Both Lawrence's ex-wife and my ex-husband are out to kill me. I just need to get away until things settle down. My life is at risk!" I told her. "I am afraid that they might come to the hospital and cause trouble here."

"You made your bed. You lie in it," she replied.

She would not give me a leave of absence, so the only solution I could see was to quit my job. My very life was at stake. When the doctors found out I had left, they were disappointed as they would have given me a three-month sick leave, but by that time it was too late. I had resigned. I never thought to go to them, since I didn't think of myself as being sick.

Lawrence and I decided to leave Breton and give them all a cooling-off period. Ten years before when I was working in the little hospital in Cassiar, I was taken to a valley where there was a formation of an eagle embedded in the rocks of a volcanic cliff. I had told Lawrence about it and we decided to go and find it. We packed a tent and camping gear for the four-day drive to Telegraph Creek.

When he picked me up at the house, he said he had everything with him that was important to him. "My pipe is my life," he said, "and that I have." I knew nothing about a pipe. I did not know why it was important to him. I didn't want to show my ignorance, so that evening when he took it out, filled it, and prayed in Cree, I could do nothing but support him in his prayers. Praying was something new for me: I had just never bothered. I just thought about how little I really knew about him.

I did know I loved every moment I was with him. He was such a mystery. He too seemed to love being with me and was not afraid to tell me. Sometimes I would catch him looking at me and he would tell me how beautiful I was, and how happy he was that I was with him. I did not even know how to respond. I was so unaccustomed to compliments. It was difficult for me to believe that he actually meant what he said. As much as I enjoyed hearing all the compliments, I would wonder when everything was going to come to an end. Even his love-making was ever so gentle and considerate. He would always ask what I enjoyed. I had no idea since my only previous experience had been so much of nothing. I prepared myself for any outcome. I was not about to get caught in a loveless relationship again. Once was enough.

I was soon to discover that he also had a great sense of humour.

Along the way we stopped in a little old variety store along the side of the road west of Prince George, British Columbia. Inside, there was a steel pole right in the middle of the floor. Lawrence had very good cowboy boots on and he gave that pole such a hard kick it startled everyone in the store. Then he pretended he was blind and said very loudly,

"Where are you taking me, hon? You know I can't see." He kept up the pretence until we were out of sight.

Our next stop was at the Hazelton tourist bureau to get more information about the region. As I went to show him the brochure, he had turned his cap on an angle. He grabbed my hand and started acting spastic and grunting. There too he continued the charade until after we left. When he got into the truck he cracked up with laughter. "You should have seen the look on your face. It was so funny!" he howled with laughter.

There was nothing he would not do for a laugh. I did not know what to think. Everything had been so serious with all that had happened. This was a side of him I was just learning about.

A few miles out of Hazelton we stopped for tea and a little lunch in a treed area along the road. We went for a walk and stumbled upon a place where there were many totem poles. Some were rotting and falling down. I wondered why they were not being preserved. We later learned that that was the natural process in the life of a totem pole. Totems are unique to the west coast people and that was the first time we had seen any in natural surroundings. It was a very spiritual place. Lawrence said prayers in his language.

We continued north. As we drove further into the mountains, the air cleared of pollution as there is no industry and only a rare vehicle on the road. The stars at night twinkled more brightly. The moon shone more brilliantly in the night sky. In that silence we were consumed by the night. I suddenly realized how much noise we are exposed to all the time in the south where there is always noise of some kind night and day. Even in the wilderness areas we would hear the sound of the oil pumps, a motor vehicle or planes overhead. It is the same with light. It is ever so rare to experience total darkness. One evening when it was cloudy we had the adventure of being in absolute darkness. We had just extinguished the campfire and headed for bed. I could not see Lawrence, but knew he was by my side as I could feel his energy. As we entered the tent there was no visual barrier between us and our surroundings. We were one in total darkness and total stillness.

We stopped in at the village of Dease Lake as this would be our last chance to purchase supplies. There was a little trading post which sold a little of almost everything. The most remarkable was their collection of jade. There was everything from the smallest to the largest. The owner told us that the Chinese people came and mined the jade, which was nearby, and brought back the finished items we saw in the store. It really was quite remarkable.

When we left Dease Lake, heading for Telegraph Creek, the mountains became higher, the pavement ended and we found ourselves on a gravel road which became narrower and narrower. As we edged our way up one side of a mountain and down the other, I started to become a bit nervous. Some places were so narrow that if we met another vehicle one of us would have to back up to one of the pullouts which were located every couple of kilometers, and it was a sheer drop to the bottom of the mountain if we were to misjudge the road. Lawrence asked me to drive. He told me he had full confidence that I would get us there safely—after all I was more accustomed to mountain driving. After more than an hour we approached a place where I could pull off the road for a stop. I needed a break. When we got out of the truck we went for a little walk. We found ourselves overlooking a gigantic gorge of a volcanic mountain formation. The Stikine River was snaking its way through at the bottom. We suddenly realized that we were on top of a narrow ridge of old lava. We then looked down to the other side of the ridge and there was another gorge with the Tahltan River running through it. Even as we stood so far above, we could hear the sound of the running water as if we were next to the rivers. I wondered if that was because the air was so clear and crisp.

When we once again hit the road, approaching the fourth big valley, we came around a sharp bend and, suddenly, there it was: the gigantic eagle in the rock. The cliff was about 100 meters high and 150 meters across. The eagle was about 75 meters across at the wing span and about 40 meters high. You could see the outline because the rocks were slightly different in color. For sure it was a natural formation as it could not be approached by man. The river was too swift and the cliff rose straight up behind it. There was only wilderness for hundreds of miles behind it.

We drove to the bottom where the Stikine and the Tahltan rivers meet. We pitched our tent and prepared a meal over the fire, without either one of us saying a word. After supper we went for a walk. The sun was lowering in the sky and as we looked over on the other side of the valley we saw a bear, an owl and a buffalo in the rock formation. As we walked past, the buffalo looked at us, no matter which side of it we were on. On the second day a group of Native people came to dry and smoke their fish on racks. They too did not say much. I thought this was like being in a time warp which had stopped before the invention of technology. The silence was so complete in that valley.

We spent four days in total silence at the eagle rock canyon. I felt a powerful energy in that valley. We had no need to speak. After the four days, through hand motions he told me we had to pack up and leave. How I hated to leave, but Lawrence had to get back to work. He had, after all, left in a hurry and he had work that had to be tended to. As we started back I had a feeling that nothing was going to be the same again, that I had gone through some kind of transformation into a different space.

To share such a beautiful and spiritual place was a perfect gift. I was feeling rather sad at the thought of facing civilization again. Lawrence was, too. Suddenly he burst into tears. When I asked him what was wrong, he just shook his head without speaking. Once again he took out his pipe and smoked and prayed. Then we packed up and left.

As we headed down the highway a black bear came running out of the bush and onto the road in front of the truck. When it was close to the other side, it literally came to a screeching halt, with all four legs stopping the run. Lawrence stopped the truck and made eye contact with that bear for what seemed like a long time. At times he would just nod and say, "Mmm hmm." After they broke visual contact he said, "Hi hi," which means thank you in Cree. The bear leisurely went on his way into the forest. We slowly went our way as well.

"Everything will be okay," he said and we headed again down the highway. He was silent for a long time as if deep in thought. I wondered who this man was. Obviously prayer played a major role in his life as did humour and now a new aspect. I had so many questions. What was the real meaning of the pipe? How did he communicate with all that was around him? Once again I was reminded of my question I got from the eagle. How can I communicate? What about us? I knew I had discovered the true meaning of love. What about him? I felt I could not break his silence. The questions would have to wait until another time.

On the way home along Highway 37 we suddenly came across a blanket of red along the edge of the forest. We stopped to investigate. It turned out to be wild strawberries. Never had we seen anything like it. There were strawberries as far as we could see. All colours in nature become more vivid the further north you go. There is nothing that beats the taste of wild strawberries at the best time, and the ones from the north have a stronger and sweeter taste. We picked our fill and then some for jam. He was one fast berry picker. One more surprise.

We arrived back in Spruce Grove and went to meet two of Lawrence's friends. Joy and Ivan owned a restaurant and an acreage north of the city. He thought that might be a good place to stay until we knew how safe it was for us to come out in the open. We had been there for about three days when Lawrence's daughter Bea showed up. He was happy to see her, but she told him it was still not safe for him to go to Buck Lake. He was very happy to see at least one of his children, but sad that he could not see them all.

I had noticed that he had a big scar on his abdomen from breast bone to pubic bone. One night I asked him what that was from. He told me he had had a gall bladder operation many years before at the Camsell Hospital. When I told him I had never seen such a scar from a gall bladder operation he went silent. He didn't want to talk about it. I did bring it up a few times after that as I wanted to investigate further. What was really done in that hospital? I could not imagine why they would cut a person open in that manner. What else was done? Was there experimenting going on or was he opened up like that for teaching purposes? Surely not! But the scar was there.

"What's done is done," he said. "It will do no good to look into it." I was frustrated. Without his approval I could do nothing. I had seen many large scars on Native people before, but never thought to question it. Now I regret not looking into it.

One day, Lawrence was sent to a youth and Elders conference near Seabird Island, which is close to Maple Ridge. He asked me to come along. I did want to see my old best friend Jean who lived nearby. It was at her home I had first met David and had my first encounter with the eagle. We had been through much together over the twenty years of our friendship. My children called them Auntie Jean and Uncle Jim. Lawrence told me not to go, but as she was my best friend for so many years I could not stay away just because he told me to. I drove into their yard as I had done so many times before. I so admired the many flowers which we could not grow in the cold inland climate of Alberta.

As I walked toward the house I felt very nervous as that was the first time I had seen her after Jack and I split and I was not certain what her reaction would be. She said nothing when I entered, but their German shepherd dog, Heidi, greeted me happily. "You have gained a lot of weight, Heidi!" I said.

"So have you!" were the first words out of Jean's mouth. I knew then it was not going to be good. She had prepared a tray with cups and tea and she told me to follow her. She took me to a little guest house they had in the back of their place. As soon as we were seated by the little kitchen table, she asked me what I thought I was doing. "You had a good life with Jack! How could you do this?"

"I did not have a good life with Jack and that is all I am going to say about it as he is also your friend."

"You have to tell me more. I want to know why you left."

"He was always so very disrespectful to me when there was no one else around. He would not even walk beside me. He always made sure I was at least two steps behind. He always got angry when I spent any money. The last time was when I bought underwear for myself. He even went to our daughter and complained about that. You know he hasn't worked for years and yet he complains!"

"I think you are exaggerating," she said. "He's not that bad."

That had been my fear all along. Even if I did try to say anything against him it would sound trivial to others and I was afraid they would not believe me. Finally I came out with it. "Jean," I said, "he has threatened to kill me."

"He would never do that," she said. "Why have you never said anything before?" she asked.

"He was your best friend, too." I said, "so I didn't want to involve you in our issues."

At that point I knew it was time for me to leave. If she did not believe me, I had nothing more to say. I got up and walked out the door without saying anything more.

"Don't tell me where you are as I will tell him," were the last words out of her mouth as I got back in the truck. As I drove along the road going back to camp, I could hardly see as the tears kept welling up my eyes.

If my very best friend would reveal my presence after I told her Jack was trying to kill me, I was afraid to take a chance on anyone else. I was afraid to say anything as it hurt too much when I was not believed.

Lawrence went back to his work at the Indian Association and I applied for unemployment insurance. The insurance people gave me a hard time because I had not applied right away. I told them that due to the threats on my life I could not apply as I could not seek work, which was one of the requirements. At first they were not going to give it to me, but when I told them the police were involved, then they approved my application. That was a big relief as I was not ready to go work yet. I was still afraid of staying in one place.

We stayed with Joy and Ivan until fall, when it got too cold at night for tenting. One day we decided to go house-hunting. There was never any discussion about us staying together. It was just the most natural thing to do. I called about several places that were vacant. When we got there and they saw Lawrence was Native, the vacancies were suddenly filled. The first few times I thought nothing of it, but when one landlord told me he had no room for 'his kind,' I began to wonder about the others as well.

One day I spotted an ad for a farmhouse just outside Stony Plain. The price was right, and the location was good as it was in the country within driving distance of Edmonton, where Lawrence was working. This time I was determined we would not be refused. As always the place was taken when we got there, but this time the woman who owned it gave many details so I felt she was telling the truth. She did tell us her brother also had a place not far away and it too was available. We made arrangements to see that one as well and when the brother said there was someone else ahead of us, I asked him who. When he turned red in the face I knew there was no one.

This time I would not be denied just because Lawrence was Native. I told him, "You have not signed papers yet, we need a place immediately, yours is available and we will take it."

"Not so fast!" he said. "How are you going to pay the rent?"

"The same way we always have, with money, in cash." I said.

"Are you on welfare?" he asked. I was boiling inside. Never was I asked that before. We desperately wanted the place, so I kept my cool. Lawrence said it was okay, that we would find something else. My head started pounding at the thought of continually facing this kind of discrimination.

"I am writing you a cheque for the damage deposit right now," I said, "and we will move in next week and you will get the first month's rent at that time." I knew he was getting very nervous, but I did not pay attention. I simply took out my cheque book, wrote the cheque, and put it in his hand. I said, "Thank you very much!" and turned to leave.

I could feel Lawrence beside me. He was so accustomed to the discrimination that he was going to accept it. I would not.

"Just a minute!" our prospective landlord said.

I turned and smiled, "Where can I pick up the key?"

"I will meet you here," he replied meekly.

"You will not be sorry," I assured him as we left, and he was not. He would come snooping around off and on and we would invite him in for coffee. He admitted that he had never rented to Native people before and he was nervous about it.

"Have you ever known any Native people?" I asked.

"No," he confessed.

"You have missed a lot!" I told him. "They are actually great people to be with. You should broaden your world, you will learn much."

After he left, Lawrence said I should really not be so frank. "Why not?" I asked. "It's the truth and it is about time some of those white people got to know that what they hear on the radio and see on television is not the whole picture. Too many understand nothing about your beautiful traditional ways. It is about time some people open their eyes!"

That night as I lay by his side I started thinking about how my life had changed so quickly. I did not ask to fall in love with a medicine man, an Elder, but I did. I asked for answers and I got those and the love of my life as well. You never know what tomorrow will bring.

I knew nothing about Native people or the Native community, only what I had heard in the media, and that was obviously not what I saw. I understood nothing of Lawrence's status, both locally and internationally. I knew him only as a man. A beautiful man with a great sense of humour, a tremendous wisdom, and he was in love with me as I with him. I did not know the depth of abuse that was inflicted on the Native community in the past and today. I did not know they were jailed without trial for practicing their religion, or for leaving the reservation without permission. I knew nothing of the 'sweeps,' where social services came in and removed a large number of children from a community all at once. I knew nothing of them being forced by the police and priests to go to residential schools. I knew nothing about what it was like to be Native in Canada. I knew I was entering another world—a world of great wisdom, of anger, of dysfunctional families, and of the struggles to find a place in this modern world without losing their identity.

One day a Native woman told me that I just wanted someone from the Hobbema reservation because they had oil money. That I found funny. Lawrence told me how much he was making and I saw how much he was giving away and when I did the math I knew he did not have money. Every member of the Hobbema reservation was getting 500 dollars per month for oil royalties. Did they think I was after that?

It did not even affect me, as I was told I could not become a band member. All his oil money went to help his children and grandchildren. That is the way he was. He, like other traditional Native people, measured wealth by how much he could give away. Lawrence always drove a new truck and spent plenty on his cowboy boots. He loved paying for everyone's meals when we went to a restaurant and most of all he loved to buy me things. He was very wealthy in every way except money. He did not receive money from anyone else except the Indian Association of Alberta, where he worked, and from those people who came for help bringing gifts.

Some people also said I was after his power. His *power*? What did that mean? I had no idea. I had never heard that expression before. I knew he had some special status in his community, but I did not really understand what it was.

Chapter 8

First Hunt

One day Lawrence said it was time to go and get some meat. Treaty Indians, Native persons registered under the Indian Act, have the right to hunt year round on crown land. There is much resentment from many non-treaty hunters. They often complain about the game being depleted by excessive hunting. Statistics do not bear that out. Numbers are sustainable in the wilderness areas. Hunting keeps the game from overpopulating and starving due to limited food supply.

First Lawrence had to buy a rifle as he had left all his guns behind when he left his home. Every firearm sold in Canada had to be recorded. He also had to have a firearms acquisition certificate (FAC), so there was also screening in place to keep firearms out of the hands of criminals. We did get his rifle.

I asked him how long he planned on being out in the bush. He looked at me as if I was not too bright. "For as long as it takes to get our meat, of course," he said.

I had hunted often many years ago as that was our basic source of meat when I grew up and during the first years of my first marriage. We would often go home empty-handed. I just could not imagine going out and knowing for certain we would get our meat.

A few days later, before sunrise, we drove west to the wilderness area where there was plenty of game. Although it is a large wilderness area, heavily treed, there were many narrow gravel roads snaking their way through the dense forest. The oil companies had put up many pumps and they all had to be serviced. Therefore it was easy to get around as long as you had a truck with a four-wheel drive to get you through the roughest areas and the mud holes that often accumulated after a rain. When we arrived at the edge of the forest Lawrence asked me to drive as he wanted to be prepared in case we saw game.

Soon, through the early morning dawn, we saw a doe with three calves. He said, "We must pay our respect to a Mom, especially when she has that many little ones." He just thanked her and allowed them to go on their way. The young would have been okay on their own, as it was late in the year and they were big. Still it was not right.

That was the only game we saw that morning. We did encounter a coyote when he crossed the road in front of us. By this time it was close to lunch time and so we decided to stop in a serene little clearing to eat our lunch and drink our tea. "There is no use trying to find game right now anyway," Lawrence said. "A coyote just crossed our path."

We put out a blanket and stretched out together. As I lay beside Lawrence watching the birds that flew above us, I once again wondered at the turn my life had taken. How wonderful it felt lying next to him in the stillness of the wilderness. I felt so at peace. Soon we dozed off. The next thing I knew Lawrence said it was time to go. I felt a little sad that the magic of the stillness was gone, but we did come to get meat and we had to get on with it.

That evening we came around a turn of the wilderness trail we were travelling, on our way to an area even deeper in the forest. Suddenly right in front of us was a nice big female moose feeding in an opening in the forest. Lawrence got out of the truck and shot her. As we watched, she slowly headed for the bush. He got back in the truck and told me to drive away.

"Why are you leaving?" I asked.

"She has to have the dignity to die without us standing and staring at her. We will be back."

We left and sat some distance away and had a cup of tea before returning. Lawrence gave a prayer of thanks. As we approached the clearing, I turned the wheel sharply and headed across the clearing toward the bush. The grass was as tall as the hood on the truck and I was very nervous about hitting something I could not see. Suddenly Lawrence shouted,

"Watch out!" I thought there was something ahead of us, so I yanked the wheel to the left, right into the water hole he was telling me to watch out for.

We were stuck. Good and proper. We went looking for the moose and found her and took care of what needed to be done including prayers of thanks to her for giving up her life so we could eat. All the time Lawrence was very gentle as he prepared her. He took one step at a time. Not once did he get frustrated. I could not do much as I was not familiar with gutting. My brother always did that on his own.

Then we went back to try to free the truck from the mud. It was stuck solid. Lawrence cut small trees and built a little bridge to climb up on. It still wasn't budging. By this time it was getting dark and so we decided to stay the night and look after the meat and the truck in the morning. I was concerned about him as I was not sure we had enough food. I was really regretting not taking more along. I should have known better. I always had in the past. As we settled the best we could in the cab of the truck, I thought about how angry my father would have been and how miserable Jack would have been in the same situation. They never would have given me a moment's peace. Not Lawrence. He was incredible.

The next morning we got out of the truck to assess our situation. He asked me to start rocking the truck to see if we couldn't walk it out. I did. Suddenly he started to laugh. I could not believe it. What could possibly be so funny? We were stuck, we had meat to prepare, we were hungry, stiff and tired as we had gotten very little sleep, and he was laughing. "The truck is not in four-wheel drive!" he said through his laughter. How I loved him at that moment. He just thought it was funny. Then I too started to laugh. I got back in the truck, put it in four-wheel drive and eased it out of the mud. Just like that.

We went to get the moose, but by that time we were both getting weaker. We drank some tea from the thermos and ate some of the crackers I had along. I suggested we go home and get some warm food and rest and return. Just then we heard wolves nearby and Lawrence just shook his head from side to side. He started running a fever and coughing. I was afraid he was getting pneumonia. He was not about to give up. That was obvious. We spent almost all day skinning, and cutting and loading. I was concerned whether he was going to make it. His fever was rising and he was getting weaker as the day wore on, but he was not going to budge until we were finished. All the time he continued to be patient. A few times tears would come to my eyes. The respect he displayed for both the animal he had taken and for me filled my heart. He was not about to leave until he could take the meat with him. Over and over he thanked the animal for giving its life for us. He would not even stop and eat. When I asked him to, he just shook his head. I was getting worried about his blood sugar levels as well, with so little food.

An eagle kept circling above our heads. This time I had someone with whom I could share. "Don't worry," he said. "We are looked after."

Totally exhausted, we were finally finished by late afternoon. Suddenly I realized I had no idea which way to go to get out. Even after all that had happened he still teased me about not being able to find my way. He had to stay awake long enough to guide me back out to the main road toward home. As soon as he knew I was okay, he went to sleep. We arrived home at seven that evening and headed straight for bed. The next morning I awoke to his laughter once again. He just found it so funny that we had not put the truck in four-wheel drive.

That was not only our first of many hunting trips, but it was also the first time I saw how he reacted in crisis. My love grew deeper that day. He always loved to tell that story. It became one for the campfires.

Chapter 9

First Ceremonies

One evening a man came to our door and called Lawrence outside. After a brief conversation he returned and told me that he had been given tobacco and that he had to go to his friend Gary's place for a ceremony and he would like me to join him.

"Can you tell me why he gave you tobacco?" I asked.

"Tobacco is a very sacred plant and we have always passed tobacco when we are requested to do prayers or ceremonies. It is our custom."

I was both nervous and pleased that he had asked. I really was not enthusiastic about spending time with other people. I was not at all sure how they would react to me. I would much sooner be alone with him.

It was late afternoon when we arrived. The house was situated close to Edmonton on a farm. It was old, warmed by an old oil heater and had a linoleum floor. The walls were panel board. The furniture was also old, but was not lacking anything. Outside there was a bonfire burning brightly. Several women were cooking food in the kitchen. Lawrence introduced me to everyone and they were all very cordial. We were invited to sit down on the couch in the living room. There was another couple who were introduced as Richard Rain and his wife Margaret. Both had long black hair. Hers was loose and his braided. There were also two other white people there named Carol and David. At least I was not the only white person present.

Richard got up and went outside and soon came back with a frying pan filled with hot coals from the fire. He put some herbs on top of the coals and soon the room was filled with the pungent odour of the smudge. I was trying to identify the plant used but could not. It was not familiar to me. There was something about it that made me feel lighter, but not as a drug would. More like a clearing of heaviness. I was very nervous as this was the first time I was with Lawrence's people at a ceremony. Everyone was telling funny stories, mainly about silly things they or their families had done at one time or another. These people sure do know how to laugh at themselves, I thought. The whole atmosphere was light and everyone was having fun.

A couple of the men spread a tarp on the floor in the living room. As soon as the women finished cooking, Richard and the young men present brought the food into the living room and put it on the tarp. Gary came to Lawrence with tobacco and said, "Ka Ka Koo, in the name of the Creator, would you please pray for us today?"

Lawrence took the tobacco and went and sat down on a cushion which they had set out on the floor for him. One of the women, Madge, sat down on his left and I was told to sit next to her on the floor. Everyone sat down in a circle, the women on one side and the men the other. Richard filled the pipe. As he did so he prayed and held the tobacco in the six different directions before putting it in the bowl.

Immediately all were very quiet and Lawrence picked up the pipe and began talking in his language. Then he started to pray. A powerful energy filled the room. The only sound was his voice as he was praying. After he was done, Richard took the pipe and passed it to the men one by one. The pipe was passed four times all in a clockwise direction. He too turned only clockwise. As I watched I realized there was very strict protocol attached to this ceremony. Everyone had a role.

After they were finished smoking, the food was prayed over. The men began passing it around to everyone. There was soup, bannock and fish as well as berries and tea. After they were done and we had eaten and drunk our fill, Lawrence once more picked up the pipe and prayed. Then he took the pipe apart and everyone got up.

I asked him why they had called him Ka Ka Koo: he told me that was his traditional name and it meant Raven. Then I remembered the white raven I had seen some months before. Suddenly I got goose bumps all over my body. I could say nothing. Others too had animal and bird and other nature names.

Again the room filled with chatter and laughter. When it was time for us to go, everyone came and shook hands with us and said good-bye. I was relieved, as I did not think I had made a fool of myself and everyone had been very gracious to me.

That was the first time of many that I sat in a sacred circle and smoked the sacred pipe. That was the first time I really felt the sacredness of their ceremonies.

What I have shared about this ceremony is only the highlights, so I ask that no one uses it as a guide. That would be bastardizing the ceremony as there is much more detail which I cannot write about. Only the keepers of the ceremonies can share more. They are the source. There is very strict protocol and much training surrounding the passing on of the ceremonies. First one must work as a helper, then when the pipe carrier feels one has learned enough to handle his own pipe, he or she will be taught how to handle the pipe and about the responsibility of living a good, clean life. When the teacher feels he can take on the responsibility of caring for the people and the pipe, then and only then will one be qualified to handle the pipe alone. That is the way I was taught.

The second time we went to a ceremony together was at the jail in Drumheller. The inmates were putting up a mini powwow which is dancing and drumming and singing in the old traditional way. There was a group of young lads sitting around a large drum. They did all the drumming and singing. Some people were dressed in regalia decorated in beautiful beadwork, feathers and jingles. All were very colorful. The sound of the drums and the jingles and the dancers' feet on the floor touched my heart. Little did I know how small it was in comparison to the powwows on the outside which may feature up to seven hundred dancers and a dozen or more drum groups.

That was the first time I heard the word 'Elder." When it was time for lunch, they said, "Elders first!" I was not sure I liked that at the age of forty-one!

Gary, the person chosen to be Lawrence's helper, explained to everyone how the Elders were so spiritually connected and told them that if they ever needed help, the Elders would always be there for them.

At the end of the day everyone came and shook hands and thanked us for coming. As they filed past I wondered what had gone so terribly wrong in their lives that they ended up here. They were all so kind and respectful to us.

Chapter 10

California Scientists

Lawrence came home one evening and told me he was invited to go to California and I could go with him. It was a group of scientists from there who were paying our fare and expenses. They had found some mysterious writing on some rocks which had been hidden with overgrowth for many years. They were wondering if it was Cree syllabics and if he would be able to interpret them. There were four of us that flew down: Buffy and Carol from the Erminskin band and Raven and me. We were hosted in a very nice hotel in Redding, California. Everything, including meals, was taken care of; Buffy had arranged it all.

Early the first morning we were picked up in a taxi and taken to a building some distance away. We were met by several scientists, who welcomed us to their meeting and expressed their appreciation for our attendance. There were also two other Elders there from the area: an old gentleman whose name I do not recall, and Flora Jones, a little woman Elder from the Wintu tribe. After introductions, the scientists explained how they had discovered this writing in the rock. They thought it must be a tribal language, but had no idea which tribe and so they were hoping the Elders could shed some light on it. They explained at great and tedious length what they assumed about the find. Finally they stopped and asked each Elder to say something in their own language. Lawrence and Flora, the Wintu Elder, did not say much, and the man totally refused to speak at all. I found that a little strange, but said nothing.

Arrangements were made to take a cab out to the site the next day. They told us it would take most of a day, so there was no use starting out now. We were served a nice lunch and sent back to the hotel. That afternoon we went for a walk. Two local Native women came to visit Buffy and Carol. That evening we all went out for dinner together. Lawrence turned the menu upside down. When the waitress came he said very loudly, "Hon, you know I can't read. You have to read it to me." From that moment on, that waitress would ask *me* everything instead of him. When she returned and asked me what he wanted to drink, everyone cracked right up. "He said he could not read," Carol giggled, "he did not say he was deaf!" Still she would not address him and we all laughed every time she asked me instead of him. She never did catch on to the fact that she was the brunt of the joke. "The lights are on, but no one is home!" Buffy kept saying.

The next day we were once again picked up in a taxi, and we four Canadians, Flora, the Wintu Indian, four scientists and some photographers headed out into the country. The old man did not show up.

The scientists led the way to the rocks. Someone had cleared away a lot of overgrowth, exposing various designs and what appeared to be some kind of writing. Lawrence said nothing. Neither did Flora. The scientists did a lot of talking about their guesses.

I asked Lawrence if it was all right to take pictures and he said to go ahead. "If you are not meant to have them, they will not show up anyway," he said, so I took some. The photographers also took many pictures with their fancy equipment. At the end of the day they volunteered to take my pictures and develop them all at once. Their pictures were blurry. Mine were very clear.

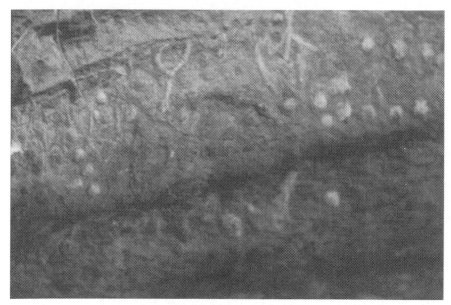

Writings on rocks

At one point we came across what I can best describe as bowl-like indentations in the rocks. Some were as big as two feet across. One of the scientists said, "We think these were used for ceremonial purposes by the early Native Americans. We think they have something to do with young girls in their menstruation time." I was so embarrassed for the scientists. They know nothing, I thought. Never would that type of ceremony be performed with the rocks. To top it off, there were also some indentations which resembled a deer's hoof prints. "We think these were made by deer," one scientist said. I just wondered how long they thought the deer had stood on one foot in order to make an indentation in the rock. I did not know what to say, so I said nothing. I was just embarrassed.

Flora Jones asked if she could come and see us that evening. She asked Lawrence if he knew what the writing on the rocks meant. He said he did not, but they agreed they were made by the little people, and they were predictions for the future. They did not know who had the gift to read the writing, but knew one day someone would come forward to decipher the meaning. She then invited us to join her for a ceremony on top of a mountain the next day to honor the rocks now that they had been exposed after many years of being covered.

After we were back in the room, I asked Lawrence why he did not say anything to the scientists. "You cannot tell anyone anything when they know it all, now can you?"

We made arrangements to meet at Flora's home. She lived with her son out in the country in a little old house. When we got there we met a nice young doctor who would also be joining us. We were to ride with him in his Jeep. Six vehicles started out from her place. Flora drove the biggest Cadillac I had ever seen. It was about thirty years old. Someone had gifted it to her in return for her help. As she was less than five feet tall, you could barely see her behind the wheel.

As we drove to the base of mountain, our doctor companion told us that he was learning all about traditional medicine from her and he in exchange was providing medical care in the western way for her. They had known each other for about two years and had become very close. He explained that we would be stopping at a stream partway up the mountain. We would have to cleanse and pray at the stream if we were to proceed to the top of the mountain where the ceremonies were to be held. He told us that many people would not be able to go past that stream. He had seen it happen before.

Soon we ran out of pavement and continued on a narrow gravel mountain road. The trees were very old and very tall. In places they formed an arch over the road. With the sun shining through the treetops, it seemed a magical place. More vehicles had joined our procession. About a half hour's drive along this road we arrived at the stream. As the pure clear water cascaded down over the rocks just above our heads, it formed a slender waterfall splashing blankets of moss which covered the dark colored rocks on either side. Flora got out and was offering prayers as one by one we pulled into the small clearing and got out of our vehicles. She asked everyone to wash in the water and say prayers before proceeding. She motioned each one in turn to approach. Not a word was spoken as she prayed silently with each person as they came forward and washed in the pure mountain water. The silence was broken only by the sound of the water and the birds. It was magical indeed.

When it was time to continue up the mountain, I looked back and there was only one vehicle behind us. Flora and her family went first. She was driving so fast we could hardly keep up to her. The road was very steep. It was gravel and all we could see was a cloud of dust from the big old Cadillac ahead of us. We wound our way around and up the big mountain. As we rounded a turn in the road near the top, we were forced to stop as there had been a rock slide which totally covered the road. Luckily the rocks were not too big and we were able to remove enough to get through. The path we cleared was still on what I felt was a dangerous slant and I was afraid we would trigger another slide or roll off the mountain. As I looked down, all I could see was the side of the mountain and the valley below. I could not see any road at all. The only reason I could persuade myself to stay in the Jeep was because we were going to a ceremony and I had to trust we were looked after, but my heart was beating so hard that I was worried the others would hear it.

The car behind us decided it was too risky, so the only ones to make it to the top were Flora, her family, the doctor, Lawrence and me. We stopped in a small clearing surrounded by stunted trees. The first thing the men did was dig a hole and build a toilet. The women put out food for a feast. Flora asked Lawrence and me to come with her for a walk. We walked a short distance through the bush to the edge of the mountain where we overlooked a cliff of sheer rock.

In every direction there were mountains and valleys. Every valley was lush with trees. The tops of the mountains were mostly rock with only sparse growth. We could not see any roads anywhere. It was pure wilderness.

Flora pointed out a natural rock formation of an elephant. That took my breath away as elephants had a special place in my heart. They had occasionally appeared as a vision. On the other side of the mountain was a rock pillar which was flat on the top. Flora asked Lawrence if he saw the young girl standing on the top. He nodded and she told us, "She always comes when we have ceremonies here on the mountain."

We went back to join the others. Flora smoked her pipe and prayed for all of us. There were songs and prayers of thanks for the food we were about to eat. When the meal was finished, everything was taken down and put away. As I turned to leave, I thought how, as soon as the trampled grass righted itself, no one would know anyone had been here. We started back down in silence. I refused to even think about the rockslide. It was too scary. We all made it safely.

The next day we went back to Flora's place for tea and she shared with us how she had been fighting Washington over the use of Shasta Mountain. "Our people came from that mountain and it is not right to build a ski run there. It is our sacred place. I go there every August for ceremonies. Many people come every year as everyone is welcome. I lost the fight with Washington and they built the ski lifts anyway. Shortly before they were to open the resort, I took out my pipe and asked the spirits to do something to stop the people from skiing down our mountain. That night the mountain shook itself and the lifts fell like matchsticks."

The following day we flew back to Canada, but I will never forget the little Wintu woman from Redding, California.

Chapter 11

First Time on the Reservation

One day a young man came to the house and offered Lawrence tobacco to do a ceremony at the Alexis reservation. Alexis is located ninety kilometers north west of the city of Edmonton on the shores of Lac St. Anne. Back in the days before borders a group of people from the Lakota Sioux nation had wandered to the area following the vision of an Elder. When the European Canadians made borders and designated land for the Native people, the Lakota Sioux group was camped at the present site of the reservation and they were not allowed to leave. That was how the Sioux got trapped in Cree country.

I had never been on a reservation before and I was nervous about the venture.

Lawrence's daughter, Beryl, was visiting but she would not come with us. She did send her 6-year-old daughter Caroline. She packed us each a bag containing empty containers with lids, a dishtowel, a spoon and a cup. This was my first time on a reservation and I realized I knew nothing about their ways. It felt like I was going to a foreign country where I knew nothing about their codes of behavior. When I asked Lawrence what was going to happen, he said, "You'll see." When I asked him what I was supposed to do, he said, "Be yourself!" When I asked him what I should wear, he said, "Anything." All my prodding got nothing more.

The three of us got in the truck and drove west toward the reservation. My apprehension grew with every kilometer. Five minutes away from the reservation we stopped for a coffee. Then he told me that women sat on one side and men on the other. "Why?" I asked defiantly. "Out of respect for the women." was his reply. I couldn't argue that. Then he told me that he would be up front and I could not go up there at all. I asked him why he didn't tell me that before we left and he just smiled.

We continued a short drive down the small paved highway and suddenly he turned onto a gravel road. "This is the reservation and this is a 'rez' road," he said. I turned and looked at him as I was not sure if it was supposed to be a joke. He just looked at me and smiled back. Trees lined both sides of the road, with an occasional house in a clearing. Some were in a terrible state of disrepair while others were well kept with the lawns neatly cut. I estimated most were built in the sixties. Occasionally there was an older, smaller home. There were no flowers or vegetable gardens that I could see. I made a mental note to ask about that another time as Lawrence had become very quiet and I did not want to interrupt him just then.

It was dusk as we turned into a clearing where there was one large teepee-like structure, which took seven teepees to cover. There were about twenty vehicles parked neatly in a row near the entrance of the clearing. We parked at the end closest to the exit. As soon as we stepped out of the truck, a young man called Lawrence, and he disappeared under the canvas. There I stood with Caroline who kept saying, "Kokum, I want to go home! Kokum, I want to go home!" (Kokum is grandmother in Cree.) "I want to go home too," I said, "but we have to wait for mushum (grandfather)." As I stood there waiting, it became evident that he was not going to emerge. I decided I needed to stop and evaluate my options. Young men were walking around carrying big sticks with feathers tied to them. I wondered what the purpose of those sticks was. All I could think about was that they did not want me at their ceremonies because I was white. I stood there wondering if they were going to send me packing.

A group of women were sitting on blankets around a nice big fire. The air was filled with the pungent smell of smoke. When I summed it up, I realized I had three choices: one—get back in the truck and wait; two—get back in the truck and leave, but then I would not know when to return, so I quickly ruled that out, as tempting as it was. The third was to take my chances and walk over to the fire. As I knew I would stay with Lawrence, and as I have a hard time with indecision, I decided perhaps the best bet was to try the fire and the women. At least if they were going to kick me out it might as well be sooner rather than later. As I approached, my knees were shaking, my heart was pounding and I was afraid. Caroline was close on my heels as she again asked to go home. I took her hand and kept walking. As I approached the group of women I looked them over briefly, picked out the friendliest-looking face, put out my hand and said, "Hi! My name is Rita." Then I held my breath and waited. She took my hand and said, "Sit down, sit down!" What a relief! I said nothing and just listened to the women chatting and laughing. "Did you bring something to sit on and dishes?" she asked. I nodded and Caroline offered to go to the truck and get them.

Soon a man came out and shouted something in his language and everyone picked up their bags and blankets and started toward the structure. When that woman moved, so did I. I followed her every move, let me tell you! As we entered, the men all went to the right and the women to the left. Lawrence was chatting with some people up front and gave me but a brief glance as I came in. There was a lot of food set out on tarps. There were pails of soup, boxes of bannock, fruit, tea, pop and numerous other foods. A fire burned brightly in the middle.

Suddenly, everyone became very quiet as the ceremonies began. Lawrence was leading the prayers, but others were also praying all at the same time. By this time it was pitch dark outside and the only light inside was from the fire. As I looked across at the men, the light and shadow danced together on their faces. I became acutely aware that I was the only white person there. Lawrence was obviously a spiritual leader amongst his people. So much mystery had entered my life. Everything I did not understand I called a mystery. This man that I had fallen in love with was an integral part of that mystery. All I could do was watch and learn.

The men's and women's pipes were in turn passed. I watched every move of the woman next to me; after she smoked the pipe and passed it to me, I smoked too. I was just hoping I did everything right. I was so nervous. After the pipe had been passed to each person four times and was once again resting in front of the Elders, the young men got up and began serving the food. The woman beside me put her dishcloth on the ground and set her dishes out to be filled. So did I. The young men filed by one after the other, first serving soup, then bannock, then tea and finally fruit, cake and candies. Soon I had so much food piled up in front of me that I felt sick because I knew I could never eat it all. When all the prayers and ceremony were completed, Lawrence announced, "Mitsuk!" which means 'Eat!' Everyone did and after they had their fill they packed up the remainder in their bags with their dishes. I let out a deep sigh of relief. One major problem solved, as it was impossible to eat it all and I did not want to offend anyone. Again there were more ceremonies. The woman I was shadowing asked me what Lawrence was saying. I told her I didn't know. That was the first time I realized there was more than one language, more than one tribe in the region. I was really embarrassed about my ignorance.

Soon the drumming began and people started dancing. Caroline kept tugging at my arm and begging, "Kokum, I want to dance! Kokum, I want to dance!" The woman I was following was not dancing and neither was I. Then she nudged me and said, "Go! It is good to dance." I thought my best bet was to oblige. I was getting embarrassed as Caroline was so insistent. As it turned out that was the best thing I could have done.

Everyone smiled at me and appeared happy that I danced with them. Around midnight the drumming and dancing stopped. The pipes were prayed with by the Elders and passed to the people once again and then the remainder of the food was passed. Then four kinds of berries were shared around. Each person took a spoonful and passed it on. When all had been eaten, everyone stood up and each went to the Elders and shook hands and thanked them for their prayers. Then all began shaking hands with one another. Soon they all left through the opening in the structure and I could hear each vehicle starting up and driving off. The sound of the motors seemed unusually loud, as if it were an intrusion on the night. Soon we too headed for the truck.

As we drove away, Lawrence told me he was so happy and proud of me that I had danced with his people. I just smiled quietly.

Chapter 12

New Knowledge, New Frustrations

As time went by Lawrence and I grew closer and closer. We became one. We were both very individual, both very different, both very strong, but both an independent part of one.

Often we would lie together on our bed and say nothing. Just enjoy the quiet of the moment. Just be, and be together. I was accustomed to always doing things or talking about something. This just being quiet was new and different.

Sometimes I would lie and reflect about my past and wonder at the changes in my life and why it all happened. It was a mystery for me. A whole new life had opened up since I started paying attention to the visions and the healing, since I allowed my world to unfold in a whole new way. Sometimes it felt like everything was out of my control, but then I would remind myself that I still had the final say over my life and whatever happened was my choice.

One day Lawrence told me that I used to play with the little people in Denmark. Some people may call them gnomes or in Danish 'nisser'. Then he drew a picture of the place. It was on Stensgård on Fyn. I remembered the place from my childhood. He drew a picture of the house where we lived, the field that I used to cross and the stone fence that I climbed over to get to the playground of my little friends. Never in all these years had I thought about them. It never occurred to me that they were real. I always thought they were a dream or a figment of my imagination. This drawing was too much for me. I did not know what to say.

"You and I have been together for many years. I have been searching for you for a long time," he said. "The Elders used to tell me that one day I would be with a white woman. For some years I thought it was someone else, but it is *you*."

I did not like him saying that. For me it implied that I had no control over my life. I told him so and he explained that we are always in control. We were given free will and the final decisions rest with each individual. "You do have a choice whether you will stay with me or not. You are given opportunities and then it is up to you whether to accept or not. You are given the guidance and you can choose to follow or not. You will however only fulfill your life mission to the fullest only if you listen and act as you are guided."

Life was much simpler before I was exposed to this new world of wisdom and spiritual awareness . . . much simpler when I thought I knew it all, had plans I knew how to fulfill and had the knowledge and drive to do so.

"How do you know all these things?" I asked.

"Many years ago when I was but a small lad, my parents would bring me to the Elders, especially to my grandmother who was my primary teacher, and I would have to sit with them. If I fell asleep when my grandmother was talking she would poke me with her cane. I had to pay attention and learn," he said. "My formal education with the Elders began when I was only four years old. My grandmother told me that one day I would speak in front of many people and I had much to learn. The education by the Elders was interrupted when I went to residential school at age eleven. All Native children were forced to go to a residential school where they were to learn to assimilate into the foreign society of the people who came to their land. My grandmother told my mother that I must learn to read and write in the white man's way as I would also need that knowledge in the future. I went to school and finished grade eight in six years. That was as much education as we were allowed."

I had many questions for Lawrence, but he would only tell me ever such a little bit. "If you want to learn more about spiritual things, you know what to do." I did not, but did not want to admit it.

Time and again Lawrence would tell me to be patient. The teachings would come. I wanted them *now*. I was willing to do whatever was necessary, but the only resources I had were the Elders. Yet I felt too inadequate and insecure to ask them anything. I could only listen and hope to learn. What can you say in the presence of the masters when you know so little?

One day a white man came to our home and he started to ask Lawrence many questions.

Lawrence said to him, "You white people want to know all about our ways and yet you do not even know how to ask. There is protocol you have to follow. I cannot speak to you of spiritual things if you do not bring tobacco. It is the key that opens the door to that knowledge. That is the way I was taught."

Suddenly the light went on. I had to present him with tobacco. He was my husband, so I thought he would just tell me. I hadn't even thought about giving him tobacco. The very next day I purchased a package of tobacco. That evening I presented it to him. I felt so nervous and close to tears, I asked, "Will you help me to learn more about spirituality and all the things you know?"

There! It was out! I thought he would be happy that I had presented him with tobacco.

"What exactly do you want to learn?" he asked. I did not have a specific question. There was so much to explore—where could I start? "I will take the tobacco this time," he said, "but only when you have a specific clear question can I give you an answer. Until you know what you are asking for, I cannot give you an answer." That was painful to hear. I did not know the questions. I knew nothing of that world. How could I ever learn?

My thirst for the knowledge was enormous. Not knowing and not understanding would almost drive me insane at times. Sometimes I would even long for the days when I had been unaware of the spiritual knowledge. Life was much less complicated then.

There really was nothing I could do but be patient. That was probably one of the most difficult lessons I have ever learned.

Chapter 13

Elder's Wisdom

More and more the Elders came to our home for ceremonies, for the latest news from their communities and to exchange medicines. There was much discussion about world philosophy and predictions for the future. For the first time I heard about the up-coming birth of the white buffalo calf. They shared the prophecy that four days after the birth the sire would die. They also said that the buffalo would change to all the colours of the people of the world.

When on August 20th, 1994, the white buffalo calf was born on the Heider ranch in Janesville, Wisconsin, I was surprised that it was born to a white man. When I asked Lawrence why she would be born to a white man when it was a native prophecy, he said he was happy she was, because if it had been born to any particular tribe they would think they were better and especially blessed. This way it belonged to all people. The Heiders named the buffalo 'Miracle.' They opened the ranch to all visitors free of charge. They set aside an area to facilitate the Native North American ceremonies. All the prophecies I had heard just a few years before did come true. The sire did die four days after Miracle was born and she did turn all the colours of the people around the world.

The Elders talked about how the time was coming near when the big shift of the 'grandfathers' would happen. That is the changing of places of the north and the south poles. They knew it had happened before and it would happen again.

They knew about a great flood in the distant past which cleansed the earth. If mankind did not show more respect it would only be a matter of time before a major cleansing would once again be necessary. If that should happen, only a small percentage of the current population would survive.

They talked about how there were wampum belts made hundreds of years ago which predicted the future. Wampum belts are made of channeled whelk shells from the North Atlantic. They were used for many purposes, from betrothal agreements to treaty agreements and celebrations of all types. They had predicted many of our modern inventions, including cars and planes. Only a few people have been gifted to read and interpret these belts. The reading is very sacred and is done with ceremony and prayers. We were to have gone to a reading, but the man who was planning to do it died. So it was never to be.

They talked about how it was predicted that when the eagle landed on the moon it would be a sign that the time for the cleansing of the earth was drawing near. When the first man landed on the moon, his first words were "The Eagle has landed."

As they sat at my kitchen table, I marveled at their wisdom and worldliness. For the first seven years I was silent. It was my time to learn. They had so much knowledge from nature and of how we are all interconnected; they had an understanding of human nature and of how we actually function in a natural way. Sometimes they would sob out loud, especially when they prayed. Sometimes they would laugh until the tears rolled down their faces. Never had I known anyone with such raw emotion, nor with such a forgiving spirit. They had no thought of revenge: they said it was not their place to judge. That was up to the Creator. They had no thought of punishment; since they knew there was a reason why a person would cause disharmony, their thoughts would go to a teaching which would restore harmony.

True understanding is not only from the head. That part is not difficult. Bringing it from the head to the heart is something else.

Lawrence often said, "From the head to the heart is the longest journey you will ever take." Even *that,* I could not fully understand. I had to find a way to deal with all that knowledge and wisdom which was new to me. There was so much I wanted to understand, but could not. I started to carry an imaginary bag and I would just put things in there until one day the understanding would come. That worked very well for me. I did not need to say I believed in something I did not understand. Nor did I need to say I did not believe. I knew that the Elders would not say these things were they not true. I was satisfied with that solution. It worked for me until one day we were visiting with my son Rocky.

Lawrence told him how many animals lived underground. They were not extinct at all and one day they would return. "Mom, you really don't believe all that do you?" That was a tough one because if I said yes, I would need to back up my answer scientifically, and I could not. If I said no, it would be denying what I was taught. Just because there is no *scientific* proof, does not mean it is not real. Many things cannot be scientifically proven, but we believe in their existence: things like love, hope, spirit, life-after-death. Even life itself cannot be either produced or reproduced scientifically. It does not 'fit' into the limited parameters of science.

The Elders too had questions, especially about their children. It never made any sense why social services thought their children were better off in our white society than with their parents. Native people were accustomed to living with many people and many generations together. They could not understand why anyone could possibly think the children were better off isolated in a room of their own. That would be much too lonely for a child. When they asked me if I could give them an answer, all I could say was that some people believe it is better for a child to have their own space. Each time they would shake their heads. That they could not understand.

The Elders spoke about the children: how they are the closest to the Creator and how we can learn much from them. They shared with me how some children have always had a special connection, a unique wisdom. They call these children 'grandfathers' and 'grandmothers.'

The Elders knew about these special children. The sack in which they lived in their mother's womb was different. When the women gave birth, the midwives and those who attended recognized them. These children were often taken from the parents and raised by the grandparents and the wise people within the tribe, as they needed special training in the ways and the knowledge of spirituality—training too critical to be left to the parents, who had not walked this earth long enough to have the wisdom required. There have always been 'special' children. We continue to hear about them in every society.

These children never fit very well into the western society we have created. They are extremely sensitive to everything around them and therefore know things that others do not. For instance, they may have 'imaginary' friends. Too often they are told their friends are not real, even though they see them, talk to them and play with them. That is very confusing for a young child. Often these children see upcoming tragedies, but they are not understood or acknowledged by others. They sometimes talk about things they know, without having been present, so are told it is not possible. These children generally have difficulty concentrating on one thing because they are so aware of everything that goes on around them. The Elders knew these things and not only acknowledged but honored and nurtured the knowledge and wisdom of these children.

The Elders shared how traditional families in past generations were much closer and smaller, and often referred to the importance of family decisions as those decisions would influence the generations to come—especially the seventh generation. Large families were non-existent until the Catholic Church taught people that birth control was not a good thing. Many years ago the Elders would give young women herbs for birth control, and herbs to reverse the effect, so children were well spaced.

I heard much discussion about visions and medicines which were freely shared. Prayers were connected with these exchanges. There is protocol the Elders strictly followed in this sharing, including the passing of tobacco. The knowledge of one medicine would be traded for the knowledge of another.

"A gift of wisdom can never be given to a person," Lawrence would say, "only shared."

I felt so gifted to have these old people share their wisdom in my home. In their presence I felt so humble.

Chapter 14

Moon Time

One day Lawrence said he had to go and do a pipe ceremony at the Sunchild reserve and he wanted me to go as there were some meetings he wanted me to attend. He was always so keen on me learning what the issues facing his people were. He was, of course, to bring his pipe.

I was in my menstruation time or moon time as they called it. On the way he reminded me that I must not be in the room when the pipe was taken out of its case for ceremonial use. I was to wait outside. As I stood outside the door waiting I felt totally humiliated. All I could think of was that four hundred people knew.

After an hour Lawrence came out looking for me. "Why did you not come back in?" he asked.

"I did not know when to come back and I thought you would come and tell me," I replied. Then he saw how upset I was and he asked what was wrong.

"Four hundred people know," I said.

"Know what?" he asked.

"Know that I am in my time."

'Chhh," he said, "four hundred people respect you and they know you respect me and the pipe, so what's your problem? I do not understand."

"In my culture no one ever knows. That is just the way it is."

I really wanted to learn more about their beliefs regarding the time of menstruation, but knew I had to talk to a woman about that. I could not ask Lawrence very much about women's business. I did ask for his guidance as to who he thought would be willing to teach me these things. He suggested that I talk to an Elder, Madge McRee, who lived in Slave Lake.

One day I journeyed the three hundred kilometers to her home to learn from the old woman (an expression recognizing her wisdom, not necessarily her age). Madge was a big woman with a very kind face. There was no way I could be sure of her age. She looked about fifty-five years old, but when she told me she had nine children and they had all left home some years before, with the exception of one who was mentally handicapped, I thought maybe she must be older. In any case she did have much wisdom and I was eager to learn.

This was her teaching to me: "Menstruation time is a time of cleansing for a woman. A woman is very powerful in that time and can obtain much spiritual knowledge if she takes the time and the quietness to learn. It is natural for moodiness to come in this modern age as many women are not taking time to care for themselves spiritually. Therefore they work against nature. Traditional women take the time to reflect, to plan and to learn about themselves as women. It is natural for a woman to want to be alone at that time. Traditionally, a woman went to a moon lodge to have time to regenerate and reflect. She took handicrafts with her if she wished, or not if she did not. This isolation was totally misunderstood by the first Europeans who came to our communities. They believed the women were banished because they were dirty. That was never the case—in fact it was just the opposite. Spiritually a woman is very powerful in her 'woman' time. Men can lose all their energy if a woman in her time enters a ceremonial place. Therefore when women go visiting in their time of menstruation they will always knock on the door, wait outside and ask politely if it is okay to enter. Those who know their Native culture understand why the women are asking and they are deeply respected by the residents of the home."

Her words reminded me how many things we see and interpret only from the perspective we know, without trying to understand the reality of someone else's perspective. There is unfortunately more 'dirtiness' associated with the menstruation time in our European culture than there ever was among the traditional people, who understood the sacredness of that time for a woman.

Madge continued: "When a young girl has her first period she is taken to an old woman to learn all about being a woman. She always stays for four days. She looks after the old woman in every way and in return she receives many teachings. At the end of the four days women's ceremonies are held in her honor. Four Elder women are picked to advise her and they will take care of her and support her for the rest of their lives. She knows she can always go to them at any time. She always has the circle of support. That is the start of a young woman's entry into the life of womanhood."

I thought how unfortunate that our society has lost the true meaning of menstruation and womanhood. When I hear the young ladies today talk so badly about their woman time, it makes me very sad. Their cycles have such a beautiful purpose and their wombs will carry the future generation. My greatest wish for our young women is that they too learn about the beauty and the power of who they are as women, and about the honour they were given of bearing children. I found that both traditional men and women understood and respected that. Now I understood why Lawrence had so much respect for women.

In the twenty years I was with the Native people I never heard one woman complain about her moon time. They were always respectful of themselves and others in their woman time, as they understood they were so powerful that they could put an Elder who was handling the pipe right down. I have seen it.

One of my biggest wishes is that our modern women of today will once again be recognized for who they are in our society—not the bra-burning hoopla, but the understanding of our true power and the humility to use it wisely.

Chapter 15

New People, Old Land

The lives of the Native people were completely altered when the Europeans brought disease, took their land, outlawed their religion and confined them to reservations where they were totally controlled by white people.

The most devastating was the introduction of many new diseases such as smallpox, measles, mumps, typhoid fever, typhus, and other viruses and bacteria, to which they had never been exposed and therefore had not built up any immunity. As a result, some communities lost up to eighty percent of their population.

In 1868 the Canadian Government passed the Indian Act, which amongst other things, identified who was 'Indian' and who was designated as 'status' and who was not. Most Indians under the Act were assigned a reservation where they were forced to live. No two treaties were identical, but most included the right to hunt on crown land.

The reservations were governed by a white Indian Agent who had enormous power, including who could live on the reserve and who could not. He was the Justice of the Peace, arresting officer, prosecutor and judge. He had control over distribution of food and supplies. He had the power to expropriate land. He had the right to depose any chief who did not follow his orders. He distributed the property of all deceased members according to his own wishes.

The Indian Agents were not abolished until 1969.

In 1884 all sacred ceremonies were made illegal. In this, the land of the free, the Native people were not allowed to worship in their own way.

European education was forced on them through the residential school program. If parents did not bring their children to the schools, police or priests would come into a community, pick them up and take them away. Many never returned to their parents. Many died and were buried in unmarked graves. In 1904 the government appointed a medical officer, Dr. Peter Bryce, to address Indian Medical Health. According to his study, between thirty-five and sixty percent of those children taken to residential schools were dead within five years. These statistics did not become public until 1922 when Dr. Bryce was no longer working for the Government. He published his findings in a book called *The Story of a National Crime: Being a record of health conditions of the Indians of Canada from 1904 until 1921*. He alleged that the high mortality rate was often deliberate as the healthy children were often exposed to those with tuberculosis.

In 1920 and 1922 Dr. Corbett was commissioned to visit the schools in the west and he found results similar to those of Dr. Bryce. In Hobbema (where Lawrence started school in 1926), he found that fifty percent of the children had tuberculosis. In Sarcee, all but four were infected. Many were forced to sit through lessons even when they were obviously close to death.

The last residential school closed in 1996.

I had not known the depth of devastation that was inflicted on the Native community.

Now hearing the stories from the people who sat in our home meant that it became personal, not just facts. Not just statistics.

My friend Henry Laboucan told me about how he and many others were not originally registered under the Indian Act as they were very isolated. After running away from residential school at age thirteen because of the horrendous abuse, he worked his way around the country. After mastering one skill he would move on to the next job. He gained much knowledge in his travels and in 1973 decided to apply for his Indian Status card. He got a big shock when he went to pick it up. On the line where they told him to sign it said 'signature of specimen.' "*Specimen?* I am not a specimen!" And from that day he started a campaign to end the term. It was eventually overturned and everyone was required to return the original cards before receiving the new ones. He kept his. When he showed it to me recently, I once more felt sick to my stomach. Does the injustice never end?

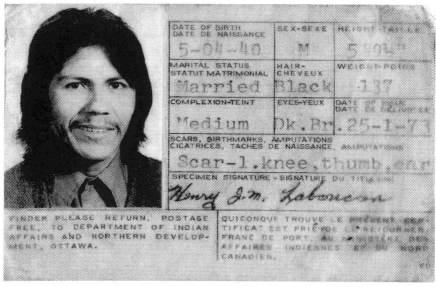

Henry Laboucan's Indian Status card

The Elders had such a deep tolerance and understanding and knew that the tragedies created by the imposition of Canadian laws were not the responsibility of the first settlers who came and lived in their vicinity. They actually welcomed the newcomers, as was their custom, and helped them survive through their first harsh Canadian winters. The Native hunters shared their meat when they hunted and the fish when they fished. Often the Native women would come and show the white women how to build drying racks, cut the meat very thin and hang it to dry. They showed them how to clean fish and to split them in half to the tail so they could be hung to dry and preserved for the winter. The early pioneers were taught which berries and roots were edible and how to dry them as well so they would not starve over the long cold winter months.

One time I mentioned to Lawrence that we had learned at school how his people had gone hungry before the white people came. He looked at me in surprise. "I do not know what you are talking about," he said, "my people never went hungry until they were confined to the reservations and distribution of food was regulated by the Indian Agents. It was the other way around. We saved many white settlers from starving."

Lawrence's grandmother, who was a midwife, helped many white children enter this world. She taught him that we were all people and he was not to discriminate. She was his primary teacher and he heeded those teachings well.

I was in awe at the tolerance and understanding Lawrence and the Elders displayed toward the Europeans. Often I would hear the Elders say, "They did their best." I doubted the Europeans would have responded in a similar manner had the situation been reversed. I was learning many new things. I became aware of how little I knew about the true history of Canada.

We have so much to learn from the traditional Native teachings. I thought that with their depth of understanding and their philosophy of life, there would never be war.

On June 11th, 2008, Stephen Harper, the Prime Minister of Canada, offered an apology for the harm done at residential schools by government, churches and other Canadians. In reference to the deaths and the children who disappeared from the schools, he made the following statement: "Tragically, some of these children died while attending residential schools, and others never returned home."

That was the first time an apology was issued. It was however specific to the government role in the tragedy of the residential school policies. It is something, but there are so many other issues: like the distribution of tuberculosis infected blankets, like the taking of the land and confining the people to reservations, like outlawing their way to pray, like taking their names, like destroying their language, like the destruction of a culture, the destruction of a people. Even today it continues. The government still uses the name "Indian" even though the terms Native or First Nations people have been used for many years. Most Native people say that they did not come from India, therefore we are not Indians. The government can't even get that right.

Recently I went to an Indian museum in Germany. Friedrich, the owner, said "We, as Germans, did a terrible thing to the Jews under Hitler's reign. We have recognized our mistake, apologized and done our best to take responsibility for what we did. I do not see that happening as far as what was done to the Natives in Canada and the United States." That, he said, made him sad.

Chapter 16

Cross-Cultural Challenges

Euro-Canadian people's cultural teachings often cause confusion with the Native teachings and vice versa.

I heard many new terms for the first time: for example, *before contact* and *after contact,* meaning before and after the arrival of the Europeans, and the expression *dominant society,* referring to European Canadian society.

The Euro-Canadian's cultural teachings are to express thoughts verbally, sometimes before giving full consideration to all the consequences. We are taught to ask questions immediately if we do not understand what is being communicated, and we expect instant feedback. It is a technique we use to share information or simply to convince others that our viewpoint is the right one.

Native cultural teachings are quite the opposite. They will take much time to reflect all aspects of an issue and will respond quietly only after they have done so. They would never feel a need to convince anyone that their viewpoint is the only or the right one. It is up to the receiver of the information to make that decision.

When Europeans raise their voices in order to convince others of their viewpoint, a Native person would interpret that as an attempt to dominate, rather than simply having an exchange of viewpoints. I grew up expressing my viewpoints loudly and clearly. It is our way.

The hesitation of Native people while contemplating all aspects of a question has often been misinterpreted as being slow to understand.

One day Lawrence, as head of the Alberta Indian Association Senate of Elders, was asked to attend a meeting with Fish and Wildlife officials at their office. Fish and Wildlife wanted to discuss a change in hunting rights they were proposing. Native people have the right to hunt on all crown land—land that was claimed by the state and not belonging to individuals.

As we entered, there were three officers dressed in green uniforms, all seated at one side of a large table. Lawrence and I were designated a place at the other side, facing them. They promptly presented their thoughts of making it illegal for Native people to hunt close to roads. They wanted to stop the practice of driving around until they saw game and then shooting it. One person presented the argument, but when he did not get an immediate response, the others in turn repeated exactly what the first officer said, only a little louder. After listening to the same thing being repeated several times by one officer after the other, Lawrence stood up and said, "I am not stupid or deaf. I heard you the first time. If you cannot take the time to listen, I may as well leave," and with that he turned to walk out of the room. One officer got up and apologized and asked him to stay, that they really wanted to hear what he had to say. After a long silence, he decided to return to his chair. Still he said nothing until invited to speak by the person who had called the meeting.

He started his sharing with: "I do not understand why you people have no patience. You called me to this meeting and yet you do not give me time to think about your proposal. You expect me to comment before taking time to contemplate the consequences of what you are proposing. That makes me wonder if you are even interested in what I have to say, or if you have already made up your mind." After another long hesitation, Lawrence was asked to continue. Now they were ready to listen.

"This issue," he said, "cannot be dealt with by you in a unilateral way. All hunting rights for Native people are under federal jurisdiction and protected under the Treaties." He suggested that if they tried to make changes to the hunting rights of treaty Indians, they would have to deal not only with the Federal Government, but would also face a lot of opposition from the Native community. "I agree with the concept and understand where you are coming from, but I think it will open up a can of worms which would cause extreme difficulty. If you do not want an uprising, I would suggest you drop the whole thing."

The officers admitted they had not thought about that. They had concentrated only on the protection of the animals. "I guess we need to rethink what we are doing," one officer said. Lawrence thanked them for listening, and they thanked him for coming in. They all shook hands and we left.

The Native Elders spoke often about how names are very important as they tell much about who a person is and how that person is recognized spiritually. Names always suited personality when passed in the traditional way from the spirit world. The taking away of the names by the 'dominant society' was but one of many devastating losses suffered through the process of trying to eliminate the traditional identity of the Native people and assimilate them into European Canadian culture.

Another teaching which causes much confusion is that we are taught to look a person in the eyes as an expression of honesty and respect. The Native teaching is just the opposite. It is to never look a person whom they respect in the eye. The eyes are the window to the soul and that is a private place. All Native people I know respect that teaching.

Whenever an Elder spoke, people would look everywhere else except at him or her. When we force a Native person to look into another person's eyes as we do in our European society, they become very uncomfortable. That discomfort has caused an immeasurable amount of grief, especially in the courtrooms and in classrooms.

One day we were presenting a cross-cultural workshop at the Royal Alexandra Hospital, one of the largest in the city of Edmonton. Chairs were placed in a circle in the room where we presented. All teachings are done in circle formation without the barrier of tables. Lawrence always sat facing south. When I asked him why, he said it was because his ancestors sat in the south and they would come and help. Every workshop was started with prayer. Then he would go on to explain how we are all equal within the circle. "We are all teachers and we all learn from each other," he said.

When we shared the teaching of no eye contact, a young man gasped. Here is what he shared with us: "I am a respiratory technician and much of my days are spent going from one patient to the next, teaching people about how and why they would continue to use medications and equipment to enhance their breathing after they returned home. I came to this workshop because I hate dealing with Native people and I do not like my own attitude. One reason for my attitude is because I never feel I get through to them no matter how hard I try. No one ever looks me in the eye or has any question for me, so I have no idea whether they understand what I tell them or not. All this time I have been disrespecting them when they are in turn respecting me. I really feel bad now."

Lawrence told him not to feel bad—that he didn't know better.

Then the young man asked how he could do better. Considering how busy his department is, it would be impossible for him to spend a lot of time with each person. I suggested that he go to the people he knew to be Native first, give them the appropriate explanation and go on to the next patient. At the end of his rounds, go back. By that time they will have had the time to figure things out. Typically they would not just be thinking about the treatments or equipment, if there was any, but also how it would affect their employment, their families and their community. Where and how would they be able to obtain supplies? Would they need to arrange for transportation? What would happen to them if they were to run out of medication? If the equipment broke down, who could fix it? They would be contemplating many things. Changes that would affect their lifestyle were important to think about. Would they be able to drive? How long could they go without treatment? In many cases they would simply give up when they could not get any answers.

This, I believe is one factor in the lower mortality age of Native people. According to Health Canada, the mortality rate of Native Canadians at birth is 8.1 years lower for men and 5.5 years for women compared to the average Canadian.

So much conflict and misunderstanding has occurred because of different cultural teachings, because we do not understand those differences.

Lawrence always used to say the road to learning is never-ending, which brings me to one big difference between our European culture and the Native people. The Natives recognize that you learn something new every day and that you do not suddenly stop at age sixty-five. All young Native people recognize the value of their Elders' advice and will ask for prayers and guidance. Here I am, just entering the time where I am considered to know a little in the Native culture and one year away from knowing much less in our European culture. I am sixty four years old.

There were so many stories about what it was like when the first white people entered the communities and all the things that were not understood about one another.

One story told to me by Norman, a man who lived up in the Northwest Territories, went like this: "The old people told me about how in the old days it was our custom that when a man came to stay with us, a woman would move in with the guest, take care of him in every way and the man would hunt and take care of the woman. When the first Catholic priests arrived it was very confusing. These men who came to our village were very strange. They not only didn't want our women, but they wore dresses. Then they started talking about this Jesus guy and told the people if they believed in him they would go to heaven. This heaven sounded like a pretty good place, so my people decided that believing was a good thing. They still did their traditional ceremonies and there was no conflict for them. Conflict only came when the police started putting people in jail for doing their sacred ceremonies, and picking up all our children of school age and taking them away to be educated far from family and friends. The loss of the children was the hardest of all for our ancestors."

Following is a poem I wrote at the time about first contact and the impressions our people left.

FIRST IMPRESSIONS

When I heard the Elder speak
about the arrival of the white man,
I learned much
about how they saw our people
and the things they brought with them.
About so many things,
They wondered!

The wise knew the people were coming
long before their arrival.
The Elders had warned about
pale-skinned people who would
overwhelm them by their sheer number.
They wondered!

These newcomers knew so little.
How could they be a threat?
We heard they'd killed their saviour.
What kind of people would kill their saviour?
They wondered!

Men came wearing long black skirts.
When we offered our women
to stay with them and look after them
they refused our gift.
How would they survive the winter?
They wondered!

They sure were strange,
these pale-skinned folks
who brought their families
but didn't know how to hunt.
How were they to feed them?
They wondered!

The Elders took pity
on the newcomers and sent
the young men to hunt,
so the families wouldn't go hungry.
How would they survive?
They wondered!

When the pioneer women had babies,
the Native women went to help
when their time came.
There were no ceremonies, no song.
What would those babies be?
They wondered!

There were no ceremonies
for hunting or fishing or gathering,
and none for the rights of passage
to the next stage of life.
What would become of the young people?
They wondered!

The people were amazed
at the things the pioneers did.
Building a house to do a two?
What were they going to do with their poo?
They wondered!

They had a cloth for blowing their noses.
They wrapped it up
and put it in their pocket.

What were they going to do with that?
They wondered!

These are the stories as told to me
by the First Nations Elders,
about the first impressions
of pale-skinned people
who came to share the land.

Lawrence made me learn everything experientially. He was good to tell me what I had done wrong, but only after the fact. How many times did I say, "Why didn't you tell me?"

"If I tell you something you would only remember the half anyway. If you learn from your mistakes, you never forget," was his reply. I guess he had a good point, but I didn't like it one bit. I began to question whether this kind of life was too difficult for me, whether I could live in this way or not.

One such incident happened on a trip to Saskatchewan where Lawrence and I went to visit some of his old friends. They lived about eight kilometers from the main highway, eight kilometers of a very dusty road with grain fields lining each side for most of the way. I was very nervous about meeting these people, as Lawrence always spoke so highly of them. Once he had helped Elmer, the man of the house, when he could barely walk.

When Lawrence used to joke with me, I often told him he was just a banana, an expression I had used for years. When we were visiting he started to tease me about something and as usual, I called him a banana. The twelve year old girl burst into a fit of laughter and the parents told her to leave the room. I was confused because I really didn't think it was that funny. The parents too were trying to hide their snickers. Later I asked Lawrence what that was about and he started to laugh hysterically. He told me it meant a man who couldn't get it up. I was humiliated that I had said that about their Elder. When I asked him why he didn't tell me that before, he just said, "It was too funny!" and laughed even harder and kept slapping his leg. "This experiential learning is sometimes too humiliating!" I said, not pleased. He just continued to laugh. Soon I too had to laugh. I just could not hold it any longer.

I just dreaded facing those people again.

One time we had finished doing a feast for a family at the Alexander reservation, about an hour's drive north-east of where we lived. Usually we were among the last to leave, but not this time. Everyone sits on the floor for a feast, the men on one side with their legs crossed, the women on the other with both feet tucked to one side under their skirts or, when the ceremony is finished, they may stretch out their legs. When Lawrence signaled me, I just got up, stepped over some people's legs as there was not much room in their small living room, and left. As soon as we got in the car, I knew he was not pleased. I asked him what was wrong and he said, "You should know better than that!"

"What do you mean?" I asked.

"Don't you even know how rude it is for a woman to step over someone?" "No," I said "It was only their feet." He just shook his head. I thought about what he had said about never forgetting what you learn from your mistakes.

I had always had so much self-confidence, but this was getting too difficult and I was losing it. There was no book to go to, I couldn't ask about such things because I didn't even know what to ask and I knew better than to begin talking without knowing what I was talking about. I had to be specific. I had to know what my problem was.

When we got home, I told Lawrence I was thinking about leaving because the last thing I wanted to do was humiliate him in any way. I loved him so much, and that was too much for me to bear. "Your people hate my people for what they have done," I said. "I don't blame them, but I didn't do it and I don't know what to say. I feel so guilty about the misunderstandings, the oppression, the ignorance of the European Canadians. I can't defend my people, but I can't carry the load any longer either." The tears rolled down my face as I was talking.

He became very quiet and said nothing. I went off by myself and cried as I had never cried before. I knew I could not stay, but my love for him was so deep it broke my heart to think about living without him.

When I finally returned to the house, he took me in his arms and I just cried some more. He still said nothing until I stopped crying. "What happened to our people is not your fault," he said. "You didn't do it. I think you are suffering from an acute case of cultural shock and I am sorry."

"I just can't do it any longer," I told him. "I don't even know how to behave properly. I am so embarrassed that I don't ever want to face those people again. I didn't mean to offend anyone. How can I sit with them after what I did?"

Again he said nothing. We went to bed and then he asked me not to leave. "I love you too much and I do not want you to go. Besides, you are just going to be miserable if you do, so what's the point?"

"The point is that I will not be an embarrassment to you again in a ceremony. I cannot live with that. It would be worse than leaving."

"You are not an embarrassment to me," he said. "I am so proud that you, as a white woman, respect our ways and you support me in every way. I have never had that much support before and I respect you and love you for being there for me."

I told him I would think about it, but I was not at all sure I could handle living this way. I shed a lot of tears the next few days. It was torture to think about living without him, but it was also torture thinking about living with him.

The Native people were always so anxious to share all the horrible things that were done to them and the few white friends and family I was seeing were just as anxious to share all the bad stories about Natives. Both sides wanted to prove how bad the other was. It was getting to be too much and I started staying away from people as much as possible. The stories were truthful. It was too painful.

I did decide to stay, but now I had to make a plan in order for me to keep my sanity. I could no longer allow the pain and confusion of others to affect my heart. I had to learn how to react in a way that was healthier for me. When the Native people would start putting us down, I started saying, "*I* didn't do it."

"No, you are white and you are nice," was sometimes the reply. That was the saddest statement ever.

"Yes," I would say, "and so are my family and my friends and most white people. Your fight is not with the average individual, but with the systems and the government. There is a difference. I know some people do discriminate, and it is not right, but most people do so out of ignorance. I wish those people would know you as I do, but sadly our people do not mix. Besides, we did bring you a few good things like bannock, horses and trucks," I said as I smiled. That always brought a smile back and sometimes we would burst into laughter. The Native people would at least listen and I like to think those types of comments helped a little to create just a little understanding.

It was always much harder the other way around. White people generally did not want to believe that Native people were not much more than 'lazy drunks and drug addicts and they take all the taxpayer's money.' Many did not believe what I said. I had never lied before, yet they thought I lied now. How could this be?

The exception is always anyone who has personal contact. Therefore, for the most part, I say the attitude is out of the ignorance of not knowing, of listening only to what is said on the news and read in papers. Good clean living never makes the news.

This is a poem I wrote one day after hearing many awful things about the Native people. We had gone into Wetaskiwin to see a white man who owned a second-hand store. He told us how he had many Native friends—he respected them and was grateful for their friendship. Then I thought about others who also had good stories and I wrote this little poem.

OUR INDIANS ARE GOOD INDIANS

We went in to Wetaskiwin,
And there we met a friend.
He told us how he did admire
How Natives a hand would lend.
Our Indians are good Indians.

We went on into Stony Plain,
And there we met a friend.
By the reserve he made his home,
For each other they would fend.
Our Indians are good Indians.

We went on into Mayerthorpe,
And there we met a friend.
He said he'd worked with Natives
They'd defend me to the end.
Our Indians are good Indians.

And so it is wherever we go,
And meet up with a friend.
If personal contact people have,
Each other they rarely offend.
Our Indians are Good Indians.

Chapter 17

Lies, Lies and More Lies

Jack was getting worse by the day. He spread rumors about how I was screwing around with Indians long before we had split and how I was brainwashed by them and they had used sweet grass to do it. As everyone trusted him in the past, many believed him now. He regularly sent nasty, threatening letters which I mostly ignored as I did not really want to believe he would harm us, but still I could not be one hundred per cent certain.

Jack even told our children that I was running around and sleeping with Indians, that I was brainwashed and evil. I tried to tell them the truth, but Margo said, "Mom, you tell me Dad is crazy and Dad tells me you are crazy, I don't know who to believe!" I could say no more. I knew it was difficult for them after having had a stable childhood with two parents they both trusted.

Lawrence kept telling me that I was right, so why should I defend myself. "Give him enough rope and he will hang himself," he would say. I had always been taught the opposite. If I was right, I should be defending myself, but my way didn't work, so I thought I might as well try his. I started heeding Lawrence's advice and quit saying much to my children, even if I was bursting at the seams, wanting so much for my children and friends to know the truth.

Jack's letters became worse and worse. He wrote and told me how he was going to ruin me no matter where I went. I was nothing but a bitch anyway and he would see to it that, first of all, every family member and every friend would hate me. Then when they did, he would kill us both. At first I thought he was just venting, but I was starting to get more concerned. Finally I showed the letters to Murray, a lawyer friend of ours. I just wanted another opinion as to the seriousness of the threats. He told me they were very serious; Jack was threatening my life and if I did not contact the RCMP, Murray would be forced to, as by law he was obliged to report any action he knew to be illegal.

I reluctantly went to the police and they said this was a criminal matter and it was out of my hands. They charged him with two counts of uttering threats, one against me and the other against Lawrence. He could get five years in jail on each charge.

The evening before the trial date the officer who was handling the case came to our home out of kindness and informed me that my brother Norman would be by Jack's side in the courtroom the next day. In a way, it did not really surprise me. My brother had refused to come to my home after I had moved in with Lawrence. In fact he would not allow me to see his children, which was also devastating. I loved them very much and they had spent many Sundays with us in the past. I just thought he was being ignorant again by being at Jack's side.

The next day however, when Jack stood up and pleaded guilty, it really hit me hard. There was my brother sitting beside and supporting the man who was threatening to kill me. When I called later and asked him why he stood by him, he told me that he felt sorry for him. After all, he had nobody and he couldn't really be blamed for what he did under the circumstances.

"So you would stand by the man who would kill me?" I asked in disbelief.

"Yes," he said, "under these circumstances I would."

I could say nothing more.

Jack's sentencing was set over to a later date as they wanted to do a psychological assessment before sentencing. The day came, and I decided to go. Again my brother was by his side. When Jack was called, I could see how nervous he was.

The judge started out by saying, "Mister Thompson, I agree your circumstances are rather unusual." I thought this was going to be another whitewash. It really hit me hard that I again could not present my side.

The following is the conversation to the best of my recollection.

"Mister Thompson," the judge said, "no matter how unusual your circumstances, your behavior is unacceptable. This society does not condone anyone threatening anyone else. It is not acceptable." He paused briefly, then said, "Do you understand, Mr. Thompson?" Jack nodded. "Do you understand, Mr. Thompson?" the judge said again.

Jack said, "Yes."

"Yes, what . . . , Mr. Thompson?"

"What I am doing is not acceptable."

"Okay, today I am going to suspend sentencing. Do you know what that means, Mr. Thompson?"

"No."

"It means, Mr. Thompson, that I will not be imposing a sentence, under certain conditions. You are not to come near either Rita or Lawrence ever again. You are not to threaten them either directly or indirectly. Not through your children, not through anyone. "Do you understand, Mr. Thompson? Repeat what I said, Mr. Thompson,"

And Jack did.

"One more thing, Mr. Thompson: if you do appear in front of me one more time I will have no pity. You will be punished to the full extent of the law. Do you understand, Mr. Thompson?"

"Yes," said Jack quietly.

"Repeat what I just said, Mr. Thompson!"

"If I do not follow your orders, I will be punished," Jack said.

"Please, Mr. Thompson, I do not want to see you back here again. Do you understand?" With that he was dismissed. I wanted to jump up and give that judge a big hug and thank him. I knew Jack would react with terror of going to jail, so what the judge did could not have been more effective. Putting him in jail would have helped no one. I just wanted him to leave us alone—which he did after that.

He did continue to discredit me, but by that time most people were getting very tired of listening to it and he could do very little to add to the harm that was already done. The death threats did stop. My truth did come out. He did "hang" himself. The lies became less believable as he embellished them in his desperation to discredit me. The children did find out who was telling the truth. The wait was ever so difficult, but my patience paid off.

My relationship with my children continued to be challenging, however. My daughter's husband gave her such a hard time and would accuse her of going to my place to screw Indians, just like her mother, so she rarely came. He would not allow his children to visit.

Rocky, my son, rarely came because there were too many 'Indians' around and he was uncomfortable with that. Both did eventually like Lawrence once they got to know him, but they told me he was different from the rest. They would not believe otherwise.

Never in my wildest dreams did I think my grandchildren would not be an integral part of my life, but my children did not allow them to come and visit on their own, and they rarely brought them to my home.

My daughter Margo called one day and asked if it was okay with me if her father moved in with them. She was expecting her second child. He needed a place to stay and she was told that she would have to stay in bed most of her pregnancy. I could see her need and told her to go ahead. I had not anticipated the consequences of that decision. Whenever I entered her home, Jack was one mass of hatred. My grandchildren felt that, of course, and were afraid of me. I could not get close to them.

I told both Margo and Rocky that I loved Lawrence and I loved the life I had with him. I also loved my children and grandchildren. How I longed for those two worlds to meet, to be in harmony in my world, but that was not to be. I was torn apart by the two worlds I so loved. They respected that I had to choose my life for myself and they wanted me to be happy. I knew it was hard for them. After all, their mother did shack up with an Indian. They could not understand this new world in which I lived. Although they loved and accepted me, they struggled with the facts of the situation.

People kept coming for help so it was difficult for me to leave the house at will as I needed to make sure that everyone was fed and taken care of. I also helped Lawrence when he doctored the people who came. With only a rare visit from my children, it was heartbreaking for me. My visits to see them were often strained.

I paid a high price for my decision to be with the man I loved. My love was so deep I could not do otherwise.

I do have to admit I was very naïve about the effect my love would have on our families. All the children were adults at the time we got together. I honestly thought they would be able to see beyond the prejudice and understand the happiness we found in each other. Not so.

Chapter 18

Name Change

Lawrence's family acquired the name Mackinaw when his grandfather was taken to residential school. His grandfather's name was Makkannaw, which means *road* or *path* in Salteaux, the tribe to which he belonged until the late 1800s when he decided to move west from the Red River region.

No one in the family wanted to be called Mackinaw, which means *a long Scottish overcoat.* One day he told me the story of how he got his traditional name, the name he was born to carry in accordance with a vision passed from the spirit world.

An old woman, who had come to his mother in the log house which they had been assigned by the Indian Agent, told her she would have a visitor in four days. "His name is Raven," she said. Four days later Raven was born. He was baptized Lawrence, taken from the church's list of approved names from which his parents were required to choose.

Every Native person was required to register under the Treaties, an agreement entered into between states under international law, and they were not allowed to register with their traditional names. Many who had not yet been given a 'Christian' name by the family were simply registered under whichever name suited the person doing the registering. Many people were named after the white settlers who lived closest to them.

Some, as was the case with Lawrence's family, were given names which sounded close to the name they carried.

On many reservations many people have the same last name, but they are not necessarily related, and it has really caused a lot of confusion. Marrying someone with the same last name has also been misleading. Marrying anyone even remotely related is strictly prohibited in the Cree teachings. Other tribes are a little more lenient with the union of distant relations.

Each time the Native people would speak of the name changes, I thought about my late brother. He was baptized Leif, pronounced 'life' in Denmark where he lived until the age of 15. He battled his whole life to keep the 'life' pronunciation. That was his name and he needed to keep it the way it was meant to be.

One day in 1990 Lawrence had been away at some Indian Association meetings. He was very quiet all through supper. That evening I served tea on the veranda, and, as we were enjoying the cool evening air and the sound of the many song birds, he suddenly said, "The white man jailed us on the reservations, they sent our children to residential schools and banned our ceremonies, but the most difficult, I think, was when they took our names, our identity." That was one of the few times I saw his pain for what was done to him and his family. Mostly he refused to think about it and would live life in the best way he could. I asked him then why he did not pick up his grandfather's name.

"Can I really do that?" he asked.

I said, "Women change their name all the time, so I cannot see why you could not change yours."

We spoke to our lawyer friend, Murray, who checked with vital statistics and found there was no record of either his birth or his marriage to his first wife. He was not registered at all. Therefore he could simply register him as Raven Makkannaw. From that day forward he was Raven. It was that easy. I was very surprised at how many people switched to his new name right away. Many did use the Cree name of Ka-ka-koo, meaning Raven, so for most I guess it was not a big change. They knew he was Raven.

Raven

I had hoped some members of his family would follow suit, but they misunderstood the intention of the name change, and thought he was abandoning them and going to the white world. His children were worried about the consequences of his not being legally married to their mother, so we had that registered as well.

The harm done to the Native people by not allowing them their rightful names has never been officially recognized. Often I would hear statements like: "They held us on the reservations, they sent us to residential schools—and that was difficult—but the worst was the taking of our identities."

One day Raven told me that I too should have my traditional name. "It will mean a lot, for you will be recognized spiritually by that name. When you know your traditional name, you will learn to understand many things about yourself. In the future you will see why you have the strengths you have and how they will benefit you through life. Besides, you already know!" he said with a grin.

The next day, Raven went to his son's place for a ceremony. When he returned, he told me this story. "When I asked who would take care of this woman (referring to me), the thunderbird came and said it would. Immediately an eagle with the whitest head I have ever seen appeared and told the thunderbird that he would. Therefore, you are now Kihiw Squew, or Eagle Woman. With the purer than pure whiteness of the head of the eagle, you may call yourself *White Eagle Woman* from this day forward. You have earned the name; the eagle will always take care of you. Know that you are looked after."

After Raven took on the name that he was meant to carry, I saw a profound change in him. It is very difficult to describe how the use of his traditional name seemed to strengthen his inner confidence and satisfaction with life. He became much more satisfied with himself and proud to carry his name.

Now that we were both birds, we could really fly together.

We had friends whose traditional names were Musqua (black bear) and Mistahia (grizzly bear). When we used to get together, we would always joke about how the birds and the bears were visiting each other.

Chapter 19

Purchasing Property

Raven often talked about how he missed having a place where he could put up his own sweat lodges. He did not feel right setting one up at the place we were renting. In order to have a sweat lodge one needs to be able to make a fire big enough to heat rocks on. I just casually mentioned that it would be very nice to buy our own place. I knew it would not be any time soon as all my money was tied up in a house in Edmonton, and he never had savings. "If you want land, we will find it," he said. We began driving out evenings. I did not really believe we would find anything, but enjoyed the drives and looking at places anyway. Raven never lost faith. He said we would find our place.

One summer evening as we were driving out west of Edmonton, we came upon an acreage for sale. The owner was outside so we stopped to chat. I knew we could not buy it—the price would be too high for us—but the chats we had with people were generally interesting. He told us about a piece of property that we might be able to deal on. The owner of that property was recently separated and he was moving back to Ontario the next morning, so if we could deal right away, we might get it.

We drove over immediately to have a look. It was an older double-wide mobile home in very good shape, situated on six acres of land. It was fenced for horses and had a little shelter for them as well. The yard was well kept. Although it was forty-five kilometers from Edmonton and a bit of a drive for Raven, it was perfect for our needs. We contacted the realtor right away and he confirmed that the owner was desperate, so if we were prepared to make the deal immediately, he would take almost anything.

We proposed a rental purchase, which meant we would not have to deal with banks. The title would remain in the owner's name until we paid the property in full, or we had the option to walk away in which case we would lose our deposit and all moneys paid into it. We offered $52,000, down from $60,000, with a $400 deposit, which was all the money Raven had, and a $2000 down payment on possession day, July 1st. By that time

I knew I would have my income tax refund back and that would more than cover it. We also requested no interest for one year and an option to continue for one more year, at which time we had the choice of paying it in full or leaving. He accepted. I never would have believed it! We had $54 in the bank and we did purchase our land.

Raven always used to say: "Don't ever worry about money. It will always be there when you need it." I really had a difficult time putting my faith in that. I did own the house in Edmonton and I thought if worst came to worst I always had that equity. In all the twenty years we were together we never lacked for anything. The money was always there.

Chapter 20

Stolen Children

The federal government had given a grant to the Indian Association of Alberta, which was a grass-roots organization formed in 1939. It was run on a one-person one-vote standard. They worked on many fronts, including research into their rights under the treaties, land claims, women's rights, damage done by the boarding schools, social services, hospitals, taxation and hunting rights.

Raven formed and was head of the association's Senate of Elders, whose services were available to anyone who requested them, including other Native organizations, government agencies and individuals. He had brought each Elder offerings and tobacco to request them to become senators and share their wisdom. It was these Elders, assembled by Raven, who reminded me of being in the presence of the Dalai Lama. They had so much wisdom about what it was to be human, how we fit in the bigger scheme of things and how we are all connected to everything that is. The Elders would gather once every couple of months and people would come and report to them and ask for advice.

The first time I attended a meeting of the political wing of the Indian association, I observed that only men were sitting around the tables, which were set up in a U-shape. Raven often spoke about how much respect there was for women and Elders. It looked to me like the men had all the say. Although an Elder was presented with tobacco to start the meeting and he or she would have some opening remarks in regard to the topic at hand, no Elders were at the table.

Microphones were set up for everyone, which was a good thing as most are so soft spoken. Whatever the topic at hand, each person spoke in turn, addressing the topics from a personal perspective as well as a professional one. Many people sat around the perimeter listening. These included Elders, both men and women, and some younger women and children. My perception of male dominance was certainly confirmed by what I observed. The men did all the talking. One person took notes. At breaks everyone mingled and I observed that the men were going to the Elders and the younger women for advice and guidance. They presented the Elders with tobacco for their advice. The Elders were all paid an honorarium and provided with accommodations and food in return for sharing their wisdom. They did not appear to have much input.

After breaks a few Elders were asked to speak. Each presented a brief summary and then added whatever he or she saw as an appropriate plan of action. Everyone was very still and did not look at the Elders that spoke. After that the meeting would resume. Everyone would thank the Elders for their input and would carry on with more clarity. They really listened and incorporated their advice.

At the end of the day, the person who had recorded the proceedings prepared a written summary of the proceedings; his report was passed around the next morning for comments, corrections and approval. The report recorded input from everyone, including the people who were not at the table. Not like I was accustomed to, where the deep thinkers often had no input as there was no space created for their thoughts and ideas.

The meetings I had attended before, all of them within the non-Native society, were generally run by Robert's Rules. First someone has to make a motion, then it is seconded, then discussion and amendments, if any, to motions, and amendments to amendments. It can be so very confusing that even the president gets confused. Time would again be wasted trying to unravel the rules. This always interrupted the flow of ideas and became very disruptive. Because discussion time was limited, many people competed with one another for attention. Some people would raise their voices in their attempt to convince others of their viewpoint. There was generally no opportunity for the quiet thinkers to have any input at all. No wonder they called us 'dominant,' I thought.

There was much discussion about land claims. After many years of lobbying, the Canadian government in 1973 incorporated a policy of addressing Native land claims called *The Statement of Claims of Indian and Inuit People*, opening the door to begin negotiations. These claims were based on the treaty obligations in effect from the 1870s to the 1920s. As more and more immigrants came, land designated as Indian land under those treaties was often appropriated by the government with promises of compensation, which were not fulfilled.

I kept asking myself how these things could have happened in Canada. I wondered why I did not know anything about them. I, as a Canadian citizen, had no idea of the history in our own country.

The first settlement was that of the James Bay Cree in 1985. Others followed with the largest being the creation of Nunavut for the Inuit people in the North West Territories in 1992. It was confirmed by referendum of the Native people in 1999 when Nunavut received autonomy.

The land claims issue finally became public knowledge as a result of the standoff between the Mohawk and the town of Oka, in 1990, followed by standoffs at Ipperwash and Gustafsen Lake. To date there are still several hundred outstanding land claims.

As I sat and listened to their stories, I heard for the first time that Native people were put in jail automatically for thirty days for things like leaving the reservation without a permit, or drinking as much as one beer. But most tragic were the arrests for practicing their own religion. In this land where we pride ourselves on freedom of religion, how could it be that the Native people were arrested and jailed without trial for practicing theirs? It was only in 1951 that the government revoked the restrictions on their religious practices. Native people were not to get the right to vote without giving up their treaty status until 1960. One man from the north told me it was not until 1963 that his people were notified of their right.

At first I had a hard time believing it. I did not want to. Many things were going into my bag of information which I could not immediately absorb. One by one, as time went by, I did learn the truth about each thing, but as more and more things came out of the bag, they were replaced with new information. To this day the information in my bag keeps rotating: some things come out while others are going in. The road to learning really is never-ending, as was Raven's saying. There were times I thought about leaving the meetings as it was too hard on me to listen to it all. Raven kept telling me how grateful he was that I stayed and listened.

"You will learn much," he would say. Sometimes I wondered how much I really wanted to learn. It was ever so heartbreaking to hear it all. As the only white person there, I began to take on all the guilt of the government-based policies of oppression.

It was the stories that put a human face to the results of our government policies.

One day old Mel Paul, a member of the senate, came calling. Mel was a little below average in height, was rather poorly dressed in old blue jeans and a faded checkered shirt. His hair was quite thin and sported two small braids which did not appear to have been combed for some days.

Over a cup of tea, he told me he was a thirty-day Indian. He just laughed about it. I asked him why he would call himself 'a thirty-day Indian.' "Well," he said, "in the old days, when I was young, we were often put in jail for thirty days. I would sneak off the reserve without permission from the Indian Agent and if I was caught it was thirty days. I would have a few beers occasionally because I did like my beer. Thirty days. We would perform our sacred ceremonies, smoke our sacred pipes, and it was thirty days."

When I asked him about court, he said, "We didn't know what that was. We were just thrown in jail for thirty days." That old man taught me lots. He and Raven had adopted each other as brothers back in the '50s when they travelled extensively together.

When Raven took up with a white woman, he could not understand it, but he always treated me well and tried very hard to accept me. At first he was reluctant to speak freely in my presence. Raven would assure him it was all right. Then he opened up. He told me how they had to hide the sacred items like eagle feathers and pipe because if the white people found them, they would be confiscated and the owners would be arrested. Most people hid them under the floor boards or set them out in the forest some place. Ceremonies were strictly forbidden until 1951. Mel was still a little afraid of getting arrested. He had a very hard time trusting white people.

As time went by he started saying, as a compliment, that I was not white. I was like them. That I would not accept. "I am white and I am like you," I would say.

One day he told me about his visit to the United Nations building in New York. He was a very eloquent speaker and was invited to do a presentation. He was told at the United Nations that the Native North Americans had the answers to save the world. "That confuses me," he said. "We are so poor. We live on these small reservations. I cannot understand why they would say such a thing." I would just nod and give him a little smile. He had no idea of the wealth of knowledge and wisdom his people had that the world could benefit from.

As I listened to one atrocity after another, I heard a totally other version of Canadian history than I had heard before. I had learned about how the children were forcibly removed from their communities and sent off to residential school far away from their homes, but I did not know about how many of them had disappeared and to this day have not been found. Everywhere I went there was much discussion about how to find these children. Some, they knew, were dead. Many were buried in unmarked graves, making it impossible to identify them. Others were adopted out and disappeared from their families. Many were found when the government allowed adoption records to be opened. Some were close by, others in far-away countries.

Mel Paul came calling one day and he could not get the smile off his face. That was ever so unusual for him as he was generally very straight-faced. "My brother," he said to Raven, "I have just found my long-lost granddaughter! About twelve years ago, when my daughter and her husband were killed in a car accident, Social Services came and wanted to know who would care for their children. It was before the burial, so all the details had not been worked out. The two oldest would go to one aunt and the two youngest to another. As for the middle one, that had not been determined. Social services took that child and she disappeared. A few nights ago two of my grandsons were driving around north of Stony Plain. The roads were slippery and they hit the ditch. They walked up to a farmhouse and knocked on the door. A young Native girl answered. They thought they recognized her as their long-lost sister, and upon further investigation we found out they were right. She lived with a white family only a few miles from us and we didn't know."

The last I heard she decided to stay with her adoptive parents, but had contact with her birth family. I never met her but always wondered how she was. It is not easy to belong to two worlds.

There were many stories of children who disappeared through Social Services. No matter how long ago they left the community, they are never forgotten. There are children from the Hobbema reservation, where Raven belonged, who have been taken into care, and no trace has been found. They have a lot of money waiting for them, as they are entitled to their oil revenues the same as everyone else.

Many through the years disappeared through residential schools and from hospitals.* Most traumatic was when Social Services did what they called 'a sweep.' Social Services would go in and remove a large number of children without doing a proper investigation of each case.

---

*   More information by searching the web on Native Mass Graves, and Hidden from History.

Then it would be up to the parents to prove they were fit. When they did not understand the language, or did not have resources or did not understand the system, that proved a formidable task, and many of these children were never returned. These families were very hurt and bitter. Many people turned to drugs and alcohol when the pain became unbearable. We never actually saw the people who were drinking, as they were ashamed of themselves and would not come near us. I certainly heard about them through others.

Because Social Services files are completely confidential and cannot be investigated, I can go only by the stories that were told to me.

One day in 2005, when I was visiting my sister in Quesnel, she told me about how she heard on the radio that seventy-five children had just been removed from a small nearby reserve. The children in that instance were quickly returned after the publicity. I said a silent prayer of thanks: that was the first time I had heard of such an incident being made public. Perhaps there was hope yet. I so want to believe that if my fellow non-Native Canadians knew of the atrocities against these people there would be a public outcry. Then perhaps it would stop.

Many of the issues of the past are also issues of the present. Problems involving the Social Services department—such as the case of the sweep in British Columbia—continue to emerge. Many times conditions for the return of apprehended children are such that it becomes very difficult or even impossible to ever get them back. One mother told me that she was ordered to complete an alcohol and drug abuse program. She did that. Then she was told to take a parenting program. She did that. Then she was told she had to prove that she was sober and straight over a period of three months. She did that. Then she was told she had to get a home of her own (she was living with her mother). She could not do that as there is a long waiting list for housing on the reservation and as long as she did not have her children, she would not be a priority. All her support system was on the reserve and she was afraid to leave. The last time I spoke to her she was still straight. Her oldest daughter of 14 years was returned to her, and she was still fighting for the rest. Her story was typical of others I heard. Native people do not dare go public, as they are much too afraid of losing their children or of not having them returned. They are not willing to take the gamble.

One day, in a gathering of the Native people from all over the province, one old woman Elder explained to the people that they were not to blame and must not be bitter over the loss of their children. "It will do you no good," she said. "You will only hurt yourself. When you are angry, you are weak. When your brain is clouded with anger and pain you will lose. When you go drinking and use drugs you have no chance of getting your children back. You must keep a clear head. You must stay smart."

I wondered if I could stay smart in that situation. I could not imagine it. When I thought about someone coming and taking my children, I could not see how I could possibly have the strength to not be angry. That was another one for my imaginary bag.

It was hard to listen to all the things that happened to Raven's people because of mine. I felt it was not fair that the Canadian people knew nothing of the truth of what it was like to be Native in Canada.

I saw the coverage on TV and read in the newspapers about Native issues. Every time there was a story about drug and alcohol abuse, they always featured Native people. The pictures they used were the worst, the most degrading they could find. There were extensive articles about the cost of the Indian Affairs department and how our tax dollars all went to supporting these people they portrayed as being nothing but drunks and drug addicts, and a drain on our society.

The general public did not understand that only a fraction of the funding filtered down to the individual people. In Vancouver alone, there is a whole office tower downtown dedicated to Indian Affairs.

When the Native people hear about how the government breaks down how much they cost the Canadian taxpayers, they get so frustrated. "We have given up surface rights only as deep as a plow will go. We have not relinquished any mineral rights. They take all our minerals and yet we have to fight to get a little funding for our various projects," is a frequent comment.

There is always so much talk from the white community: "Why can they not just integrate? Why can they not be just be like us?"

To my white brothers and sisters I will tell you: most do not want to. *They do not want to live like us.* They do not respect our way of life, our thought patterns or our greediness. Ownership of things is not important. Family is.

There is so much we do not understand about each other and I took on the burden for it all. I did get sick. I started to have headaches, which I had never had before, and I was sad much of the time.

Raven tried everything to cheer me up. He bought me things and joked around and told me funny stories. One day when all his effort was not making much difference, he asked me what was wrong. "Now that I understand so much more about the history of your people, I am so disillusioned with my own. I cannot understand how this could happen without my knowledge. I feel I need to do something, but I have no idea what I can do. I feel so helpless and so guilty. I have tried to talk to some of my people, but they don't believe that it is that bad. That means they think I am lying or at best exaggerating. Never in my life have I been accused of either, but now I am!"

"Do not take this on, you did not do it. You have always been good to my people. Why on earth would you feel guilty for something you did not do?" replied Raven.

This is the poem I wrote when I was at my lowest.

A White Woman's Guilt

I felt so guilty for what was done
To the Native people one by one
My people took their babies away
And left the mothers without a say

I felt so guilty when I sat
Listening to where the Natives were at
With all their pain I could not cope
Many had so little hope

I felt so guilty when I would hear
How Indian Affairs were never clear
On their rights under the treaty
Of how they were treated in the city

I felt so guilty for freedom lost
How the police would them accost
They were arrested and put in jail
For as little as drinking a bit of ale

I felt so guilty for the oppression
Trade was forbidden off reservation
Government policy kept them dependent
As they would bring in another amendment

I felt so guilty for poor education.
In public schools they faced rejection
Grade eight was as far as they could go
In education they could not grow

I felt so guilty for spirituality
Jail time for prayer time, a reality
How could this be in the land of the free?
How could this be their reality?

I felt so guilty as day after day
I'd listen to what the people did say
One day I became so dreadfully ill
My body with poison began to fill

To help me out, the Elders came
They told me I was not to blame

It wasn't my fault these things went wrong
Government policy is very strong

For me they started to sing a song
Amongst our people you do belong
In any event what's done is done
The process of healing has begun

So please my child do not fret
Our destiny is already set
There's a reason why you've come to us
So please don't cry and make a fuss

Why your people have come to this land
Is something I honestly don't understand
The Creator has guided you all to be
Joining us here around our tree

My healing began that very day
As the Elders there did quietly say
Nothing can ever change the past
But for the future we have a forecast

One day we'll all live in harmony
You'll learn about spirituality
Your people will come from far and wide
Our differences we will set aside

About my brown brothers today I write
It's not to offend or start a fight

It's so all people can understand
And to each other offer a hand
To once more bring the harmony
Peace and respect as it's meant to be

From that day forward for a long time, whenever the Elders came, they
always began their conversations about the problems with white people

with: "I know this is not you. Our issues are not with white people, it is the government policies and agencies we have trouble with, not you. You have come to us for a reason." How did they all know I was having such a hard time? I had only told a few. It was a mystery! "You will help others to understand, and when they do, harmony will be created between our people." I would just smile inside at their kindness, but I could not see how I could possibly be of help.

The effects of past oppression are certainly evident and affecting all Canadians in many ways today. The rate of fetal alcohol babies born today affects us all with the cost of care, as does the high crime rate among fetal alcohol affected people. The high cost of treatment due to diabetes-related complications is a *today* problem. The proportionately high rate of Native people incarcerated is a *today* issue. The number of apprehensions of children is a *today* issue. For all those people who say they are not responsible because it is in the past, it is not. It is *current*. It is *now* and much of the problem is due to misunderstandings and lack of information *today*. Not in the past. I believe if more people really knew the truth they would not be so judgmental; they would be much more open to the fact that we all share some responsibility for each other as Canadians. Our ancestors were a big part of the problem—we can be a part of the solution. We vitally need to be informed of the truth.

One thing about the Native people, they know how to laugh. Many times I heard them say that their humour got them through all the discrimination, the theft of their children, their confinement to the reservations, their jail time for prayer time, and all the other things that happened to their society. They know how to have fun, no matter how extreme their conditions.

One time Raven and I were camping up at the Alexis Reservation, where I went for my first ceremony. We had erected a teepee up against the trees overlooking an open field. Raven needed to stay there as he was to conduct some upcoming ceremonies. My sister Karin came for a visit. She was very nervous right from the time she got there and asked several times if it was okay for her to be there. She had never been on a reservation before. I assured her it was fine and reminded her that I was white too.

Suddenly an old station wagon came roaring around the corner and came to a screeching halt not far from where we were camped. Out stepped Percy Potts wearing old track pants and a t-shirt full of holes. He had not combed his hair. He came toward us with long strides and hollered, "What is all that white trash doing on my reservation?" I knew Percy and I knew he was joking, but when I looked over at my sister, her face was sheet white. I laughed so hard and told Percy he was scaring my sister half to death. "Is she your sister?" he asked. When he looked at her he realized I was right. He truly had frightened her. He apologized profusely, but had a hard time keeping a straight face. We really had a good laugh over it. She, however, never did come back to the reservation again.

Chapter 21

At the Bank

After two years, our contract on the acreage was up and I was still not working. We could not prove most of Raven's income, so I was concerned whether the banks would finance us anyway. He was also disappointed that he could not keep his horses there, as it was in a sub-division and he had too many for the size of the property.

We decided to sell, pay the balance out, and use the rest of the money to purchase more land if we could find a rent-to-own or someone who would be willing to carry our mortgage. We found the perfect place up at Sangudo. There were 180 acres with two sheds, a house and lots of space for his horses. They needed $11,000 down and the owner would carry the mortgage for three years. Three years gave us time to finish renovations, which were well under way. I knew I could get work in that area, so we decided to take the gamble. During those three years we made a lot of improvements. I was working part-time and we were able to get letters to prove much of Raven's income. We had an appraisal done on the property and needed only sixty-five percent of the value. Payments were well within our means and we both had a very good credit rating, so I expected no problem at all.

We approached several banks—and we were turned down on the spot. I could not believe it. Their reason was that Raven did not pay income tax on a large portion of his income. He worked on the reserve and as a treaty Indian working on the reservation his income was not taxable. They refused to take any of his income into account. I thought that would be a positive factor as there was more disposable income. After we had put so much time and money into the place to make sure it was secure, they did not even take an application. I was sick. We were about to lose it all.

Then just twelve days before we were to turn it back, a neighbor came over and offered to carry our mortgage for us. I could not believe our luck. The rate was high, but not atrocious. It was not a bad deal, so we took it. The second time I delivered a cheque to him, he told me he needed to cuddle and I should come inside. I told him I was very married and had no intention of cuddling with him or anyone else. I could see he was not happy. I made arrangements with him to make a deposit directly into his account from that day forward. This incident upset me so much that, knowing how tight he was and that he would be checking his account on the first of every month, I made deposits on the second or third day just to be a tease.

A few months later, we were returning from Slave Lake, about three hours north of Edmonton, where we had been participating in a youth and Elders get-together. It was Friday afternoon and we were much later departing than was our plan. We had a flat on the horse trailer which we used to carry the teepees and rails. Therefore we missed the bank payment, which meant that by Monday it was four days after the due date. As I was walking out of the house to make the deposit I got a call from our lawyer: he asked me what was going on with our payments. I told him what had happened. He told me they had put a foreclosure in motion. I was in shock. Murray told us that by law he had to give us time to pay, so we were okay, but then I realized what a vulnerable a position we were in.

I decided to try a different bank. I had heard that the CIBC in Onoway treated Native people like everyone else, so I went there. They did at least take the application and send it in. A week later we had our mortgage through them. I finally felt safe. Later I spoke to one of the top officials for the Bank of Montreal. He said we could get a mortgage from them with no difficulty. I have wondered if the barrier was due to bank policy or if it was the decision of the staff that was to submit the application. In any case it certainly shook me when I thought how close we had been to losing everything.

Chapter 22

Gifting The Enemy

One day a woman who was not happy about Raven being with a white woman and did not like me being around any of their sacred ceremonies phoned. Dorothy was not shy about letting everyone know her feelings. I rarely knew who was for me and who was not, but her I knew. She made no secret of her attitude, and she had a lot of influence in the Native community. Dorothy even tried to keep me away from the ceremonies. She wanted some medicine from Raven. I was very nervous about her coming to our home.

When she and her husband arrived, Raven said, "Newa (wife), put food on the table! We have visitors. Find the best we have!" I said nothing, just served them lunch, the best we had.

I was laying new carpet in one of the bedrooms and had a large piece of carpet left over. Dorothy complemented me on the job and said the carpet was very beautiful. Raven immediately told her she could have it. I had plans for that carpet and was not pleased that he gave it to her, but said nothing. I was still in my silent days. "Thank you," she said.

Then Raven took them to see the out-buildings on our farm. There were many things left behind by the previous owners. When I looked out the window I saw them loading their truck with a heater that I had plans for. He also gave them lumber and tools. I was totally confused and not happy. They came back in the house and she told me how happy she was for all the things she was given. They were looking for a heater as they had just renovated their house and needed one. The carpet was also much appreciated.

As we were eating lunch I listened politely to all that she said and acknowledged whatever she said. I saw Raven do this many times and so I thought I would follow his lead and see what happened. It was a new way of doing things for me and let me tell you it was not easy, but I thought I would give it a try.

When they were ready to leave, he reached in his pocket and gave them our last hundred dollars. That took my breath away. We had no money for gas or groceries and it was another week before he got paid. After they left, I asked him, "What are you doing? Why did you give our last dollar to someone who has harmed us so much? Now we do not even have enough money to go to town. How are you going to get to work?"

"Don't worry," he said. "It will come. We will get back all we need and more."

"But why did you give it all to her after what she has done to us?"

"It will pay off. Wait and see. She will have a different attitude from now on."

I was still worrying about how we were going to get to town when there was a knock on the door. It was Percy Potts. He handed Raven one hundred dollars which he had borrowed from him at the powwow, a gathering of dancers and singers, in Kamloops a few weeks before.

We had stopped in at the powwow and Percy had asked him if he could spare a few dollars. Raven gave him a hundred-dollar bill which was all he had then too. When I asked him how he thought we were going to make it home without money for gas he just said, "Don't worry! We will make it." I did not think we could.

When we reached Jasper, the tank was getting low. We dug in every pocket and the cubbyhole and checked the seats and the floor and found enough change to put a little more gas in the truck. I drove ninety kilometers an hour all the way, as at that speed we should get the best mileage. The gauge went to empty when we were still an hour away from home. I held my breath, and prayed. It was getting very late and I did not want to sleep on the road, but we still had no money for gas. To my amazement we made it home without incident and then, laughing, he said "I told you so. I knew it would be okay."

And as for Dorothy? She became as supportive for me as she had been against me from that day forward. No matter how large the crowd, she would come and give me a big hug. She never tried to keep me away from the ceremonies again and became a regular visitor to our home. She became one of my teachers.

Chapter 23

Raven's Family

As time went by and still Raven's family did not come to visit, with the exception of one of his daughters, Beryl, I felt very bad. Beryl told us the family was very angry about us being together. Not everyone was close to their father.

Up until he reached the age of forty, he had been drinking heavily. He told me how Johnny, his son, came to him one day and said, "Dad, don't you think it is time to begin the work you are supposed to do?" "I just looked at my boy and immediately knew what I had to do. It was time to stop drinking and start doing the sacred work I was destined for. I told him to go and buy four pieces of broadcloth, two meters in length. When he returned, I took out my pipe and smoked. I have not touched a drop of liquor since that day. That is over twenty years ago."

One day the oldest girl, Shirley, came to visit. She wanted to see her father and meet me. We had a very good visit and when she left she gave me a hug and said, "Thank you for taking care of my dad." I invited her to come any time she desired. I liked her very much.

About a year after we got together, Raven's ex-wife died. Some family members blamed the fact that we were together for her death. That was hard, but there was nothing we could do about it. They also thought he was abandoning his family when he took up the name Raven Makkannaw. For him it meant so much. He was so proud to carry his grandfather's name.

Sometimes Raven would lie in the bedroom in the dark. When I asked him what was wrong, he would say, "I am waiting for my children to come." Often I would suggest he go to them. "They do not want me right now," he would tell me. "The day will come when they will. I just have to be patient. When they do come, then it will be okay." I could not understand that way of thinking.

Almost a year after Annie's death we decided to get married. The families and communities needed to know this was serious, that we planned to stay together for good.

We actually had two weddings, the first one with the justice of the peace, followed by a nice intimate dinner with family and a few friends.

The second was a blessing by the Elders with a pipe ceremony, and then a traditional round dance in the evening, which was open to everyone. Many drummers from the Native communities came.

My non-Native friends and my family had never seen a round dance before. A round dance is a gathering of people who all come together to dance and celebrate for a purpose such as weddings, anniversaries, graduations and holidays. In a round dance everyone forms a large circle, holding hands, around the drummers. Then the people move sideways in a clockwise direction. They dip slightly at the knees, in time to the drums, so it is like a wave going up and down.

I told all the non-Native people that it was not very polite if they did not dance. "It is very simple," I told them. "Once you have watched it you will see. Then it would be good if you would dance."

Exchanging Wedding Vows

That was the only time in all the years I was with Raven that there was nearly half and half Native and non-Native people together. When all the non-Native people had watched for a short time, they too got up and joined the dance. My Native friends and family were ever so happy and grateful that they joined in.

Out of the seven daughters, the only one who came to the wedding was Beryl, who brought her children. It seemed as if his children were finding pain in everything we did.

Late in the fall of 1992, nearly two years after we were married, Raven got a call from his son Johnny who asked if he would join them for a hunting trip. Many of his children would be there. He was ecstatic. He had recently purchased a brand new 4X4 Ford half-ton truck and this was the first time he had the opportunity to take it hunting. As we were packing he hardly stopped talking about previous hunting trips with his sons. That was the first time I heard about those early hunts and the first time I realized just how high a price he was paying for his life choices.

I had never seen Raven happier than he was that day. He made arrangements to meet the children in a clearing in the wilderness west of Buck Lake where they had hunted in the past. By mid-day we arrived at the designated meeting place. It was a cool crisp fall day and the leaves were already turning a bright yellow and red.

There were four or five children running around and laughing merrily. Johnny had parked his large camping trailer along the east side of the bush. To the north stood a trapper's tent (a tent built like a house with a peak, always made of canvas), which obviously belonged to Grant, another son. He kept going in and out as he was setting up his air-tight heater, a wood burning heater which is easy to transport as it is very light in weight and will keep a tent cozy even in the cold of winter. He was cutting and gathering wood for the anticipated cold night. Next to his tent was a large grey and red nylon tent. Raven's daughter Katrina was busy bringing in a lot of bedding for her and some of the children. Next to her was a small nylon tent, which Shirley, the oldest was preparing.

In a moment everyone stopped what they were doing and came over to greet us. Both Johnny and Shirley immediately expressed their gratitude to their father for coming. After Raven introduced me to those I had not previously met, everyone began unloading our truck and in a matter of about fifteen minutes our large canvas tent was erected and our supplies were all in our tent. Hardly a word was exchanged while they were setting up our camp; each person just did what was necessary.

Soon one more truck pulled in. It was Shirley's son Bobby and his family. After a brief greeting they too got busy and set up camp.

Once everyone had their camp set up, the women started to prepare a meal in Johnny's camper. I decided to join the women. They kept saying that this was the lazy man's way of cooking and tomorrow they would cook everything over the fire. I did not want to offend anyone and as I did not know their ways, I felt the best thing to do was to be polite and say as little as possible, only listen.

In the meantime the men were busy getting a good supply of wood, and cutting poles which they used to set up tarps so we could sit under them should it rain or if the sun got too hot in the middle of the day. Everyone had something to do and everyone was happy.

A table and chairs were brought out and placed under the canopy attached to the camper. Soon we women set out dishes and condiments followed by steaks, potatoes and turnips. All the adults came and sat down to eat. The mothers prepared plates for the children, who took them to a log where they sat and ate. Everyone was talking about the funny things children do and reminiscing about past hunting trips.

Johnny told us that he had smoked his sacred pipe and prayed for a good hunt the evening before. Everyone nodded in respect.

After the meal everyone went to their camp, relaxed a little and then began preparing for the evening hunt. Raven said we had to go soon as the sun would be setting in about an hour and a half. That would give us time to look for game. The animals feed just before sunset and just after sunrise. At that time they move around and are easier to spot, so that was the time to hunt.

One by one the trucks headed out in different directions. There were many small gravel roads leading to the oil pumps which dot the country. We headed straight west and soon arrived on top of the bank of the North Saskatchewan River. We got out of the truck to scan the valley below. The bright yellow and red leaves contrasted with the blue of the river below. We saw no game, so we wound our way southward for the next half hour, but once again there were only tracks, no game. At one point when Raven got out to check, with me following as I was anxious to learn all I could, he turned to me and said, "Can't eat tracks, we may as well go back. Maybe we will spot something on the way."

We turned around and headed back toward camp.

It was dark by the time we arrived. A campfire was burning brightly as we pulled into camp. Everyone was sitting around the fire. Johnny and Grant were there ahead of us. They hadn't had any luck either. As we joined them, Shirley immediately poured us a cup of tea. The warmth felt good in the cool evening air. Just as we settled, Shirley's son Bobby arrived. He'd had no better luck than the rest of us.

That evening around the campfire they told stories around the campfire of other hunts. They told one story about a time some years back when a white man came into their camp at Kootenay Plains. They invited him to join them as they always did when visitors came. As he accepted a cup of tea, he said had seen hundreds of buffalo in a valley close by and told them how lucky they were to have so many. They all looked at each other, and said nothing. The buffalo had long since disappeared from that area. After he left, everyone agreed he had seen the buffalo come out of the ground as they sometimes did. I said nothing, but remembered Raven telling my son how the animals lived underground.

The next morning Raven woke me up very early. It was still totally dark and it was cold. The temperature had dipped well below freezing in the night. We had brought a camp stove which he lit to warm the tent and heat water for tea. I made him a bowl of instant porridge as he had to eat because of his diabetes. He grumbled and said he was not used to eating before a hunt. I told him he did not look after himself properly and now with his diabetes he had to eat. In the meantime he went out and started the truck to warm it up and melt the ice on the windshield. After preparing a thermos of tea and packing some cookies, we headed out. By this time the light was just beginning to appear in the eastern sky. Raven asked me to drive. He pointed to the south and I turned in that direction. We were silent as we drove. Soon we came to a crossroad and once again he just pointed in the direction he wanted to take. That morning Raven spotted a grizzly bear off in the distance. He just pointed again and said nothing. We spotted one moose, but it was an old bull and he said the meat would be too tough. We also saw several deer but they were too far away for a sure kill. He would not take a chance on just injuring an animal. About eleven o'clock we returned to camp. Shortly after, Bobby arrived and proudly announced that he had shot a nice young bull moose.

Shirley and Katrina were busy preparing a late breakfast of bacon and eggs and home-fried potatoes. Soon it was time to eat. Everyone present thanked Shirley and Katrina for cooking such a fine meal for us. For some reason, food cooked over a fire is so much tastier. Everyone ate in silence as we all enjoyed our food.

After everyone had eaten their fill, the men prepared to drive the four kilometers down the bush road to where the fallen moose was. Raven told me to come with him as he wanted me to drive. As we approached the moose everyone was silent in respect for the animal which had sacrificed its life so we could live. In the meantime, the women cleaned up in camp. When we returned with the meat everyone took a rest.

After about an hour and a half, we once again gathered as we began cutting and wrapping the meat. Everyone constantly thanked the animal for the giving its life. The moose's nose and heart were put aside for ceremonial purposes. Shirley and Katrina cut meat for drying. The pieces were cut very thin and hung over racks built for that purpose. A fire was lit under them and they were smoked and dried. That would take two days. Dry meat is one of the staples of a traditional diet. It is one of the ingredients in pemmican. When it is crushed and mixed with berries and moose fat it will never spoil. Some has been found that is estimated to be one hundred years old. Pemmican was the favorite food of travelers. It has all the ingredients needed to sustain a person indefinitely and it is delicious.

That evening we went out again. We saw a beautiful big female moose with two calves. Raven said we could not take her because of her babies.

When we returned the campfire was already burning brightly and we enjoyed a cup of tea boiled on the open fire. In the darkness of the night, the light of the fire danced on everyone's faces like ghosts. It was like magic as we all enjoyed the sharing of stories and the laughter of the children. No wonder Raven had missed this.

Making moose drymeat.

I wondered at many things. We had always hung our meat for a few days before cutting it. I had learned that if we did not it would be tough. Here they were cutting it up immediately. When I mentioned it to Raven he said he had never heard of hanging meat. It would be very difficult to keep the flies away, and their meat was never tough.

They would not shoot an animal that would have tough meat. Not like the white people who shot bulls in rutting season. Maybe that was why they hung the meat.

The next morning Raven and I saw a nice big moose buck standing in the middle of the road. I stopped the truck. Raven got out, put his rifle to his shoulder and shot. The moose took a little jump and slowly began walking toward the trees. Raven got back in the truck and motioned for me to drive away. "He is a three-year-old and will be good eating," he said, "but for now we must have respect for him and allow him to die in peace. We drove about a kilometer and then stopped and had some tea and cookies.

That was so different from the way I was taught when I used to hunt so many years ago. We would never have left an animal; we would have chased it and then perhaps have shot it in the head if it was not dead. Never would a traditional hunter shoot an animal in the head nor put their foot on top of it. They would never shoot a female who might be with young, or a bull in rutting season (when they are looking to mate). For one thing, the meat is stronger and for another, nature must be allowed to take its course. Native people really think that opening hunting season for bulls in the time of the rut is ridiculous.

Although they have no written laws in regard to hunting, Native people have laws all the same. Preservation and respect is very much practiced by all traditional hunters even today.

When Raven was satisfied that the moose was probably dead, we went back to look for it. As soon as we found it, Raven prayed, thanking the animal for giving its life, cut its throat so he could bleed it properly and then turned back toward camp. Later that day the young men came and loaded the moose in the back of the truck and took it back to camp where they skinned it and took the meat off the bones.

Altogether, in the four days we were there, four moose and two deer were taken. Dry meat was made and it was all cut and wrapped and then Johnny shared all the meat amongst the people there. We broke camp and loaded everything into our trucks. As we were ready to leave

I looked back: the only signs that there had been anyone camping there were the ashes of the cold fire and the flattened grass. There was not a scrap of paper, not a can, nothing that did not belong in the wilderness.

On the way home Raven told a story about a young man who came and asked if he could help him as he had been unable to find game for the past two years.

"Why?" Raven asked, as he knew the young man was a good hunter.

"I did something very bad two years ago," he said. "I did not take proper care of an animal I had shot and the meat went bad. Since then I have not had the privilege of even seeing an animal when I go hunting. I know what I did was wrong, and I deserve this drought, but can you help me? My family is yearning for wild meat. They do not like to eat store-bought."

Raven did help him. The next time we saw him, he'd had a successful hunt. He was so grateful.

What a nice time we had that weekend! It was a successful hunt, for there was meat enough for everyone, but much more important, Raven had time with his family. He was happier than I had ever seen him.

For the next few years I said nothing when I was around Raven's family. There was so much to learn, so many things I knew nothing about, the hunting trip being but one.

Raven had thirteen children: most of them were married and had children of their own. It was hard for me to figure out who was who and how they belonged. Then I would hear someone refer to a Kokum (grandmother) So-and-so, or Mushum (grandfather) So-and-so, who I knew were not their actual grandparents. One day I asked Raven, "Why do your grandchildren call your sister Kokum? She is not really their grandmother."

"Of course she is!" he said surprised.

"I have also noticed that they call a lot of people sister and brother, and I am totally confused as I do not think some are your children. I am so mixed up about the family!"

"In our society everyone in one generation is the same. All my brothers and sisters are Kokum and Mushum to my grandchildren. All the cousins are not cousins like you say. They are brothers and sisters. There is no difference between those that are born of the same parents or those born to ones brothers and sisters. Many other people also come into our lives and we adopt them."

"Now I understand why I have been so confused." I said.

"You will catch on," he said.

I did not want to make a fool of myself, or offend anyone, not being able to figure out who was who or how to address the different relations. That was another reason for saying nothing of significance when I was with the family.

There were so many differences, and often I did not understand their ways, and they often did not understand the non-Native perspective on many things. I did not want to get into any discussions that might disturb already fragile relationships, and I really did want to learn from them, therefore the silence. I also knew from past observations that if I said too much I would leave the impression that I thought I knew something. Then they would just clam up and I would learn nothing.

After seven years of this relative silence, Raven and I were invited to his daughter Katrina's place for supper. I was still trying to figure out where everyone belonged in the family. I do not know how many people were there, as long before I had been taught not to try to count family members. "What if someone dies?" he had said. "You cannot count." Anyway there were more than a dozen. We were all sitting around the table when Katrina's son Charles suddenly said, "I stole."

"Who did you steal from?" asked Katrina.

"We wanted some booze so we broke into these people's house and stole some," said Charles.

"You know better than that, my boy. You are not supposed to steal," she said.

"Jeffrey made me," he said. "He should not have made you do that," said Katrina and nothing more.

That time I could not hold back any longer and I said loud and clear, "And if he would have told you to shit your pants, would you have done that too?" Everyone turned just looked at me. I looked at Charles and he looked back at me.

"No," he said meekly. No one else said anything more about it. After a long silence the chatter continued.

After that first time I was no longer silent around the family. Most did show me respect and some became very good friends, but it took seven years. Seven years of listening and learning.

Chapter 24

Karen and Kathy

One day thirteen-year-old Karen, one of our grandchildren, came to us and asked if she could come and live with us. The first time I met Karen was about three years before at a rodeo at the Hobbema reservation. She came and put her hand in mine and we were just together at every opportunity. Now she was struggling, as her mother had problems providing a stable home for her. She had not been in school on a regular basis and she wanted her education. We agreed for her to come, and took her home with us. First off, we had to buy her school clothes and supplies as she had none. Then Karen and I went to get her registered. The principal told us they had no other Native children at the school and he was thrilled to have her. We were getting known in the community of Sangudo where we lived and, as was the case almost everywhere he went, Raven was immensely popular.

On the 15th of September, Raven, Karen and I drove to Buck Lake. We found that Karen's eleven-year-old sister Kathy was not yet registered in school, so we picked her up as well. It was a Sunday afternoon. Kathy was dressed in a man's t-shirt, runners that were two sizes too big, and shorts. It was very cold that day. When I told her to go and get her things, she came back with a tiny bundle which contained a couple of t-shirts. That was all.

I knew we had to find a store and get this poor girl some clothes. On the way home she asked if she had to go to school the next day. I told her firmly that she had to go to school every day. I could see her in the rear-view mirror and she just gulped.

We stopped at the Saan store in Spruce Grove. I told her she had to go and buy some school clothes. We went to the rack of outfits and I told her to pick one she liked. The first thing she did was look at the price tag. I told her not to do that as I would make the decision as to whether I was willing to pay for it or not. Nothing was too expensive in the Saan store anyway. When she had finished picking an outfit, I told her to go and find undies, shoes and socks. Then she had to try them on. It was a joy to see her eyes sparkle. I thought the look on her face was worth every penny I would ever spend on this young beautiful girl. Then I told her to pick out another outfit.

"I don't believe it!" she said.

"You can't go to school in the same outfit every day," I told her.

She did pick out another outfit. I had it in mind to get her three outfits and so I told her to go back for a third. I was really surprised at her reaction.

"I can't! Please don't make me!" she begged. It was too much for her all at once.

Off we went. I was so grateful to have youngsters in my home again. My heart was full of gratitude.

'Give children at least five compliments a day and they will live up to their full potential' is a policy I always lived by. These two girls really needed to learn what their full potential was, I thought.

Both girls were fully welcomed into their school. The teachers were terrific and did a great job with introductions. They both made good friends right away and were very happy.

Then they wrote their first exams. There was not a mark over 30 percent. I knew there were holes in their education, but I did not know they were that big! Their teachers called me right away; they asked me why I thought the girls were not doing better. Both teachers said they felt the girls were very bright, so what was this about? The principal also called and asked if I would come in and meet with him. He told me they could test them.

"What are you going to use the tests for?" I asked.

"We want to know if they belong in a regular class," he replied.

"No, you cannot," I told him. "These girls are very bright and they will not be sent to any special class. They have had enough of that from their previous school. Their marks were at least partially as a result of the 'special' class. There has to be another way and we will find it."

The principal was very surprised and explained that they would like to see if there were any learning disabilities for which they needed some help. I then agreed to the tests, but only if they did nothing with the results until they talked to me. They agreed. The only thing they found was that Kathy had a problem with short term memory and so if she said she forgot to do her homework, she probably did. Her teacher simply set up a homework list for her and that solved that. It did help to know about it, as we could adjust learning methods to accommodate that. We just had to make sure she could keep a teaching long enough to put it into long term memory. Then she did fine.

We set up a homework schedule. One hour every evening. No more, no less. First was assigned homework, then the rest of the time would be spent catching up on what they were missing. They were to pick their own hour. They totally supported it and committed to working hard, and they did.

Kathy was so funny. A thousand times she exclaimed, "I'm not stupid!" She was on a discovery journey.

Karen also worked very hard. She could not understand ratios and fractions. One evening we took a deck of cards and we did fractions by placing the cards in squares on the table. When she understood how 1/2 was the same as 2/4, it was a beautiful moment. She just kept saying joyfully, "This is easy!"

I kept laughing with her and saying everything in school was easy as soon as it was understood. The hard part was getting the understanding. Ratios we worked by using pens and pencils. I asked her to tell me how many pencils there were in comparison to pens.

"There are two pencils and three pens," she said.

"So the ratio is two pencils to three pens or 2:3." She caught on immediately and was more joyful than I had ever seen before. We danced around, laughing, as I used more examples and she got them all. By Christmas time both girls were passing their exams. I had expected that they would by the end of the year, so they far exceeded my expectations.

The fun and laughter of these youngsters in our home was such a blessing.

We were not without problems, however. Karen started making phone calls and charging them to other people's phones. When the phone company began receiving complaints from their customers, they investigated and the source was traced back to our phone. We got stuck with phone bills totaling $1200.

After a lot of discussion and many tears, we set up a work schedule for her to pay it off and also cut her allowance in half for a while. That one backfired—we had worked out a budget which included all her needs, and so I ended up paying for many things anyway.

One thing I found very difficult with Karen was, whenever I complimented her, she would often get angry. I thought if I only kept it up she would realize that I meant every word I said. She was pretty and smart and had a nice personality and I loved her laugh.

One day Joe Couture, a Native man who was a child psychologist, came and stayed with us as he wanted to learn from Raven. I spoke to him about her anger and he told me she had created a block of ice which was her protection. The compliments were like an ice pick to her. When I asked him what I should do about it, he told me to keep it up, but expect her to break. "When that happens, you need to be there for her. She will need you more than ever."

Joe's stay was very challenging as well as enlightening. One evening, after Raven had been very quiet all day, he told me he was not pleased at the way I looked at Joe and how we talked together. My heart sank. I could not put up with jealousy. It was not the first time, but this time was different. Before, he had just expressed his displeasure and we were able to come to an understanding. This time he became very angry. Much of the problem was because I am an outgoing person and accustomed to looking at people when I speak to them or they speak to me. He had interpreted it as flirting. After that I closely observed what other women did and changed some of my mannerisms as I did not want to hurt him.

I continued to compliment Karen, although sometimes it was very difficult.

We took the girls along when we went to ceremonies and traditional dances. They learned a lot about the spiritual practices. One day Dorothy, the Elder who had come to our home and to whom Raven had given our last dollar, came for a visit. She had much experience in raising children as she had cared for probably fifty. Some were brought by Social Services and some were her grandchildren and of course she had her own as well. I gave her tobacco and offerings to do a sweat lodge for us. After that everything went much more smoothly.

That Christmas my granddaughter Theresa, from my first husband, came to stay with us through the holidays. Theresa's father had become violent with her. She did not want to stay in a shelter for Christmas. Her mother Bev had called to ask if we would take her, and of course we would. My own children had no time for me as their father was being so pathetic that they took pity on him and invited him to spend Christmas Eve with them. They were going to their in-laws for Christmas Day, hence no time. When I commented about that, they told me that I had many people in my life, while he had no one. Karen and Kathy's mother was drinking, so they did not want to see her.

There was not one person in our house who was not hurting real bad.

One evening I said to the girls, "How would you like to go on a ski trip to Jasper for Christmas? That way we can all have a good time and do something different." I definitely wanted to put something good in our lives to replace all the misery, at least for a while.

Jasper is a picturesque town nestled in the Rocky Mountains. It is home to Marmot Basin Ski Resort, which has hosted numerous international ski meets. I told them they would have to keep their eyes open for celebrities up there. You never know who you will see in Jasper.

All three girls loved the idea and so I called to see if we could get accommodations. We were in luck! Someone had just cancelled. We booked a suite, packed our food and off we went. We cut a little tree on the way and bought all edible decorations. Christmas Eve we cooked a goose and Christmas Day we took the girls to the ski hill. When they'd had enough skiing they came to the clubhouse. All three girls were laughing so hard that it was totally infectious for everyone around us. When they could finally collect themselves long enough to tell us what had happened we got the story. Poor Kathy had got caught up in the very tree they had already coached her past. They could not figure out how she had managed to go back up the hill to hit the tree. They could not stop laughing.

The next day Karen, Theresa and I cross-country skied from Jasper to Alexandra Falls, about seventeen kilometers away. The mountains in winter are breath-taking with their blankets of white and the frozen waterfalls. There had been a snowfall two days before and the only break in the flowing patterns of the pure white snow cover was the animal tracks, a reminder that we shared this fantastic land with our four-legged friends. The trees too were decorated in white. It was a cold crisp day and we could see our breath as we glided along the mountain trail. About halfway there we stopped for a break by a river. We did not say much, just enjoyed the winter wonderland it was.

As we were getting ready to continue, I whispered, "Shhhhh! The world is asleep!"

We all looked around and said nothing more, just donned our skis and continued on.

It was a most special Christmas that year.

Jasper Christmas with Karen and Kathy
Left to right: me, Kathy, Raven and Karen.

As the end of school drew near we got a letter that Kathy was getting an award and we were being asked to attend the ceremonies. When it came time for 'most improved student,' I knew she had that one. The teacher who was doing the presentation praised the new student who had come to their school. He talked about how hard a worker she was, how she was such a happy person, and how she brought joy to the class. He told everyone how bright she was to be able to bring her marks up as she had done—how in just one short year she was able to raise them by over thirty percentage points. He said he felt privileged to know her and hoped she would be back next year. Kathy's friend kept poking her and saying, "That's you!"

Kathy whispered back, "No, I'm not that good."

Finally he said, "That young woman is Kathy Mackinaw!"

I have never seen anyone jump so high in the air from a sitting position on the floor. Everyone laughed.

Karen in the meantime was doing extremely well, but for whatever reason decided to fail her final exams. The teachers said she knew the work and that she was very bright, so they could not figure it out. Neither could I, but I told them I would talk to her. I made one fatal mistake. The kitchen area was small and U-shaped. She was sitting on the cupboard and without even thinking I was blocking her way out. From previous experience I should have known better, as she could not handle being trapped, and she lost it. She screamed some not nice things and rushed past me, almost pushing me down. I decided it was best to let her cool off a little before trying to talk to her again.

I felt so bad; and decided to go for a walk to plan how we could get back on good footing. When I returned, I saw her sitting up at the cabin which was on our property. I decided to wait to try to talk until she returned to the house. When she had not returned an hour later, I started to get concerned and went to search for her. Kathy told me not to bother, that she was at her friend's place. I called there immediately and the mother told me that Karen was sleeping and I had better leave her there until morning, which I did.

The next morning Karen and Kathy's mother and Raven's daughter Katrina showed up and told me they were taking the girls. Legally, I knew they could as there were never any papers drawn up, but I did not want them to go until we had the opportunity to talk and bring things to a good place.

I told Katrina to stop badmouthing, which I knew she had been doing as several family members had told me so. "It is not right," I said. "You know nothing about me." She tried to deny it, but I told her not to bother since I knew every time she said something bad. There are always people who like to share bad things. "All I ask is that it stops

NOW! Got it?" She left the house in tears. On her way out she told Kathy to grab her things and run to the car. Kathy did and they were gone. My heart was broken. Never did I think it would end like that.

Later that same day there was a knock on the door. It was two people from Child Welfare. They had come to investigate as they had a complaint against me. I could not believe it. I told them the story of the past year.

I swore I would never again take on anyone else's children. It was too hard to lose them like that. Tears flowed for days. It was a nightmare the way such joy could turn to such pain.

I was also afraid I had 'child welfare status' and that could come back to haunt me. Child Welfare kept a record of any children removed from a home. If that ever happened, they would put your name on a 'status list' and you would be restricted from ever working with children again.

I was heartbroken about it all, but realized there was nothing I could do. I had no legal leg to stand on and I could not fight Raven's family. That would bring too much heartache to too many people. Especially Raven. Besides, it was much too hard to put the girls in the position of making a choice against their mother. I knew they could not. I have a saying: 'If you know you cannot win the battle, why start it?' I really feel it was the case with the girls.

Chapter 25

Sacred Ceremonies

As time passed, I attended all the ceremonies by Raven's side, and went alone to many others that were specifically for women.

I cannot, however, write about the actual process of the ceremonies that I attended. I was told that I was given much knowledge and wisdom to share with all people for peace and understanding, but not the ceremonies. Although I attended hundreds, they are not mine to share. I am so grateful to all the Elders for their teachings and the guidance and healing they gave me and I will always respect their wish. If anyone has a desire to learn more, they must do the proper protocol for one who has been passed that gift. I will however, share about some things that were *my* experience.

On a cold winter day in February Raven told me someone would be coming with a pipe. I felt it was something important, but did not ask because from past experience he would just tell me to wait and see.

A few days later, a group of men came to our home from the Alexis reservation, (where I had been for ceremonies). They brought a pipe and offerings. Raven sat cross-legged at one end of what we called 'the big room' of our home. Danny, who was obviously the leader of the group, put his hand on Raven's head and asked him if he would put up the sun dance for them on the Alexis reservation. Tears came to Danny's eyes. He was obviously very moved. The sun dance is the biggest ceremony of them all. Raven took the pipe and they all joined him on the floor in a circle. Then he said, "I am with a white woman and she will be by my side throughout the sun dance ceremony. So take the pipe back to your people and if they still want me to put up the sun dance, bring it back next week."

The pipe did come back. They had discussed it with their people and they said everything was about the spirits and the Creator, not the color of someone's skin. Raven accepted the pipe and said he would do it for them.

This was the middle of February. The first round of ceremonies was to be completed by the end of the month. Let me tell you we got busy! There are many things that need to be acquired, including a heart sac from a moose and a moose hide, tanned in a special way. We had to travel to pass tobacco to helpers and Elders. There was food to prepare for many people and I did not know how many or what was needed. Several women said they would come and help, but as his woman I was responsible and was expected to steer the whole process. But I knew nothing!

Gary and Bob, on different occasions, told me that if I went ahead with the ceremonies, one of Raven's family members would die because a white woman had no place in their ceremonies. Every time I talked to Raven about it he said, "Don't worry! It will be okay." I thought that it was easy for him to say, he knew what he was doing. I didn't.

A few days before the first singing (a preparation ceremony), I got a call from his daughter Beryl who told me that I had better not go up there if I knew what was good for me. The family would do the cooking and if I was there they would kill me. Not again! I thought. I wanted out and I told Raven so. I did not think I could do this.

"I need you there, and I do not think my family would come anyway," he said.

"I was told that if I participated one of your family members will die," I reminded him. "I cannot be responsible for that!"

"Whoever told you that does not know what they are talking about. I know you. Do not worry. It will not happen."

I reluctantly decided to continue, as I knew how much it meant to him and he could not do everything by himself. I was not certain that any of his family would show up, but was certainly prepared to leave if they did. I wanted to be there both for him and for myself, but neither would nor could fight his family. For one thing, they were bigger and meaner, and there were too many of them. For another, it would be much too difficult for Raven at this time of preparing for sacred ceremonies. He was much too tender to enter into any kind of conflict. Every time he prepared for ceremonies he would open up to the spiritual world. That also meant he was open to all other energies around him.

Finally the day arrived.

Some weeks before, Beryl had told me that I would need to start the cooking at six in the morning in order to get it all done in time. The food cannot be prepared until the day of the ceremonies, so we started to cut meat into bite-sized pieces right after midnight. We crawled into bed exhausted two hours later. We didn't wake up until six. Did we ever scramble to load everything up and get on the road to Alexis! The crunch of the snow under our feet broke the stillness of that quiet cold morning. Every breath looked like a cloud of smoke as our warm breath met the cold air. I was not sure if the car would start, but it did. We reached the reservation at seven-thirty. I was getting in a panic. Already we had lost one and a half hours.

As we drove into Danny's place, where we were to pick up the keys, I saw his wife, who had said she would be there to help, run for the bedroom and I never saw her again. She was the person I had counted on to guide me. Now I had lost the support of both Raven's daughter and the woman I thought was my friend.

Danny couldn't find the keys to the building where we were to cook. He drove to another man's place, no luck there either. Finally at about 11 o'clock the keys were located. By that time I was beyond panicking. I knew I would be humiliated in front of his people. There was no way we could be ready in time, so I would just do the best I could, but my heart was heavy. I had heard that when a person did a lot of spiritual work they would be rewarded. I wondered about that, too.

His family, at least, were not there. I almost hoped they were. Then it would at least fall on their shoulders when the food was not ready.

The building where we were to cook was situated on the shores of Lac St. Anne. It was a bi-level with about eight steps going to the upper floor and eight to the lower. The kitchen was on the upper level. There was no sign of any volunteers. They had agreed to be there at nine o'clock, two hours before our arrival; I had no idea if they had been there and left.

As Raven was unloading the groceries, an eagle appeared out of nowhere and hovered above him. The bird's eyes were level with mine as I stood on the upper level of the bi-level. That eagle had the purest white head I had ever seen; the white was whiter than white. It hovered there for what seemed like a long time. Our world came to a standstill. Then slowly the eagle flew off. At that moment I *knew* everything would be okay! My heart was light again. I was singing inside.

It was not five minutes before Angelique arrived. The first thing she said was: "I know nothing about this, so tell me what to do!" I had thought all Native women knew all about these things. I asked her if she could make deep-fried bannock and she nodded. Thank goodness! I had tried a few times and it was not good. I put four pails of water on to boil for the soup while she made the first batch of batter for the bannock. There were only four burners so I knew this was definitely going to be a challenge. Just as the last pail was placed on the burner, two more ladies showed up. They too said they knew nothing so I would have to tell them what to do as well. "This is a case of the blind leading the blind for sure," I said. "No one seems to know what to do!" We all started to laugh and called Raven. When he heard our dilemma, he joined in the laughter and reassured us: "That's okay. We will get it done."

Raven, although very busy with the many people who were coming to him, was in and out of the kitchen all day coaching us along the way. We women were laughing all day about our ignorance and other things or nothing. Every time we added rice to a pail of soup we would have a discussion about how much. To top it off, we had no idea how many people would show up, as the idea of having a white woman there was not acceptable to some.

The Royal Canadian Mounted Police did stop in and they told me they were surprised at Raven's request to check in as they were usually told to stay away from sacred ceremonies. I didn't know he had talked to them. He sounded so sure there would be no trouble, but yet he called the police?

It was mid-afternoon when the old man, Red Bear, showed up. His role was to be a support and teacher to Raven and the head helper, Danny. I did not know how he felt about me, but knew his support was crucial. I immediately got him a cup of tea and shook his hand. He took my hand in both of his and bowed ever so slightly to me. My heart was lifted. He was so respected and the wisest of them all. Tears of relief were on the surface of my eyes. The other person from whom I needed support was Mary Mae Strawberry. She was the old woman whom Raven had asked to lead the pipe ceremony for the women. When she arrived I went to her with tea as well. She just said, "Thank you," and tilted her head to the side and down and gave me a little smile. That was enough. It did not matter what anyone else thought. With Mary Mae, Red Bear and Raven's support I had everything.

Just as we were done with the four mandatory pails of soup, Raven told us we should cook another. Just in case. We had finished making one large box of bannock and we thought that was enough, but no. He brought us another big box to fill. Just in case. We just looked at each other, shrugged our shoulders, and started again. By six that evening we had two tables, each three meters long, full of food. We were not only ready in time, but were early. Was it divine help? What else could it possibly be? We washed up and changed clothes to prepare for the feast and ceremonies. Our job was finished. Now it was up to the young men to bring everything to the hall across the street where the ceremonies were held. There they smudged it all by passing it through smoke from a burning sweet grass braid and set it in order on a large canvas spread out on the floor. The young men were to do all the carrying and the serving.

Adding to the race factor, we were also dealt another whammy: the thermometer dipped to minus thirty. I wondered how many people would show up.

Slowly people began to trickle in. Then suddenly, as if on signal, the hall filled with people. Some people also brought pails of soup and bannock. They stood by the door and waited for a young helper to come and get it. The women went to one side, the men to the other. Besides Raven and Red Bear, five more men sat in the front, to Raven's left. Mary Mae sat to his right. Everyone sat on the floor around the perimeter of the hall. Raven was obviously thrilled that so many came. I was happy too.

They started with the smoking of the sacred pipes. Then everyone took out dishes and set them out on the floor in front of themselves. The young men got up to do the serving. They passed the soups we had made to the Elders and helpers first. Then, starting at the far right, they moved along serving one person after the next. We were sitting on the far left of the Elders. Not one spoonful of our soup came our way. As we were not to taste any food while we were cooking, we never did find out how we did.

Then there was singing and drumming, and blowing of whistles. Many people came to Raven for prayers. About one o'clock in the morning, everything was done and the people got up off the floor. I admired the old people for sitting on the floor for so many hours. There were always many people ready to help them to stand. I thought about how close the people of the community were, how the spiritual ceremonies filled my heart. How grateful I was to have played a small role in something so sacred. Life, although ever so hard, certainly had its rewards.

All through the rest of the winter and early spring Raven prayed morning and night over the offerings, the cloth or flags as they were called, that were brought by the people for prayers. They were tied in a very large bundle and hung on a tripod, set up beside the house. There were many more ceremonies and more flags brought for prayers. The load of the people got heavier and heavier as Raven carried the weight of each person's request for help. That is the burden the sun dance maker takes on.

By April, when it was a little warmer, we had to move up to the Alexis Reservation where the big sun dance lodge would be erected. It would be located in a field away from the town site. Raven packed the truck with all the supplies we needed, the tent, the teepee and food. We drove up to the Alexis reserve late one morning. Raven pulled into a yard and honked his horn. Out came Francis Alexis. Raven told him he needed help. As Francis said, "The young lads are ready for you," about eight of them came out and jumped in the back of the truck. We turned west down a gravel road. After a short distance we turned left again onto a small two-track trail. We followed that up a hill and across a field to a stand of trees on the other side. The trail was barely visible in the grass. As we approached a stand of trees, Raven stopped the truck and told the boys where he wanted the teepee and tent to stand. They reminded me of little beavers, busying themselves with the cutting of the poles for the tents and unloading the teepee rails. It was not long before we had our camp set up, the airtight heater (a wood burning heater made of aluminum) assembled in the tent, and wood for cooking and heat piled up. When they were done, our young workers just jumped in the truck and we drove them back to the house.

When we returned, the stillness consumed us. I prepared our beds, one on each side of the tent. We were not allowed to sleep together. I wondered about that too: it was a long time until the big lodge in July.

Raven unpacked the rest of the supplies and by that time hunger pangs were beginning to creep in. It was time to think about supper. Raven made a fire pit and placed rocks all around it and laid a grill on top.

In the meantime I prepared the meat and vegetables for a good hearty soup. I found the tea and the kettle. Soon we had hot water for tea. That first cup was the best tea I had ever tasted. There is something different about tea that is made from water heated on an open fire.

One day Raven asked if I wanted to fast for the sun dance. He told me it was up to me, but it would be good if I wanted to as I would probably learn things from the spirits. If it was good, I certainly wanted to. That day I committed to fast for four days during the up-coming ceremonial time.

People really looked after us in the months we lived at the grounds. Every day they brought fresh fish or meat and whatever other supplies we needed. The men would always make sure there was enough wood.

The old women of the tribe came and talked to me about proper dress and behavior for this sacred time. They talked about the meaning of the ceremonies. They always said, "Even though you are white, the ceremonies, the feasts and protocol still have to be done the right way. There are no shortcuts." I had many teachers and I was grateful for them all. In my mind I thought of them as my Moms because they taught me as if I was a child, and I was. I had much to learn. Let me tell you I followed every step just right!

The thought that one of Raven's children might die because I made a mistake was not far from my thoughts. The warnings of the young men still haunted me even if Raven had assured me it would never be my fault. I was afraid I would be blamed anyway, were it to happen. I have never prayed so hard or so much for so many people that I didn't even know than I did in those five months. I could not handle being held accountable for a family tragedy.

One day in May, I had to make bannock for a ceremony to which many people were coming and there was no one else to make it. It was a windy day. Ella and Gwomans, two of my friends, came early. They started laughing so hard that tears were rolling down their faces.

When they could stop long enough to talk they told me I had flour all over my face and that I looked like the Pillsbury dough boy. I had been very tense with the responsibility I was carrying, but I too had to laugh. That story has become a campfire story and it has been retold time and time again. Whenever I visit Danny and Ella we still laugh together about that.

The days of the big lodge were fast approaching. One day Raven's adopted brother, Mel Paul, brought us some fresh fish. We knew there was a Catholic priest coming who wanted to dance. As Mel was cleaning the fish, he asked, "You are not really going tofeed the priest fish soup, are you?"

"If he does not want to eat fish soup, he can go to the restaurant," I replied.

"You sure are a brave woman!" he said. I guess he would never have fed a priest fish soup. I chuckled and thought I did not feel my bravery was challenged by feeding fish soup to a priest. Especially after all I had gone through the past five months. When Father

Noel did arrive, I served him the fish soup and he enjoyed it. Mel just sat and watched.

My two Moms, Nancy and Marceline Potts

He was amazed as he never thought a priest would come and share fish soup with them.

As more people arrived and set up their tents for the preparation of the big lodge, many sweat lodges were done and that priest never missed a one. On one occasion he came over, obviously highly moved as tears were welling up in his eyes. He took a deep breath and then told Raven, "I think I saw Jesus in the lodge. Is that really possible? Would he really show himself in a sweat lodge?"

"Why not?" was Raven's simple reply.

When the time for the big sun dance lodge was drawing near, many people came and camped. Everything was to be done at precise times, not by the clock, but by the sun. My four-day fast was to start the day the lodge went up. Father Noel decided to join me and I was grateful for his support.

Very early in the morning there were ceremonies by the men who built the lodge. The tree of life, which was to be the center of all, was to be selected. That was done by a group of young men led by the head helper. There were stories and songs which were a part of the ceremony of the selection. Poles and rails were cut and erected for the framework of the lodge. Willows and poplars for fences and coverings were cut. The offerings people had brought since February had to be prepared and prayed over. All the people who worked so incredibly hard had to be fed. We extended the fire pit so I could make more soup and stew and cook tea and bannock all at the same time.

Everyone came from miles around and brought offerings for prayers. They erected tents and teepees around the perimeter of the lodge. There was dancing and drumming in the lodge from sunup until sunset. Then the young people took over. They are called 'sevens.' That is where they get the beginning of their sun dance experience. Four campfires, one in each of the four directions, were kept burning all night by the fire keeper. There were dances for the sick. There was a big giveaway, where many people brought gifts for the sun dance maker, the helpers and the community as a whole. There were fasting and prayers and visiting and sharing. The children played non-stop but if they got too loud they would get "the look" from an Elder and immediately they would lower their voices. Not one person showed anger or raised their voice. There was harmony in that camp.

When the ceremonies were done and everyone had broken their fast with the water which was blessed by the sun dance maker's prayers, we all ate together one last time. Father Noel shared his dreams of being a true help to the people. He told us that he would be bringing many of the teachings to his congregation, especially about respect for personal beliefs and ways. He really gained an understanding of the traditional wisdom of no conflict between organized religion and traditional ceremonies. He could integrate the Native beliefs with his. That was his gift that week—his reward for all the sacrifices he made with the fasting, the dancing, and the lodges.

Soon everyone but us packed up everything, including every scrap of garbage, and left the same way they came. The grounds became so silent. There was a stillness that was more intense than anything I have ever experienced.

We had made it. No one died. No big disasters. Even the crops in the fields grew tall that year, the game was plentiful and all was as it should be.

Raven and our friend Bob had also left to take back some teepee rails that we had borrowed. There were two large picnic tables full of dirty dishes from the feast. I was extremely tired as I looked at the formidable task ahead of me. I decided step one was to warm some water over the fire which was still burning brightly. As I started to pack up our camp I avoided looking at the long row of dirty dishes. It was too much to even think about. I decided to start tackling the job one little step at a time. I could think only about the little steps. When the water was hot enough I set two basins at the end of one table, one for washing and one for rinsing. I decided to simply wash one dirty dish after another. As I was concentrating on the task at hand and thinking about all the things I had experienced over the past five months, I was suddenly filled with gratitude. Everything had gone well. I had done my best and it was good enough. I overflowed with the love I had for Raven; I was overwhelmed that he put so much trust in me. In those five months I learned *who* I was and how much I could accomplish. As tears of gratefulness for his and the spiritual help I had received filled my eyes, I looked one more time at the big lodge.

Surrounding the lodge was a ring of pure white smoke. It was about a meter high and solid. I saw a stream of smoke from the cooking fire going east, in the direction of the exit to the grounds, then turning south to join the ring around the lodge. This is not possible, I thought, but quickly remembered not to question. It was real and it was special, but I could not understand it. As I stood there in awe, I heard Raven's truck coming. I was so pleased, as now he too would see, but as he drew nearer the smoke suddenly dissipated.

When he got out of the truck, I described the ring of smoke to him. He said, "Good! It was a gift for *you*. Not for anyone else." He later shared the story with other Elders: All gave the same response as his. Each time tears would well in my eyes—tears of humility, of gratefulness, of something much bigger than I understood.

Many people came to Raven with tobacco, prints (two meters of broadcloth) and gifts to do healing and sweat lodges for them or for their family members. He was taught never to sweat with women as they are too powerful and he could get hurt. He never went against any of his teachings. He did, nevertheless, appreciate the women's presence and their prayers outside the lodge and always let them know that. He had a very deep and genuine respect for all women. He knew their power and appreciated their support.

As I sat outside the sweat lodges, and helped Raven with prayers and helped the sick people, I so felt the sacredness of the space. Many times the spirits would come and sing with us. I heard their songs. They also came and helped the people. I saw the changes in their faces. They would suddenly relax. Deep worry lines would disappear; some would just smile and others broke into tears of gratitude. Sometimes the lodge shook in ways that could not be created by those inside. My heart was at peace, even though the work was hard with so many sick people to help, so many to feed.

I became an expert in one-pot cooking. I had big cooking pots which I used to make moose stew or fish soup or smoked-meat soup with rice. Everything had to be cooked before the participants went into the sweat lodge. I was always there to help Raven with prayers and healing. Everyone pitched in to help so it wasn't too hard. I knew I was protected, and, most important, we never lost our sense of humour through it all. Someone always had a good joke; sometimes we would go into competition until one or the other would say, "Okay, you win! I can't top that one!" We had joy and laughter, hardships, and challenges, but most important we had love in our home, especially between Raven and me.

Too many white people had come, learned but a little, and then had done their own version of the ceremonies and called them Native American. Native people who lead ceremonies must train as helpers for many years before they are passed the right to do them. Then they sit with the Elder for another year or more before they sit alone. There is much more to it than process. There is a knowing of spirituality which takes many years to understand well enough to lead the ceremonies.

Many would write about these ceremonies, having no idea of the depth of spiritual knowledge required to perform them. I was taught that the ceremonies cannot be put on paper and I could not even begin to capture the reality if I tried.

I did feel some people's resentment, but they were still were gracious to me, as they would never go against Raven in any way. He really wanted me by his side and it was his guidance I always took.

One of the most memorable ceremonies I attended took place one day when a man, who I will now call Terry, told Raven his sister was very ill, and out of her mind. He gave Raven offerings for her healing and then went off to the reserve to build the lodge. However, it was late in the fall and rather cool, so they decided to use the sweat house which had been erected so they could do lodges all year round. Built in a little clearing at the sun dance grounds, it was about four meters across and eight meters long and had one large window on one side. There was a wooden floor in one half of the building; the other half, where the sweat lodge sat, was dirt. Terry was busy taking care of all the details, and there were many. After everything was prepared and the men got ready to go into the lodge, he brought in his sister. She was screaming, "My eyes, my eyes!" and started rolling along the walls. Raven asked us to set her in front of the door of the lodge with her back up against the canvas so he could doctor her from inside. She was fighting so hard that it took three of us to hold her down. When Raven doctored her, she suddenly settled. An hour later she was cooking us dinner, laughing and joking. To me it was a miracle, to the others, not surprising.

Soon after, Raven told me we were doing a sweat lodge for a man who had just come out of prison after a twenty-year incarceration for a heinous murder. Many thoughts went through my mind as the day approached. I was not sure I wanted to be in the presence of someone like him, but then I thought about the Elders' teachings about harmony and not to judge. I was not sure if my heart was big enough to accept him in my home without prejudice, without judgment.

When the day came for the sweat lodge, the ex-con arrived with members of his family and as they approached I thought it strange that I did not know which one he was. When they entered the house everyone introduced themselves and shook hands. It was then that he was identified to me, but as I looked at him and his companions I thought once again that he was no different from the rest. Then I chuckled at my ignorance. Why would I think he would look any different? I invited them all in for tea. Lawrence as usual joked around with them and teased the ex-con about how good it would be to have a woman again. They drank up quickly and went out to where the sweat lodge was being prepared.

While I was preparing the soup and bannock we would share afterwards, I watched the men working around the lodge. A couple of women also showed up for support. When the cooking was finished I joined them all at the lodge. By this time there were perhaps a dozen people present.

Soon the men entered the lodge and the women took a place on the grass outside. Raven asked me to keep the door and I in turn invited the other women to help. Then the people in the lodge smoked pipe and Raven took offerings and prayed. When that was complete he said, "I want to thank you women for coming and praying with us today. When you are outside helping you get as much benefit as you would in here. I would just like to ask you to help me with your prayers. You are very powerful and I appreciate your support." With that we closed the flap for the first round.

After the sweat was complete, everyone present went in turn and shook the hand of the fellow the sweat was for and thanked him for coming . . . thanked him and wished him luck in his future. One of the young fellows came with me to the house and we brought out the food. As we all shared together, everyone was chatting and laughing. My heart filled with gratefulness that I was in these people's presence and had the opportunity to learn a big lesson about judging others.

We were very busy in those days with Raven's work for the Indian Association and with so many people coming for help. He was always allowed the time off from the Association work, because the lodges were help for the people. The sweat lodges, which were a vital support for the people, had to be built, the people had to be fed, and time had to be put aside for counseling those in need. It was hard, but also a time of much learning.

I began questioning why I felt so at home and at peace in this culture of the First Nations people. Why was I there? What was my purpose? I was Danish/Canadian, not Native. In fact I never felt more Danish in my life than I did with these people, maybe because I was most often the only white person present. Everyone spoke about the importance of knowing *who* you are.

Some people did not like me being at their ceremonies because they did not trust white people. I understood their mistrust, but felt I could do nothing but follow Raven's direc- tion. I often said a silent prayer for tolerance and understanding.

Raven was frequently called out to do opening and closing prayers for various groups, conferences and meetings. People would come and bring him tobacco and ask him to come. He could never refuse the tobacco. He was often called by the Royal Canadian Mounted Police.

Every Native youth gathering was always opened with prayers from the Elders and they remained throughout the conference to give presentations, and, more important, to have one-on-one talks with the young people.

Raven was often called to open international gatherings. One time he was called for a big gathering of railway people at the Hotel McDonald, one of the fanciest hotels in Edmonton. We were met by one of the organizers, who directed us to our room and then told us he would come back as soon as we had a chance to get settled and talk to Raven about what was to happen.

He came back with a sheet of paper on which he had something written. He told him where to be and when. Raven did not look at it until after he left. When he did he threw it on the bed and said, "Newa, this is no place for me. Let's get out of here." I picked up the paper and saw that the organizer had written what he wanted him to say, word for word, in large letters. "They are counting on you, we can't just walk out!" I said. "I will call him and tell him it will not happen the way he wants, that you will do it in your own way." Raven hesitated. "Just give me a chance, and if it is not okay we will leave. He probably thinks that he is doing you a favor." As I went to the phone, I was debating whether I should ask him to come to the room or not, as I knew Raven would not be kind. I decided to do just that, as he might as well learn something about Elders and prayers.

Raven Leading Opening Prayers at RCMP Change of Command
Ceremonies

When he arrived, Raven threw the paper at him and said firmly, "I do not ever write my prayers. How can anyone do that? The prayers are from the Creator, not from a piece of paper. I can pray for you. You need it, but I will not say your words in front of all those people."

"By all means go ahead in your own way," said the organizer meekly. "I am so sorry; I thought I was doing you a favor. How much time do you think you need, then?" he asked. I held my breath as I knew he was about to get blasted again.

"How can you ask how long the Creator will take? You white people surprise me. You know nothing about prayers!" replied Raven, and he turned away.

"It will take the time it takes," I told the organizer. "You really cannot set that. That is the way it is. If it does not work for you, we will have to leave." He asked us to stay and assured Raven that he could do it in his own way.

"Okay, now can we go and have our dinner? Would you like to join us?" Raven asked our host.

"No, thank you," he replied. "I have much to do to prepare. I do not have time."

"I understand," said Raven.

The next morning I saw they had changed the time slot for Raven's opening prayers from before all the political welcoming speeches until after. "That's okay," Raven said. "It works; all those politicians have to be so precise."

The most memorable opening prayers were in 1993 when Edmonton hosted the world triathlon games. Raven was asked to do prayers for their wrap-up awards dinner. He was dressed in full regalia and as the minister of Indian Affairs, Pearl Calahasen, escorted him onto the stage, he received a standing ovation from the approximately 5,000 people in attendance.

As the applause subsided, he said, "I would like to welcome each and every one of you to our country of Canada. I am humbled to stand before you today. I know you have all been taught different ways to pray. I would like to ask you to pity me and help me with your prayers. Pray in your own way, the way you were taught, the way you know how. I will be praying in my language, the way I was taught. I am sorry but I cannot use the microphone. It is the way I was taught. Hai hai." (meaning *thank you* in Cree)

Once again everyone got up and gave him a standing ovation. As he stepped away from the microphone everyone remained standing and soon there was total silence in the room. As Raven stood on that stage, praying in his language, I could feel the energy of his prayer and those from the audience. It was indeed a magic moment. When he was finished, again everyone clapped for him and continued until he left the stage.

Chapter 26

My Danish Elder

As I participated in more and more ceremonies, I felt more and more at peace in my heart, yet there was one question that kept haunting me. I was Danish, with not one ounce of Native blood. Why was this happening to me? I had asked for answers to my own experiences, I had not asked for this new world I had entered. I began praying about it all as it too was too confusing for me. Praying was also new for me; and I had not thought about it before I was woken up.

In 1992, four years after I met Raven, I was sent a vision. It happened one night in that beautiful space between the two worlds of asleep and awake where you learn much. I saw a group of Danish women building a sweat lodge. They were ever so joyful in their task. They had gathered the willows and were trying to set them up. Rocks were collected and ready for the fire, but I was uncomfortable, as they were not doing it quite right. I watched in silence for a while, not wanting to interrupt their joyfulness, but then I could not hold it any longer. I went over and said, "What you are doing is very good, but it is not quite right." I was very afraid they would not be happy with my criticism and I did not want to interfere with their happiness.

'Okay," they said. "Then how do we do it?"

I explained it to them and we all worked together in complete harmony, joy and laughter.

When the lodge was finished, I saw Madge McRee, the Elder who was my main woman teacher, standing there calling the spirits as she always did.

The following week I brought tobacco to Madge, as she had been in my vision. She took the tobacco and prayed silently with it. Then she said, "You are to build a lodge. Just you and I will be going in."

"Okay," I said.

The next weekend I built the lodge. That was the hottest lodge either of us had ever been in. Although it was burning hot, we did not get burnt. After the lodge was finished, Madge told me that there was a woman in Denmark I was to find. "Some people will come in the spring to help you. You are to wait for them," she said. I was so happy.

That was in the fall. I waited impatiently all winter; spring came and nothing happened, no one showed. I was so disappointed. I had waited longingly for the connection. That was confusing, as I had seen so many people receive what they asked for, and I began to question why I did not. Had I done something wrong? Was it because I was white? Was I not deserving? All kinds of questions crossed my mind.

By fall I decided to put it out of my mind, as it was too painful for me to think about it. It was taking up too much of my time and energy. I could not do anything about it anyway.

The people who needed our help kept coming and I needed to do something about them.

Winter came and went. One day in spring, while we were in Edmonton for a meeting, we went to West Edmonton Shopping Mall. There I saw a young couple together. The young man had a Danish flag on his sleeve. Raven told me to go and talk to them. I wasn't going to, because we were in a hurry, but he insisted. "Maybe you can talk your own language," he said. That has so much importance as Native people believe there is a connection between language and culture and *who* you really are.

I reluctantly went over and introduced myself. They introduced themselves as Anders and Berit and confirmed they were from Denmark. I invited them to come to the hotel where we were staying that evening, which they did. They told us they had landed in the States and had bought an old van, which they lived in as they toured North America. We invited them to come home with us, to the reservation where we lived at the time. They were in dire need of a shower, a clothes wash and a warm place to be as it was early spring and nights were still very cold.

I really had put the thought of finding my connection in Denmark out of my mind. It was not until they had been there for nearly a week that it re-entered. I told them about the lodge and the message. I did not know if they were my connection or not. When they left, I told them we would try to come to Denmark and would look them up.

Later that summer, my cousin Margit and her husband Jens came from Denmark for a visit and I told her the story as well. Margit was so thrilled and was sure that she was the connection.

The next year, in 1993, Raven and I took a trip to Denmark. My cousin Margit had several people lined up for us to meet, but one after another cancelled and once again doubt began to creep into my consciousness. We journeyed up to northern Jylland to meet with our two young friends, Anders and Berit. After introductions and coffee, Berit told me that she had talked to a woman named Florence, but Florence couldn't come to meet me. Not again! I thought. Will this not happen? I was so disappointed as that was my last connection. I got very nauseated and actually threw up. It was just too devastating. Time was running out and I knew I would not be returning to Denmark any time soon. Then a call came from Florence. She had a phone number for a woman I might want to see. When Anders asked if I wanted to follow up, I just took a little time to answer. I felt a stillness come over me. I just nodded. That night I slept very little. Butterflies were having a field day in my stomach.

The next day we headed for Vestbirk where she lived. We were met at the door by a little woman with braids and a narrow red scarf on her head. She introduced herself as Gudrun Von Benzon. The house was very old, as were almost all the houses in the village. The room we entered was almost filled with a big table. One wall was totally covered with shelves of jars with all kinds of herbs.

"You have braids," I said.

"Yes," she said, "our people also had braids many years ago and I have always kept mine. Indicating the red scarf tied around her head, she told us how she always wore red and her sister had blue. "I have something for upset stomachs," she said and proceeded to mix me a potion. It was only later that Anders told me he almost left at that point; as it was just too much for him when she offered something for my stomach without me telling her I had a problem. I never thought anything of it, as I was so accustomed to that from home. Raven always knew what was wrong with someone before they came.

"Why have you come to see me?" she asked. I told her how I had been living with the Native people in Canada and for some reason everything seemed so right to me, but I was Danish. My question for a long time had been "Why?" Why would I, a Danish woman, feel so at home with these people, with their spirituality, with their life philosophy? I then told her about the vision and the lodge and how I ended up at her house that day. "That is the story of why I am here," I said.

She told us how many years earlier her husband was stricken with Alzheimer's disease and she had to figure out a way to generate some income. The old women in her family had taught her about the herbs and what they were for. She started collecting and selling them. Eventually she went on to teach others and was now giving presentations in many places.

I told her we would be in touch again and we left. We did return for a brief visit the day before we were leaving Denmark. Raven gave her his bear claw necklace, which she wore until the day of her death.

Gudrun with her herbal medicine

I really felt I needed to learn more from her, but was not sure how that could happen. My family would never understand if I came back to Denmark and spent all my time with a stranger.

One day the idea of asking her to come to us for a visit in Canada suddenly popped into my head. That way I would have her undivided attention. I called her immediately. When I asked her if she would consider coming over, she was so surprised and said," I am not sure I am hearing right. Phone me back in three days if you are serious!"

I did and we made arrangements for her to come later that summer.

The weather was perfect the day Gudrun and her daughter Pia arrived in Edmonton. The sun was shining and the temperature was at a comfortable twenty-one degrees. As soon as I saw her in her red scarf, braids and black cape, I knew she would make an impression.

The next day we were to have a blessing ceremony for the new teepee we had just erected at the University Hospital in Edmonton. We invited them to come and they were honored.

The next morning we drove a half hour through countryside then into the city. Traffic was heavy and it took another half hour to arrive at the hospital. The teepee was erected in a small grove of trees in front of a six storey building spanning at least three city blocks. When we arrived, two ladies, Liz Harding and Ella Arcand, came with soup and bannock and tea. When I introduced Gudrun, Liz turned to me and said, "She is an Elder."

I said, "Yes, she is, but she speaks only Danish."

"Please ask her if she would do us the honour of accompanying us for the grand entry at our powwow next weekend," said Liz.

Of course Gudrun agreed.

Every year the Alexis Reservation, as well as many other communities, hosts a powwow. Dancers and drummers come from far and wide. The people all camp together and the whole event is a wonderful celebration of culture, dance and community. Raven was doing the opening prayers for them.

At the powwow everyone we introduced her to asked if she was my Elder from Denmark. Everyone welcomed her. They recognized Gudrun as one of them. She was an Elder.

On Monday, Madge McRee, the Elder who had put up the lodge for me the year before, arrived for a visit. As soon as she saw Gudrun, she knew she was the woman she had seen in her vision. The three Elders—Madge, Gudrun and Raven—spoke of many medicinal herbs which they had in common. All were used for the same symptoms. It was another 'magical' day. When Raven and I retired that night, we just lay together and recapped the whole experience. My heart had rarely been happier.

Gudrun, Pia and I planned a trip to the Rocky Mountains. Raven would not come with us.

"You need time alone; you need to talk your language," he said. We were disappointed, but there was no changing his mind once it was made up. We were going to take a tent, but he said it was too risky because of the bears. "How are you going to defend yourselves?" he asked.

"I will figure it out," I said. "Besides I do not expect bear problems. You know I have a healthy respect for them. I do not put bacon in my bedroll!" (That was what we used to say about ignorant tourists who did not know protocol in bear country.)

"I do not like it one bit. You three women should not go out and sleep in the wilderness by yourselves with no one to protect you. I do not like it one bit," he said. I decided we had better listen as perhaps he saw something which we needed to avoid. I had seen tragedies happen before when people did not listen so we decided to stay in motels along the way. The trip was fantastic and I did have a chance to share many things with Gudrun about the old Danish history and more about her work with herbs.

The day after we returned home we took a drive to Buck Lake to visit Raven's family and pick some sweet grass. It was growing at the site where the teepee village was set up. I was a little ways from Gudrun and I could see she was getting frustrated. When I asked her what was wrong, she said, "I cannot see any sweet grass and I so wanted to pick enough for a braid to take back with me."

"Have you offered tobacco?" Raven asked.

"No," she said, and immediately took one of her cigars, crushed it and prayed with it. After she did that, she saw there was sweet grass everywhere.

Later in the afternoon we headed over to visit Raven's son, Jack. The young people immediately brought chairs for her and Raven. I went to the kitchen to greet the women. This is the story Gudrun told me about what happened next.

She offered Raven a cigar and he took one. Raven never smoked, so that was quite unusual. She was the cigar smoker. She lit his cigar and her own and they sat there and smoked together. Everyone quit talking and just looked at them. That was the first time they had ever seen a woman smoke a cigar and it was doubtful if they had ever seen Raven smoke one either. Of course they were too polite to say anything. Gudrun thought they stopped talking because they thought it was a ceremony where the two old people smoked together. Raven soon threw his cigar in the fire. She followed suit.

It was wonderful to see the closeness and understanding between the two Elders and suddenly I understood why I felt so at home with the Native people.

We are no different.

We are all the same after all.

Language is not a barrier, only a challenge.

My heart was at peace. The world of my birth people and the world of my adopted people came together for just this brief period of time.

Even into her eighties, Gudrun was one sharp bridge player. She taught me how to play bridge. I saw her often. We went for drives and shared many things about spirituality and life philosophy until her death on January 13th, 2009.

Chapter 27

Legal System

There are some very important differences between the western and traditional beliefs in the whole concept of crime and punishment and correction.

In Canada when a crime is committed it is considered a crime against the crown and the crown will punish the perpetrator.

In the traditional system crime is committed against a person, a family and a community. When laws, minor or major, are broken, disharmony will be the result, and harmony needs to be restored.

In the western system guilt or innocence is determined through a court system which gives the perpetrator the opportunity to hire someone to manipulate his or her way through the system. Only the people who are directly connected to the actual crime are heard from.

In the Native traditional justice system, the Elders determine how harmony can be restored, after hearing from all people who are directly or indirectly involved with not only the crime, but with what had happened leading up to the crime.

In the western system, the judge and/or jury decides on punishment for the offender.

In the traditional system punishment does not exist, only consequences which serve to restore balance for the perpetrator and the community. The worst consequence in the traditional system was banishment. It was rarely used and only when there was consensus that there was no other way to restore harmony. Those who were banished could return after many years, but they had to bring many gifts and persuade the people that they had learned their lesson and would no longer cause trouble.

In many ways their laws were much stricter than those in our society as they also included codes of behavior, like misbehavior of young men and women flirting at ceremonies, or inappropriate dress. Each tribe had a little different process, but all had the same goal of harmony. At their gatherings someone who was not following the proper code of behavior might be called to the middle and would be talked to by the Elders about proper behavior. Then they would be told how they must change. If they did not learn from that, which rarely happened, the Elders would sit again and decide the next step. The person could be forced to serve someone such as an Elder. In return the Elder would pass teachings to the perpetrator which would enhance his or her life.

There were no jails. The belief was that locking a person up was inhumane, that it would cause damage to the spirit. It is difficult to bring harmony to a person with a broken spirit, but it can be achieved through ceremonies, support from the family and the community, and learning from the Elders.

In the traditional system, the community sits together in a circle and discusses what actually happened. They hear in turn from everyone involved or affected in order to arrive at the full picture of what happened and why. The background leading up to the disruption has a big part in the deliberations. Knowing the cause is believed to make the final decision much more effective.

There were many people lobbying to at least incorporate a community circle after the courts had determined guilt or innocence. Everyone was aware that the court system was too big to budge significantly, but perhaps in the sentencing aspect they would allow the Native traditional system to have input. In the early 1990s the sentencing circle was incorporated, but only as far as making recommendations. According to Canadian law, the judge has the final say, so the recommendations of the circle are not binding. To begin with, almost every Native convicted would opt for the circle, thinking it was an easy way out of jail, but soon word got around that it was much harder to face the people than to go to jail.

The following are two cases where the sentencing circle was utilized:

One circle involved a case where two boys, who were best friends since childhood, had been out drinking. The boys were fooling around with the car and Kyle accidentally ran over Andrew, killing him. Kyle was charged and found guilty of vehicular homicide. Alan Balser, the father of the deceased, requested a sentencing circle and it was granted. The families sat together in that circle. The family of the deceased then had the opportunity to question the perpetrator about their son's final time on this earth, his last words, his frame of mind, and so on. They had the opportunity to come face to face with each other to see how they all suffered terribly because of the loss.

After everything had been said, after the confrontations, after many tears, after much heartache, Alan finally told everyone that there was no point in losing two fine young men. One was enough. He requested that instead of being sent to jail, Kyle be made to finish his high school and that he was not to touch drugs or alcohol. He was also to accompany Alan to a school on a regular basis and tell the students what he had done and talk about the consequences of drinking and driving. Even in light of such tragedy, everyone was able to once again come together, and together bring an important teaching to the young people.

Everyone was white.

In January 2008 two little girls were found frozen to death in -30 degree weather on the Yellow Quill First Nation Reserve, 260 kilometers east of Saskatoon, Saskatchewan. Christopher Charles Pauchey, their father, was subsequently charged with failing to protect Santana Pauchey and Kaydence Pauchey from exposure to the elements which caused their death. According to his sister, he was trying to take the children to a relative's house 400 meters away because there was something wrong with one of them. The father too suffered severe frostbite and was taken to the hospital. He was obviously intoxicated. He pleaded guilty and requested, and was granted, a sentencing circle. The case received a lot of attention in the national media as well as in the community.

Included in the sentencing circle were Christopher's father, step-mother, mother, interpreters, a band councilor, a mental health therapist, two surrogate victims, a probation officer, a court worker, police, mother to the children, crown prosecutor, Elders and Judge Barry Morgan. Christopher showed deep remorse and sorrow at the loss of the two deceased children, and the subsequent removal of his third child. Social Services took his daughter from its mother after she took the child to visit Christopher. The Elders' recommendation was that he and the mother take counseling together and work toward eventually reuniting the family. They also recommended that Christopher serve the Elders for life, a life sentence that, in the words of Mr. Francis Nippi, "would serve as a reminder that the Creator has not left him."

The courts sentenced him to three years' incarceration, the reasoning being: 'the principle of denunciation and the need to foster respect for the judicial system mandates a significant response.'

One day I asked Raven why he thought so many people would commit crimes again and again. "Sometimes after a person has been locked up for a long time they will leave part of their spirit in the facility and they will go back and commit a crime just to get to their spirit. They most often never understand why."

I heard so many stories from people who did not receive fair treatment from our Western legal system. When I first started hearing about them, it was very difficult to believe, but as time went by and I heard more and more stories, I started to pay more attention to details of reports in the media and compare that with the information I got from the Native people.

The first story was told to me by a young lad who had been arrested for being drunk on the street. When he came home the next day he had a broken arm. I asked him what had happened and he said, "The cops broke my arm."

My immediate reaction was that he had resisted arrest. He assured me he did not. I then asked him what he was going to do about it.

"Nothing," he said.

"Nothing?" was my reply.

"Nothing," he said. "If I say one word I will be harassed for the rest of my life, and not only me but also family members and friends." I was very upset to think the police could get away with this, but he was not willing to do anything and without his support I could do nothing.

One fellow told me about how he ended up in jail. He was served with a warrant and as he couldn't read very well, he asked the police officer to read it to him, which he did. He was charged with indecent assault against a thirteen-year-old boy. He had no idea what the word 'indecent' meant, but with the word 'decent' in there, it couldn't be too bad and so he pleaded guilty. It was only after he was sent to jail that he learned the meaning. By that time it was too late. He had pleaded guilty.

Another fellow, whom I will call Bob, told me this story one day: Bob's identification papers had been stolen and the person who had taken them beat a man almost to death. He was arrested and charged with attempted murder. The problem was that he used Bob's stolen ID. Then he jumped bail and soon the police came and arrested Bob. He fervently denied any connection with the beating and told them about the stolen ID, but they kept him in jail anyway. No one, it seemed, checked the picture of the person they arrested with that of Bob. He continually proclaimed his innocence but no one would listen. He did not have a lawyer so the courts appointed one for him. They had their first meeting one hour before trial, which is very common for court-appointed lawyers. He told him his story. His lawyer left the room and came back with the RCMP. Both his lawyer and the police told him that the charge of attempted murder could get him twenty years. He had a family of four small children and he went into a panic. Twenty years without seeing his children was too much to bear. He knew there were many people in jail for things they did not do. They offered him a deal: six months if he pleaded guilty to common assault. That way he did not have to fight the courts or risk a very long sentence. He would be back out in three months anyway. He took the deal.

One fellow told me about a baseball brawl between two teams, one mostly Native, the other white. One of the Native boys got a broken leg. No one else was hurt badly. Some of the Native boys were charged. The white boys were not. The fellow with the broken leg was the only one sent to jail.

Stories of people being taken for a ride and left in the snow and cold by the police are not uncommon. These rides are so common that they even have a name: 'Starlight Tours.' Some, like the case of Neil Stonechild, who died November 25th, 1990, at age seventeen after he was taken by police, driven to a remote area and dropped off in a field outside Saskatoon in -28 degrees Celsius, are now coming to light. Ten years later, two more bodies were found, within a week, close to the same area.

The cases that are heard about in the media are but a tip of the iceberg, but at least the tip is finally being seen.

On September 4th, 1995, about 35 unarmed Native protestors occupied Ipperwash Provincial Park to draw attention to the lack of action by the government to act on a land claim. The Stony Point reserve had been temporarily appropriated by the Canadian Government under the War Measures Act in 1942. The Native people never got their land back, nor were they compensated. On September 7th the Ontario Provincial Police opened fire and killed Dudley George, one of the protestors.

In the summer of 1999 a Native university student told me that one night he got tired of studying and went for some fresh air in the middle of the night. He was stopped by the police, who beat him up. After the beating, they checked for a criminal record. There was none. "You are one of the few!" they said and drove off.

In the winter of 1999 Social Services went to apprehend Connie Jacob's children on the Tsuu T'inaa reservation, near the city of Calgary. She became very irate and the social worker went for police escort. They were met by one irate mother who fired some shots above their heads. Common practice was backing off and calling in the SWAT team. Not in this case. The pregnant Connie Jacobs and her eight-year-old son Ty were killed. Why would a police officer shoot to kill when there were children in the vicinity?

In 2003 a single mother moved back to the Saddle Lake Reservation when the Edmonton City Police began to stop and search her fifteen-year-old son on a regular basis when he was walking to and from his friends' houses. She left behind a good career. He was doing well in school and had his circle of friends.

When it came time to go to court, many took what they considered the easy way out and pleaded guilty when they were innocent. No one was willing to do anything as they said time and time again that it was easier to go to jail and be done with it than fight a losing battle. They did not feel they could win.

The Native community in general has no respect for the legal system. They do not feel they can get justice.

At first I did not want to believe the stories and tried to make excuses and explanations as to what might have happened, but as time went on and more stories kept coming, I had to admit they indicated serious problems.

Some people within the system did recognize the seriousness of the problems within the legal system for the Native people and wanted to bring improvements. Corrections Canada, headed by Ole Ingstrup, in cooperation with Native people, including chiefs and Elders, built a facility at the Hobbema reservation designed to help people who were in trouble with the law to heal. The philosophy of that institution was that of the old ways of healing and harmony as opposed to punishment. The inmates were allowed and encouraged to do their healing, which included prayers and ceremonies. The Elders were an integral part of their healing process and continued to be available after release, for as long as there was a need.

The Indian Association of Alberta and the RCMP began talking. Commissioner Norman Inkster, top officer in Canada, Assistant Commissioner Gordon Greg, top officer in Alberta, and the president of the Indian Association, Roy Louis, set up a conference. Raven was responsible for bringing in the Elders. It would be the first time ever that there was an official gathering of the two groups. History was about to be made. In 1990 the 'Sharing Common Ground' conference became a reality. It was held in a big hotel in Edmonton. There were about 400 people present, with about two-thirds police officers and one-third Native people, including many Elders. Everyone gathered the first evening for an opening dinner.

Raven did the opening prayers that first day and he said, "We are all gathered here for a very important purpose: to create understanding between our people so things can be better in the future. Now I ask each and every one to stand and pity me, help me with the prayers. Pray in your own way, the way you were taught, the way you know how. I will pray in my Cree language."

He did, and as I stood there feeling the energy in the room, I swear the Holy Spirit entered there as so many people prayed together.

In his opening speech Commissioner Norman Inkster of the RCMP acknowledged that there were many problems, but since they had only one weekend together, everyone was asked not to spend the time on the past problems, but to focus on the future and try to find ways to do things better.

The late Norbert Jeubeaux also had an opening speech, where he too acknowledged that his people had lived through many injustices. He also encouraged everyone not to use this time on raking over "what has happened in the past and is still happening. The stories are important, and they need to be told, but that is not the purpose here this weekend. The purpose is to create a better way for the future."

One officer shared with the group how he never had any greater problems dealing with the people on the reserve where he patrolled than with any other community in which he had worked. His 'magic bullet' was Juicy Fruit gum. Every time he had to go to the reserve on business, he always brought lots of Juicy Fruit gum for the children. The first time he could not get one child to come to his car, and he had to throw it to them. As soon as they figured out why he was calling them, they surrounded his car every time he went to the reserve. He would also bring tobacco to the Elders in their homes and they would give him tea and advice.

As a result of that conference, federal and provincial advisory committees were set up to meet on a regular basis all over the country. Cross-cultural education was incorporated with local First Nations people doing the educating. Now we often see a police officer at community events.

One police officer came to a round dance, the community gathering where everyone dances together in a circle to the beat of the drums. Immediately a little girl came running to the officer, who picked her up and starting dancing with the people.

Raven was appointed to the federal committee and I always travelled with him.

One time when we were in the east, we read in the papers and saw on TV about the Indian smuggling problem over and over again. There is a reserve, Akwasane, located on both sides of the St. Lawrence River. The boundaries of the reservation cross into New York State and Quebec and Ontario. Because the reservation is partially in the States, the residents can purchase tobacco products legally from there and bring them to the Canadian side. On the news we would often see the RCMP boats chasing Native boats on the news.

When I got into a discussion with the RCMP, they told me no one had ever been charged with smuggling, so how could they call them smugglers? Do you call a person a murderer if they have never murdered? Too strange, I thought. I spoke to some of the people from the reserve and they just laughed about the whole thing. They were hoping someone would get charged as they knew they would win in court. They knew their activity was not illegal. They had the right to move tobacco products anywhere within the reservation. No one was ever charged. They thought the police were using them as a good photo opportunity.

The Canadian public was not pleased that a few Native people had an advantage because they could buy cigarettes at a lower price in the United States. The government lowered taxes on all tobacco products and lost millions of dollars. Go figure!

Raven was getting a lot of complaints from one particular reservation about a certain officer and so as a member of the advisory committee he went to talk to the head of the detachment about it. When Raven told him about the complaints the corporal just laughed. "He does not discriminate," he said. "He is an asshole to everyone." We all laughed about that one and passed the word. He was transferred shortly after that and I heard he was sent way up north. I hope the Elders up there had a chance to give him an attitude adjustment.

Once when we were at a national committee meeting in Regina, Saskatchewan, we all gathered in the big foyer of the hotel for drinks and snacks. There was a mix of police officers, their wives and Native committee members and their wives. As usual wherever there are native people gathering, everyone was laughing and having a good time. At the other end of the foyer was a group of people wearing suits and ties. Very serious conversations were taking place. Raven poked me and said, "Look at those people. They are so serious. I bet they are talking about money. We talk about sex. Much more fun!"

Chapter 28

Life on the Reservation

One day in 1993 Raven got a call from Johnny Erminskin, the chief, who asked him to move back to the Erminskin band at the Hobbema reservation where he came from. "We need you here," he said. "We will give you a house and work. We need someone to work in child welfare."

Raven told him he would not have anything to do with outsiders and he would not be a party to any children being removed from their homes. He had done that previously in Rocky Mountain House and he quit there because it was too inhumane and he would have no part of it now.

The chief told him that he would be responsible for helping people on welfare. He would be able to make the decisions and have a free hand in who would get welfare and who would not. He would also be involved in helping people to become gainfully employed. He decided to take the job as he was hoping to make a difference. The funding for the Indian Association of Alberta had been cut off completely at that time so he had no outside work at the time. Many people were still coming for healing, and he was doing consulting, but that was not generating enough income to keep us going. I was just working casual at the Mayerthorpe Hospital, so altogether it looked like a good solution.

Raven knew the job would be very challenging and he was not sure if he could adjust to life on the reservation again, as he had been away for over forty years. In the early sixties, about 140 members of the Hobbema band, including Raven and his family, had moved up to the Rocky Mountain foothills where they could live a more traditional life.

I too was apprehensive. To move to the reservation would be like moving to another country. I was not very good at the Cree language, which was the primary language spoken. The first item on my agenda was to take a Cree course.

We were given a nice three-bedroom bungalow in the country to live in, and so we made a rental purchase deal on our farm.

I was well on the way toward a degree in administration with Athabasca University, which offered correspondence courses, so my plan was to continue my education. I knew how much resentment there was when white people were given jobs on the reserve, so studying for the first while would be a good option for me.

Hobbema reservation consists of four bands, all with their separate governing bodies and land base. There are the Sampson, Louis Bull, Erminskin and Montana bands. Raven was a member of the Erminskin band. Total population of all four bands was in excess of ten thousand people. Each band has its schools, medical centers, seniors' centers and band offices. There are also service stations, grocery stores, clothing stores, banks, hairdressers, and numerous other retail outlets and services available from one band or the other. There are ball diamonds as well as an arena. In other words, the reservation offers all the services you would expect in any community anywhere.

Of all the communities we lived in, I found relations between the band members and the nearby city of Wetaskiwin, with its majority of Euro-Canadians, were the worst. Although they had a relatively high percentage of Native people living there (twelve percent), very few people mixed. There was much resentment on both sides. The Native people felt they were looked down on and discriminated against.

Wetaskiwin has many bars, which were an attraction for band members. They had to go into town if they wanted to drink as there are no liquor outlets on the reserve. It was not uncommon to have many alcohol-related disturbances, some between the Native and the white population.

The white people resented the fact that the band members got oil money. The bands at Hobbema owned the oil located under their reservation and occasionally there would be a distribution of profits to the people. Every Christmas and sometimes at the annual powwow a lump sum payment would be made to every band member. The funny thing about it was that within a day the merchants had most of the money anyway, so what was their problem? At one point the discrimination got so bad that all band members boycotted the businesses in Wetaskiwin.

Wetaskiwin has the highest per capita vehicle sales in the province, which is credited to good advertising, ignoring the fact that most reserve members buy their vehicles in the city when they receive their oil money.

Raven and I felt very bad about the breakdown in relations. Together we had worked hard to bridge the differences and bring understanding and respect between our people.

No one would hire us to do cross-cultural workshops even though they admitted there were many problems and we were really good candidates as we both understood both cultures. We did have our ways of teaching a little here and there.

When we entered a restaurant we could always feel the discomfort of anyone who had an issue with Raven and me being together. Then Raven would be even more gentlemanly than usual. He was always a gentleman, but he would really overdo it. He would ask me if the table was suitable, he would take my coat, he would pull out my chair and then ask if everything was okay. Often waitresses would ask if we wanted separate bills, which never happened when I was with a white man. Raven would always have a smart remark about me being his wife and we had not fought all day, so it was okay—he would pay the bill. I always said, "No one ever asked me that when I came in with a white man."

The waitresses would often be embarrassed. We had great fun with that. One day he decided to change his tactics and told the waitress to give me the bill. "This nice woman picked me up on the road and now she is feeding me." The waitress did not even blink an eye. She gave me the bill. Raven cracked up in laughter.

During Raven's first days with the Department of Welfare, he let it be known that cash would not be so easy to get any more except for single mothers. He would buy fishing nets for the able-bodied men to feed their families. The men would have to begin providing for their families either by catching fish or working. Every man, woman and child was receiving five hundred dollars a month in oil revenues at that time, just enough to keep them in poverty, not enough to starve. Many able-bodied people decided not to work. Those were the ones he was targeting.

There was not enough work on the reserve, however, and with relations as bad as they were with their non-Native neighbors, it was not easy to find employment off the reserve either. From what I saw, the Cree people did not have any problem giving an honest day's work and more. They did, however, have a problem with the lack of respect and discrimination they often faced. Mostly they did not apply for jobs as they believed they would not be hired anyway.

When he turned down some people, they went to the band Chief and council and got letters to give them the money. It was devastating for Raven. He did not want to be there simply to authorize welfare. Now we had sold our place and moved.

One day Raven was asked to sit on a committee to look at diversifying the economic base of the community. That he enjoyed; they had a very good committee, who presented a solid plan that would have put all band members to work. When the report was done, they were thanked and paid, but nothing was implemented. He was so discouraged.

Many people were dysfunctional with alcohol and drug abuse problems, while others, who knew *who* they were as Native people and understood and lived the traditional philosophy, were strong.

Many had been off-reserve and some were well educated, and have made their mark locally, nationally and internationally. Willie Littlechild was the first Treaty Indian in Alberta to receive a law degree, in 1976. He was a leader in the sports world and also went on to become the first Native member of Parliament in Canada, from 1988 to 1993. After one term he decided not to run again. He went on to work with the United Nations and was one of the founders of the International Organization of Indigenous Resource Development. He was instrumental in getting the acceptance of indigenous people's knowledge and medicines protected through the UN. I could say so much more about this remarkable man, but what has impressed me more than anything was how he always knew *who* he was as a Cree man. He brought the wisdom of the past with him to the present.

Higher education was a big challenge for those living on the reservation. The members had to leave the security of the reserve in order to go to university. They had to face discrimination, but one of the most difficult challenges was that the standard of education on the reserve was so much lower than provincial standards. They did not have the preparation needed for a university education even though they had graduated from high school. A course to prepare them for further studies was developed. Most were not aware of their lack of knowledge until they entered university. It was devastating for many as they thought they had done so well.

One day Raven's daughter decided to move off the reserve. When some of the grandchildren were transferred to a "white" school, I asked them how they liked it. They said it was actually okay, but they were not sure they were as smart as the white kids. I knew these children and saw how they played games and strategized. I knew they were both intelligent and capable. I had also seen their report cards and they were doing very well. When I asked them why they thought white kids were smarter, they replied with big eyes, "We have to finish all the books. In the reserve school we only had to do half." That was the first I heard that the standard of education was lowered to such an extent.

The eight-year-old also told me, "Whities steal!"

I asked her if someone had stolen something from her.

"No," she said, "but we have to buy a com . . . com . . . something lock so we can lock up all our things. Otherwise someone will steal them."

"You mean combination locks?" I asked.

"Yes," she said, "otherwise the whities will steal."

They were behind, but did eventually catch up and discovered they were as smart as the white kids. They graduated.

After we had lived in Hobbema for a year, the people reclaimed the house we were living in. We were then given another home with forty acres of land. This time it was put into our name.

We always hear on the news about the violence that happens on the reserves, and it does. Most often it happens when people are partying and someone gets jealous and gets stabbed or beaten up. Alcohol and drug related violence has always been an issue, but never has it been as bad as it is today. It is a major problem, for sure. In all the years I was with Raven I heard of only one act of random violence, and it was condemned by everyone I know. I used to be nervous driving through the reserve but now I always know someone will stop and help. They do look after both their visitors and each other when there is trouble. It is much safer to walk on the roads on the reserve than in the city. Everyone had so much respect for Raven, being an Elder, that we had no personal exposure to the abuse or violence.

Once when we were driving home a man hit the ditch close to where we lived. It was late in the fall and very cold. He had been drinking. Raven told him to get in the car. He just shook his head from side to side. He was freezing, but he didn't want to be near Raven when he was drinking. Raven insisted. I could see the poor man was not happy, but Raven was an Elder and no one would challenge an Elder. Just before he got in the back seat, he took a deep breath. He held it just as long as he could. Then he opened the window only a little and blew out through the crack. Then he took another deep breath. I have never known anyone with such a big lung capacity. He held it each time for about three kilometers.

It was a luxury for me that when anything broke down we just called and someone would come and fix it. No bill was sent. The band also paid for the utilities for all the Elders. We had virtually no housing expenses, and we did not have to pay taxes on any items purchased on reserve nor on anything delivered to the reserve. It is against the law to tax treaty Indians on the reservations.

Big ticket items we never paid taxes on, but we did have to pay delivery charges. The merchants' books were always scrutinized and if they did not have an official receipt from a commercial carrier, they would be charged the goods and services taxes and could also face penalties. The store could not even deliver the items themselves. The exception was vehicles, where the recipient was allowed to take delivery on the reserve as long as the dealership had a copy of the Indian Status card and signed for the delivery. There was no trust on the part of the Canadian Government. Their vigilance bordered at times on harassment. Regular taxes were paid on most items as the stores did not want to be bothered shipping to the reserve. It was a lot of trouble and, unless it was a big ticket item, not worth it.

Often staff in the store would say, "Send in your receipts for a refund." When we told them the government did not refund GST, they were surprised. One clerk asked, "They do have the right to shop tax free, right?"

"Yes, it is against the law to tax anyone with treaty status, but when they make purchases off the reserve the government will not reimburse the taxes."

"Doesn't make sense to me," she said.

"Not to me either," I replied.

Raven never complained about paying the taxes he did pay. All acquired revenues off the reserve are taxable as are property taxes, and he did pay GST on the majority of his purchases. He is the only Canadian I know who was happy and proud to pay. "You can't run a government without revenue, so why shouldn't we pay?" he used to say.

The interpretation of the tax laws is an ongoing issue between Ottawa and treaty Indians.

I learned many things about Native politics and politicians and understood much better how the politicians could get away with the corruption that occurs at times. There are few laws governing distribution of band property, therefore all decisions made by the chief and council are considered a political rather than a legal matter. For instance, if a decision is made to close a business owned and operated by a band, such as a ranch, and the chief decides to keep all the cattle, he can do that, with no laws stopping him or her. This actually happened, and our family met with the police, who told us it was a political matter and if we wanted changes our only recourse was at the polls.

"So you are telling me that politicians can legally remove band property and just keep it? Are there truly no legal repercussions to such an action?"

"No," was the reply.

Local governments could pass resolutions on the reserve, but Indian Affairs in Ottawa had the final say as whether to approve them or not. That often tied the hands of chief and council and at the very least delayed most projects and at the worst stopped them altogether since Indian Affairs had veto power over band law. Long before I met Raven, the Enoch reserve tried to get permission to build a casino. Twenty years later, after two non-Native casinos opened in the vicinity, they finally got theirs.

The closest description I can come to the reservation type government is a communist system, where the central government rules all. We all know that does not work, so why are we surprised that it does not work on the reserves? The government created a system that forces people to be dependent because they cannot get mortgages or borrow money to start businesses. At the same time there is great resentment from the general public that they are dependent and have such a high rate of unemployment. That cycle of dependency I cannot see being broken at this time.

Life on the reserve was like life in another country. I do not want to call it foreign as I was the foreigner, not them. It was hard to get a decent education, nepotism among politicians was rampant, and although the morality of that is questionable, it was also in conflict with traditional beliefs where every family took care of each other. It was next to impossible to start new enterprises without access to financing.

Banks could not legally repossess property on the reservation, so there was no security for them. The risk was too high. That law, as set down by Indian Affairs in Ottawa, is the main stumbling block to economic development on the reservations. There are other constrictions, such as the lack of qualified people, and the federal rules and regulations which are in some cases too lenient and in others too stringent. It was difficult to watch as time and again I saw people who had very good ideas not be able to fulfill them because of insufficient funds or business savvy, or not having the knowledge to fill out required paper work. In any case, time after time viable business ideas did not get off the ground, so unemployment was rampant. Alcohol and drug abuse was a constant problem. Living off-reserve was also a difficulty as housing would have to be paid for. People would have to leave family and friends and cope with a world of discrimination and all the challenges that present themselves in Canada today. I always told anyone who managed to get to university that they were ever so brave—and they were! They had to face people on the reserve who were so against white people and felt they were just trying to be 'white.'

Personally, I liked living on the reserve. No one bothered us there. It was so peaceful. I never had to worry if my car broke down. I knew someone would always stop and help.

They are proud of the fact that visitors and neighbors alike will be taken care of on the reserve. Not like in the cities and on major highways.

Raven however struggled with many things, including the dependency syndrome many people had developed from the days when they were not allowed to work or trade off the reserve. He had a hard time with those who were hanging on to blaming the white people for everything. "Yes," he would say, "there was a time we were tied down, but it is time to move on."

He believed in the power of learning and encouraged everyone to get their education. "We now live in a world where it is necessary," he would say.

Higher education is now made available on the reserves and in Native-run institutions off the reserve, so things are improving, but it takes time. It took us a thousand years to develop our western society the way it is today. We should not have expected the Native people to make changes in only a few years. Taking their children away for eight years and teaching them our language and reading and writing and arithmetic could not possibly prepare them for life the way we live it. It only resulted in mistrust, pain and anguish at families being torn apart and children disappearing.

I saw the devastation caused by government policies which created so many road blocks—road blocks like not being allowed an education past grade eight, like not being allowed to go to a regular school, like not being allowed free movement to work or trade, like not being allowed to perform their ceremonies, and many others.

There has been progress in many aspects but in attitude between our peoples I saw only slight changes in the twenty years I was with the community. Sometimes I wonder if we will ever establish good neighborly relationships, but there must always be hope.

One misconception that the non-Native people seem to have is that Natives get a lot of money from the government. In actuality each individual is entitled to five dollars a year—the only people I know of that have not received a pay raise in over one hundred years! Any other money they get is from oil revenues or welfare, the same as any other Canadian.

A treaty is an agreement between two nations, two peoples. Treaty 6, under which the Hobbema bands are governed, was signed in 1876. The Natives received the five dollars, housing, medical and dental care and education and protection from white people taking that particular piece of land.

It was a foreign life for me on the reserve, but I am so grateful for living with the people and sitting with the Elders and learning from them. It took many years before some band members trusted me. I guess I cannot blame them, considering their experiences of the past and the present with white people.

When I lived on the reservation, many told stories of how the people lived before they were forced onto reservations. At that time there were chiefs who inherited the title. It was only after the government forced the new system on them that there were elections.

Young people who showed natural tendencies were nurtured. Some were born horsemen; others were teachers, athletes, story tellers, hunters, fishermen, gatherers of food and medicine. There were doctors and spiritual leaders who said prayers for the people. There were camp criers who went around the village announcing whatever message the people needed to know and there were warriors who were often in competition with other tribes to see who could steal the most horses and women from one another. In those days, before contact, people were not voted to any position, they simply took their place in society and everyone contributed in their own way to the whole tribe. It was a natural process. They could attend any particular gathering they had interest in. No one was ever kept away. All input was appreciated.

Elders were an integral part of society; they were recognized as having wisdom that others needed. They were always called on for advice. Elders would never call themselves an 'Elder.' It was up to the community to recognize one as such. Even today it is so.

Time in the days before contact was measured by the sun, the moon and the stars. Meeting places were identified by the natural surroundings, such as bends in rivers, certain unusually shaped trees, hills or mountains. When I asked Raven if it was really effective, he just said, "Of course," and gave me a puzzled look that I would even ask such a question.

Everyone always knew the time and the place of gatherings. When they spoke of an event in past years, it would be linked to a special event—a natural disaster or a man-made event, such as when they first made contact with Europeans.

One day old Mel Paul was visiting and he started to explain about a past event. This event happened some years after the Euro-Canadians came to their territory and outlawed their ceremonies. "It happened the year after they arrested eight sun dance makers," he said. That caught my attention as I still had the question about arrests for religion in my imaginary bag. I asked him what had happened. Here is his story:

"Many years ago, when I was a child, we had all headed out in the wilderness to put up the sacred sun dance. The police found our hiding place and arrested the sun dance maker, who could best be compared to a minister of a church. Another sat in his place and did the prayers. He too was taken away for the mandatory thirty-day sentence. Another took his place and they carried on. In total eight people were arrested before they could complete the ceremony, but complete it they did. This, however, discouraged them so much, that they gave up on doing the sun dance ceremony after that."

It was Raven who brought it back to their reserve in the early 1980s when it was allowed once more.

Ownership of land was another unknown concept before contact. It would be like us saying today that we owned the air and we would not be allowed to breathe in certain locations without permission. Land was there for everyone's use. There was plenty to go around. It was inconceivable that anyone would not be free to move from one place to another. Different tribes did live in specific areas, but there were no defined borders. Everyone just knew whether they were in Cree country or Blackfoot country or Sioux country, and there was respect for one another's territories. "You walk lightly on their land" was the expression used to describe that respect.

Traditionally the Native people lived the life many people work all year to experience for three weeks when they go hunting or fishing or camping.

Such is the cost of 'progress.' Is it any wonder they yearn for the ways of the past? They knew how to live in harmony, respecting other people's ways and allowing everyone to be *who* they are, *who* they are born to be.

Chapter 29

Teepee Village

One day in mid-May, one and a half years after moving to the reservation, Raven came home and told me he was really getting fed up with his work as everything he did went against his philosophy of self-reliance and self-respect. It really hurt him to see so many people not looking after themselves financially and spiritually. The next day he approached the Chief and council to see if they would provide some funding to set up a teepee village to be used for a cultural camp. Not only would it be a place for band members' use, but we would also be able to do camps for all the people who were requesting them.

We had started to receive phone calls from many people, including the Royal Canadian Mounted Police and non-Native parents of Native children as well as educational institutions. Many people from all over the world expressed interest in learning about the connectedness of the Native people to everything in nature. The Royal Canadian Mounted Police were requesting cross-cultural workshops to help establish better relations between the Native community and their officers. The non-Native families of Native children wanted to learn about everything so they could give their children a better understanding of their heritage. Almost everyone wanted to participate in a sweat lodge and other sacred ceremonies.

The band council agreed to purchase whatever we needed as long as we would become self-sustaining after that. Raven decided to set up the camp at Buck Lake. The band had purchased land in the area and most of Raven's family lived nearby. About forty acres were set aside for recreational use. The location was very good as it was just over an hour south-west of Edmonton.

As we drove into the grounds, there were baseball diamonds and open fields to the right, and to the left a stand of trees which were far enough apart to accommodate many teepees. As each teepee is about five meters across at the base, we required space between the trees. A building large enough for a camp kitchen and dining area was also nestled in the trees. There was an artesian well with plenty of fresh, clean water situated on the edge of a grassy area. It was perfect.

With Raven's family living close by we could provide employment for them and it would be a perfect opportunity for us all to work on a project together. The building needed a coat of paint and some new windows. We had to do the work and the band provided the material. We decided to paint it a bright red on the outside.

The University of Calgary, which was hosting an environmental course for people from all the Pacific Rim countries, requested a weekend with us as part of their course. The head of the program, Tim Bryce, called, asking if we could be ready in one month. Raven just said, "Of course!" There was so much to do before the first camp. I could see we were strapped for time. Raven was not concerned at all. He said it would all come together as it should. "Something very special will happen in this camp," he said. "We will be ready."

I was ecstatic about the camp and had endless energy. It was an opportunity for many more people to learn a little of the beautiful traditional knowledge of the Elders and create understanding between the non-Natives and the Native People. There were so many injustices that the white people knew nothing about, and I felt that a lack of knowledge was a major factor for much of the animosity and a stumbling block for many things. Sometimes it was a little lonely as my two worlds just did not come together at all. This was an opportunity for that to change, maybe just a little.

First of all Raven and I had to go into Edmonton to purchase canvas. The best place we could get that was at a fish and netting supply company where Dennis, the owner, would order canvas by the roll. We needed to make ten teepees, each requiring about forty meters of canvas, so we ordered 500 meters to make sure we had a little extra in case we decided to make liners. In any case we knew it would come to good use. Then it was off to the wholesalers where we could buy the thread the shoemakers use. Next stop was a camping supply store to buy loops that didn't rot in damp weather, for the bottom of the teepees.

We then headed to a hardware store to pick up rolls of clear plastic for ground sheets so the bedding would not draw moisture from the ground at night. We also purchased the largest tarpaulin we could find to spread out on the ground for cutting the canvas for the teepees, and fifty white plastic chairs.

The next day it was back into Edmonton to a store that sold used restaurant equipment. There we found dishes and, most important, a big propane stove with four large burners, two ovens and a large grill. It was perfect. Raven was ecstatic as he exclaimed, "Newa (wife), now we are rich!"

The next stop was Chinatown in the center of Edmonton: the Chinese stores carried the big eight-liter tea kettles and the big pots we needed to feed up to forty people at one time.

Then it was back to pick up the canvas. We were all set to begin with the sewing. Katrina offered to help and to use her place to sew the teepees. She had a good old treadle machine and Raven and I brought ours which we had purchased a few months before. The next day Raven's children—Johnny, Gregory, Shirley, Katrina, and Adeline—and Raven and I all got together to start making the teepees.

First we spread out the big orange tarp we had purchased the previous day. Then we spread an old teepee on top of that for a pattern. The men began to roll out the canvas and cut it, all under the watchful eye of our expert, Katrina. She herself then cut the fronts, which is a little tricky and she did not want anyone else to do them. Each panel was numbered so we would know which ones fit together. As soon as the first one was completely cut, Adeline and I began sewing together the long seams. The cutting went on all that first day until we had ten piles of canvas ready to be assembled.

Early the next morning Katrina began assembling the front panel where the door is located. By early afternoon we had the long panels assembled so we could sew the body of the teepee to the front. Then it was hemming and loops to sew on all around the bottom. As we sewed everyone shared stories from other sewing bees and powwows where they had lived in teepees.

Now the handwork needed to be done. Each teepee had twenty-four holes for the pins which hold the teepee together above the door. It is called the breast of the teepee. There were also four at the bottom of the door that had to be done, all of which had to be sewn like button-holes. More people arrived to help with the handwork. For the next week everyone worked from early morning until midnight every night. With all that help we actually sewed them all in one week.

Raven got a permit to cut swamp spruce, which grew tall and thin enough for teepee rails or poles. It could also carry the weight of the canvas without bending. Raven, Johnny and I went out west of Buck Lake to cut them. Each one was six to seven meters long. Luckily we had a horse trailer long enough to carry them.

The next step was to peel all the bark off each rail. We purchased two draw knives for that purpose. Raven built stands to lay the rails on while we were peeling them. There were two hundred in all. Looking at the stack of rails I wondered how we could ever be ready in time for the first camp, which was now only two weeks away. Supplies had to be purchased, the teepees put up, firewood cut, the grass mowed, and willows and tarps for the sweat lodges gathered.

I wanted to stop and draw up an agenda as the participants were with us for three days; we had to know *what* was to happen *when*, so I could prepare. Every time I would ask Raven about developing an agenda he would always give the same comment: "Don't worry. It will be okay."

"How are we going to assign teepees? These people do not even know each other."

"Don't worry. It will be fine."

"Who is going to teach what?"

"Don't worry."

"How are we going to run the program?"

"Don't worry; it will take care of itself."

I was getting more and more worried every time he would say that. Finally I just threw up my hands and said, "At least let *me* worry!"

He just laughed and said, "If you want to."

Then I realized how foolish I must have looked to him. And then I remembered my late mother's words. "Why worry?" she used to say. "It is such a waste of time and energy if nothing happens. If it does, you will handle it the best possible way and you cannot do more. So why waste your time and energy on worry?"

When we began peeling, Raven called his adopted son, Richard, and his wife Margaret to help. They drove all the way from Paul Band, over an hour away. They did not ask for any payment, but we gave them gas money and groceries. I used to marvel at Richard. Raven would call him up and the conversation would go like this:

"Richard, I need you."

"Okay. I'll leave right away." He would not ask anything. Raven needed him and that was that.

We worked from sunup until sunset every day peeling rails, getting pins and pegs, and erecting the teepees. Richard brought a big propane tank and fire wood.

Two days before the first people were expected, I sat down and made a grocery list. Raven asked me what I did that for. I looked at him as if he had lost it. "You're going to forget some things whether you have a list or not, so you are just wasting your time," he said calmly. I made my list and I did forget some things. The next camp, I decided to try without the list and he was right. Either way I forgot some things, but actually fewer when I did not have a list.

Finally the big day came. We were ready. It was a dream come true. There were fourteen teepees—the ten we had made, plus our own teepee and three that Raven's children had loaned him—set in the little grove surrounding our bright red camp kitchen.

A big bus pulled into camp at noon. Raven and I greeted the people and told them the first thing to do was to have something to eat. We immediately served a lunch consisting of moose stew and bannock which had been prepared by Shirley and Beryl, whom we had hired to cook.

The people were here and we still had no plans, no agenda; I still did not know what would happen or how.

When everyone had finished eating, I told them they could just go over to the teepees and select their home for the weekend, then lay out the bedding which they had brought with them. I reminded them to be sure to use the plastic for a ground sheet if they did not have one with them.

The Elder Madge arrived with Carol Dillman. I took them directly to the kitchen and served them their lunch. I cautiously approached Madge on her thoughts for the program. She looked at me with just a little grin and said, "I don't know yet. Don't worry; it will come together as it should." Not again! I thought.

While we were eating, Richard made a fire and set the chairs in a circle in a small clearing close to the camp kitchen. Raven went off for a quick little nap while the participants were making their beds. Soon he came back and I saw he had a rock and a braid of sweet grass, which is a type of grass used as a smudge, in his hand. He called everyone to the circle of chairs for the opening session. When they were all seated, Raven lit the sweet grass and began with an opening prayer. As he was praying, I looked into the fire and there I saw four faces of Elders. They all had deep wrinkles, and as I watched them they seemed to smile with their eyes rather than their mouths. That was when I stopped worrying. Months later, Madge told me that she knew everything was going to be very special when she saw the faces of the four Elders in the fire at that first circle. We both had seen the same thing. I silently thanked the spirits and Creator for their guidance.

After prayers Raven said, "We are all here together for the weekend and I would like to ask everyone to share with us what you are here to learn. What are your wishes and your expectations? That way we will know what to talk about for the rest of the weekend. Today we will set the agenda. I will pass this rock to each person in a clockwise direction. Only the person holding the rock may speak. The rest will listen. We are all teachers within this circle. We all share our thoughts and feelings when we sit together. No one is more or less important." With that, he handed the rock to the person on the left and motioned for him to start with a nod of the head.

Everyone shared their purpose and their expectations, but, as the rock went around from one person to the next, it was obvious they were very tired as they were constantly yawning. Raven saw how tired they were and told them to go for a sleep. We would gather again later. Someone asked what time and he replied, "You will know. Just sleep as long as you need to."

I reminded myself that had we had an agenda, an afternoon sleep would not have been on it. We probably would have carried on the way the schedule was 'supposed to be' and chances were no one would have remembered the teachings anyway as they were too tired. Everyone gathered about three hours later ready to learn.

The next morning when we started with the circle again, one poor man from Thailand said he did not sleep a wink. He was so afraid he would freeze to death in the middle of the night. Never had he experienced such cold. That night we all tucked him in with extra blankets, top and bottom, a toque, mitts and a warm sweater and sweat pants and assured him we had never heard of anyone freezing to death while sleeping in a teepee and Native people had slept in them summer and winter for many years.

Many things were shared that weekend: how we are all connected to each other, to all in nature, to the Creator and the spirit world; how Native people learned many things from the animals . . . .

Madge shared how in the old days they would watch and see what the wild animals ate when they became ill. "That is how we learned our medicines. The bears told our Elders how to doctor people. From the wolves we learned how to create harmony in our camps. The trees taught us about strength, and the grass about patience. Even if grass is trod on, stamped down or even burnt, it will always come back stronger than ever. All the animals and plants are teachers. We can learn something from them all."

Raven shared the following: "All the plants and animals do not mind if we use them as long as it is for a good purpose and we give something back. For instance, it is okay to cut trees to build houses or make teepee rails, but at least we should appreciate them for giving their life for us. That is the reason we have protocol and prayers for all that we take. We thank the plants for giving up their lives so we can nourish our bodies or doctor us when we are ill. We always do an offering of tobacco and only take them the way we have been taught. That is the way it is. We are all sharing a common experience, so now we too are connected to one another through this experience."

On the last day of the camp we put up a sweat lodge. Richard came to help.

A so-called miracle happened to a man from the Philippines in that lodge. When it was time to go into the sweat lodge and they closed the door, he panicked. He had not realized it would be dark. Fortunately, he was sitting beside Raven, who calmed him down and told him he would be able to go out when the door opened. The young man managed to make it through the first round and then took on the second and then the third and fourth. After the sweat lodge he went directly to his teepee and we didn't see him again until the evening, when he shared this story:

"I am from the Philippines. I was captured and tortured under the Marcos regime. They kept me in a dark hole for many months and I never saw light of any kind. I, until this day, could still not be in the dark. I would panic even at the thought of being in the dark.

I have been to every kind of treatment I could think of and nothing helped. I have even tried hypnosis to no avail." Then he started to cry and through his tears continued: "Here I come to this little camp in the middle of nowhere in this huge country called Canada. Today in the sweat lodge all the weight I have carried for so many years was lifted from my shoulders. Today in the sweat lodge I got cured. I feel so light and I am happier than I ever thought possible. I thought my life was over, but now I know that today it has just begun again."

Our next camp was a group of non-Native parents with their Native children. These were not foster parents. Their children were adopted. Everyone had the children because they loved them very much, and had actually given up a lot of money when the adoptions went through.

Mel Paul brought his family out and they set up camp at the edge of the village. The way everyone learned from one another in that camp was a great gift for us all. The Native people discovered the love those white people had for their children. The parents met beautiful Native people and discovered the reality of what traditional people were really like.

After everyone had settled in, we had an introductory session with the parents and their children. Raven just welcomed everyone and gave a little background on himself and the

Mel Paul and family camp

work of the Elders. "One thing I want you to know which is most important," he said, "is that the Elders will always be there for you and for your children."

I looked over and tears were streaming down one woman's face. After we were done, she came to me and said, "I have adopted three boys, all brothers. My husband and I went looking for a ready-made family of three or four siblings. One day I found my family when one of the boys was featured on a TV program called 'Wednesday's Child.' It features hard-to-place children who are in need of a home. Marg the hostess said he had two brothers and I knew in my heart I had found our children. My husband and I have given them all our time, provided them with everything they needed, yet I knew there was something missing and I could not figure out what it was. We gave them so much, but in my heart I knew it was not enough. Today I got my answer. They needed to be exposed to their traditions. They needed their Elders."

Circle Teachings by the Elders

The next year, when they came back to our camp, she came over to the picnic table where I sat and shared this story with me: "Our oldest son became very bitter. He faced discrimination in school and had difficulty adjusting to a new home, a new kind of life. The most difficult for me to watch was his low self-esteem. Whenever my husband or I would try to help him through any problems he would just tell us that we didn't understand because we were not Indian. He was right, of course. We are not, and he blamed everything bad in his life on the fact that he *was*. One day things got out of hand with shouting and the oldest boy even pushed me.

"My husband and I decided to take the boys back to the reservation where they came from and talk to their grandfather. That was the lowest we had been since we adopted our sons. We were even questioning whether we were good enough to be parents to these boys or not. We made arrangements for the whole family to stay for the weekend, and as much as we loved our sons, we prepared ourselves to leave the boys there, if that was what the old man suggested.

"When the weekend came to a close the old man called us all together and told us that he could see we loved his grandchildren very much and that they were getting an education and had a good life with us. He asked if we were willing to keep them. My husband and I just looked at each other and nodded. Then he told the boys that their parents loved them very much and they were to respect us more from now on. It has made all the difference in the world to our family. That day our family really came together. It was like magic," she told me.

Later that day, Raven explained how traditional names told much about a person and which spirit was looking after them. One mother, who had adopted two sisters, resolved that her daughters too should have a traditional name. She wanted to make it very special for them, so she spent the next year preparing them for the big day. The Elders are always gifted by the people who receive their name, and so she had her girls make a gift for Raven. The little eight-year-old had embroidered a teepee with a buffalo on a piece of burlap. She had fringed it with beads and embroidered a sun on one side. She had asked her mother what she should put on the other side, in the sky. Her mother suggested a cloud.

"No," said the little girl, "I want to put a blue eagle there." And she did.

On the last day of the camp, when we had the sweat lodge, the families gathered around. The mother of the two girls had previously given Raven tobacco to ask him for a name for her daughters. Now it would happen. The father, along with other men and boys, joined Raven in the lodge; the women and girls all sat outside beside the lodge. When the ceremony was finished, Raven emerged from the lodge and told the youngest girl that she was Bear Child and the oldest was Blue Eagle Woman. Their mother started to cry. How could he know? How could she know?

The Royal Canadian Mounted Police also hired us to run cross-cultural camps to help them understand the native community better and give them some guidance to make their job easier.

Raven and I were staying at the camp between sessions. Four days before the members of the force were scheduled to arrive, an officer came to see Raven. I poured him a cup of tea, as we always did for all guests. He told Raven that he was looking for someone and he wondered if Raven had seen her. He had not. That officer was very angry and resentful that he was being forced by his superior to come to the camp that weekend. "I have to take time away from my family to live in a teepee and learn what?" he said angrily. "I have worked with Native people for many years and I do not need this," he complained. I tried to assure him it would be worth his while, that he would learn much that would help him both personally and professionally.

After he left, Raven became silent and I knew something was bothering him. After much prodding he finally came out with it. "You did not have to flirt with him like that," he said.

"I did not think I was," I said.

"I am not pleased with you one bit," he said.

I was devastated. How could he accuse me once again? With the heavy workload and responsibility of looking after everything, I felt I could not carry that too and I broke out in tears. "I can't do this!" I said. "I cannot look after everything and have you angry as well. I did not flirt with him, I do not even like him and why would I do such a thing when I love you so much?" As the tears just kept coming, he told me to forget it. He had. He would not bring it up again. All through that camp I was very cautious about who I spoke to and when. It was very difficult.

In the first opening circle, that same officer told everyone how angry he was about being forced to come to the camp. He had dealt with Native people for many years and he knew them all right and he had no use for them. Good! I thought. We have honesty.

Many were obviously in agreement with him but others also shared how grateful they were to be there—they knew things were not good and they could not seem to find a solution. It was good for everyone to hear each other's views. Everyone is a teacher within the circle.

That weekend the Elders shared much about protocol and how to integrate in a good way into the community: how they would always be welcomed at the round dances and powwows and treaty days celebrations, how the officers would be welcomed by the Elders in their homes and how they would always be open to share if they brought tobacco. The officers were also offered the opportunity to participate in a sweat lodge, which almost all took advantage of.

At the end of the workshop, we once again had a sharing circle in which we used the eagle feather to pass from one person to the next as they spoke. That same angry officer took the eagle feather, but when he started to talk he choked up and broke down in tears. As everyone sat in respectful silence, he gathered himself enough to say, "I am one person who has made a one hundred and eighty degree turn." He was too choked up to say any more. He did not need to. His tears said more than words ever could.

Tim, the professor from Calgary, called one fall day and asked if we were willing to put up a camp as part of their continuation courses. We agreed and scheduled one for the next spring. His department was taking care of registrations. We had told him we needed a minimum of twelve people as that was our financial break-even point. Three days before camp Tim called and told us that he had only eleven registered. I asked Raven if he still wanted to go ahead with it. He became very quiet. After a few moments he said, "This is going to be a very special camp. It does not matter that we lose money. We will do it anyway."

When everyone arrived for the camp, we discovered that none of them knew each other, as they had all registered separately. That first evening, as we were all sitting around the fire, one person asked if she could bring out her drum. Raven said, "You can all bring out your drums, if you wish." My eyes opened wide as every person simultaneously left the fire. All came back with a drum, some large, others small, all different one from the other. We spent the evening singing and drumming.

That night Raven and I retired early. We went to sleep to the sound of the drums.

In the fall of 1989 we took down the teepees after what was to be our last camp. We did not know that at the time, but there were new adventures, new challenges coming into our lives.

Chapter 30

Combining Native Traditional and Western Medical Models

In late fall of 1989, Dr. Tom Noseworthy called and asked if he could come out to the reservation to meet with us for a couple of hours. Dr. Noseworthy was the CEO for the Royal Alexandra Hospital in Edmonton. The Royal Alex, as everyone calls it, is a very large active treatment hospital employing 4,000 people. It is situated in the center of the city of Edmonton, Alberta, Canada.

He was acutely aware of the discrepancies between the health standards of Native Canadians and the rest of the Canadian population and wanted to do something about it. They had just closed the doors at the Camsell Hospital, the only place where Native people felt some degree of safety as at one time it was an all-Indian hospital run by the federal government.

He also saw a special camaraderie between patients and staff and a pride in working at the Camsell, which was unique to that institution. He hoped to bring some of those qualities to the much larger hospital of which he was in charge.

Raven and I were hired on as consultants to that process. For me to be combining the western medical model which I had been a part of for

25 years, with traditional healing was a dream come true. Raven and I would be working together to fulfill a vision we both shared.

Dr. Noseworthy asked us to go and learn about other Native programs in health institutions in North America. Together we travelled extensively in those first months. On our return, Dr. Noseworthy called us to his office and asked Raven to share some of his findings.

Raven began to speak in his slow deliberate way: "I do not like most of what I saw out there. The programs were mostly set aside from the rest of the institutions and there is much conflict between the staff of the Native programs and the rest of the people within the institution. We need a program of cooperation rather than confrontation. We need to understand one another much better. It is the only way we will succeed." Dr. Noseworthy listened attentively as Raven continued: "I cannot speak for all the people, so we must have Elders from the various communities we serve to advise us of their needs."

The establishment of an advisory committee representing all the people the hospital served was the first order of business. It was from their guidance and their wisdom that the entire program was developed. Therefore everyone agreed to call it the 'wisdom committee.'

At the very first meeting of the wisdom committee, the Elders wanted to be sure they would be heard and their advice considered. They did not want to sit as 'token Indians,' meaning Native people who were assigned to committees, but not heard from—as was often the case elsewhere. Dr. Noseworthy assured them that their contributions would be taken seriously.

Another request the elders had was that they did not want the program's precious funds spent on research. We needed to help the people, not study them. There were so many studies and so little help.

They also expressed fear that as soon as the hospital administration learned a few things they would take it over, and run it their way. That had been the pattern in the past for so many programs.

"Not on my watch!" Dr. Noseworthy promised.

"Not as long as I am here!" I affirmed.

This was *their program, for them by them.* My role was to see their resolutions incorporated in the hospital, and to be a bridge between the two worlds, creating space for each to function as they must.

The foundation, as identified by the Elders, was to be one of cooperation as opposed to confrontation. Therefore all programs were to be developed in cooperation between the Native community and the medical community. Both needed to be in harmony and supportive of the programs.

First the Elders requested to be able to utilize burning substances for prayer and for spiritually cleansing of the rooms the patients would occupy when ill.

Workshops were established to help staff understand the special issues facing some Native people coming to such a large and frightening institution. There were many issues, with the biggest barrier being communication.

Fear was also a huge issue. Fear of getting lost, fear of having treatments they did not understand forced on them, fear of their children being taken from them, fear of the food, fear of separation, fear of being treated with disrespect, fear of dying in the hospital.

There was much work to do to create understanding of and respect for 'otherness' within this huge institution. We needed to create a comfort zone for all people to be allowed to be *who* they are, to pray the way they were taught, the way they knew how.

It was a daunting task, but we had good support from hospital administration and from the Elders.

With regionalization in the works, the program was expanded to encompass the whole Capital Health region in Edmonton, but we lost

Dr. Noseworthy in the shuffle. It was a great blow to the program and we feared for the continuation in the same light of cooperation.

Diabetes is pandemic in the Native community. Reported rates of the incidence of diabetes vary greatly, but a screening by means of an oral glucose tolerance test of the Ojib-Cree Sandy Lake people in 2000 found the prevalence was 25 percent among adults and 80 percent among women between 50 and 64 years of age.*

So many Native people with diabetes go undetected because they rarely go to doctors. If they are diagnosed, they often go into denial, so nothing more is done and testing is not completed. These would not necessarily be included in the statistics put out by other institutions such as Health Canada. I feel the Sandy Lake study is much more accurate because they screened everyone.

Raven too had diabetes and he certainly would not have been counted in the statistics; he had previously told me he had been diagnosed with diabetes thirty years before I met him. "I don't believe it!" he had said.

"Why do you think they would say that if it wasn't true?" I asked.

"I guess you have a point," he said. "But I didn't feel anything."

Raven was so typical of many, many people I spoke to.

From the Nova Corporation, an international company which specializes in building projects for special data base and electronic needs, we were able to secure a one million dollar grant to develop a diabetes program specifically for Native people.

Some of us travelled to Manitoulin Island in Ontario where the western and the traditional medicine were utilized side by side for healing, including the treatment of diabetes.

* see more www.cmaj.ca/cgi/reprint/163/5/561.pdf

There we met with Dr. Taylor, who spearheaded the project from the western side, and Elder Ron Wigijig and his assistant Honorine Wright, who guided the traditional approach; they shared with us how they worked together to develop the concept, design the building and develop the trust necessary for success.

The clinic was set up so that when you entered you could go to the right to see the Elder or go to the left to see a physician. The room where Ron Wigijig, the Elder, practiced was round and about ten meters in diameter. In the center was a fire pit. Many educational sessions presented by Ron and/or the western medical staff were held there. The physicians, the Elder and all the clinic staff worked in harmony, with each referring to the other and combining traditional treatments and western medicine. The Elders do play a major role in the acceptance, or rejection, of western medicine.

After the information-gathering trip to Manitoulin Island, a committee consisting of Elders, nurses, a program coordinator and me was set up to develop our program. The focus was on *balance* in every way: balance between western medicine and traditional medicine, and balance of the physical, mental, emotional and spiritual being.

Every session was to be opened with prayer, every person was to see a physician and a specialist as required, every detail of understanding what diabetes is and how you can be well was up for discussion, and the emotional ups and downs that are associated with the condition had to be addressed.

Because a person with diabetes can be well as long as you keep the glucose levels within normal range, the committee decided to call it the "Aboriginal Diabetes Wellness Program."

You can be as well as anyone if you know how. That, above all, was the message we wanted to convey. The utilization of humour was of utmost importance. Utilizing the traditional sharing-circle format, everything from the most technical to the most personal aspects of diabetes care was a shared subject. Even difficult topics such as sexual dysfunction could be shared in that format.

One old woman shared this story. She had been married for over fifty years. Her husband had passed away the year before from complications due to diabetes. Now she too had diabetes. When he could no longer have an erection, he would say to her, "Hon, I know it won't come up any more, but could you please hold it down just in case?" Everyone got a good laugh and others began to share.

The staff also utilized games and skits for better understanding.

Dr. Voaklander did scientific studies with base-line measurements when those diagnosed with the condition arrived, and three-month and six-month follow-ups. Every parameter showed overall improvement. We had a completion of percentage attendance rate in the high nineties. At the request of the participants, we established outreach and follow-up sessions. All in all it was a complete program with cooperation between participants, the community and the medical professionals.

We went on to develop programs for healthy babies and support for women's health. In 1998 we developed a program to help mothers who risked losing their newborns to Social Services. The development of this program was particularly difficult and emotional. I wrote the following poem shortly after we had completed setting up that program.

LOVE FOR THE BABIES

They're stealing our babies, Aboriginals cried,
And making good money on the side,
Making money is their primary goal
Forgetting about the children's soul.

We love our children, don't you see?
When you take them away, what will they be?

How it happens we don't understand:
Everything is done with such underhand.
To give birth and for help we come to your place,
Before we know it we're just another case.

We love our children, don't you see?
When you take them away, what will they be?

We're social workers and really care.
What will happen to children there?
How they'll survive is such a worry
So away to safety we must hurry.

We love your children, don't you see?
To leave them with you, what will they be?

And so we take them into care.
Their lives with White folk they will share,
An education they will all achieve,
Life will be better we believe.

We love your children, don't you see?
To leave them with you what will they be?

It's been going on for so many years,
We've shed at least a million tears
At the loss of our children one by one
Our little daughters and our son.

We love our children, don't you see?
To leave them with you, what will they be?

We come here to request support,
To keep the babies out of court.
To find out more is our request
Before taking the babies from the breast.

We love our babies don't you see?
When you take them away, what will they be?

Child welfare is such a frightening place,
I don't know how to plead my case.

All my options I do not know,
They've taken my baby and I hurt so.

The pain is almost unbearable,
I've never felt so terrible!
In court I am supposed to appear,
But all I do is shed another tear.

I feel like I don't even have a chance.
White people have their circumstance
Which the courts will naturally understand.
But our spirituality? They just can't.

And so our children one by one,
We find that they are really gone.
Our grandmothers grieve, when our babies you keep
And the communities continue to weep.

We're social workers, we're starting to see
The harm that we have done to your wee.
But how can we help to make this better?
When the system makes us follow the letter.

We have to abide by confidentiality
So how can we show hospitality?
The system demands we do as they say,
So how can we help to save the day?

Is an oath not something a worker can take?
As all other staff had to make
When they went to work in the helping field,
With goodness and kindness intent to yield?

From the start of the process it took one year,
To work out the bumps and quiet the fear.
There were tears and frustration on many an occasion,
But the Elders, invited in, saved the situation.

> The rate of lost babies drastically dropped
> When families were appropriately propped.
> And the glue that kept us all together?
> Was love for the babies, the storms we did weather.

There were many tears along that trail, but in the end we triumphed. Once the social workers really understood the harm done by the apprehensions, they were ever so supportive and worked well together with Marty Ouellette, the Native worker. They would stand by the mothers whenever possible. It was a pilot project and after ten months we had to do an evaluation. Apprehensions by child welfare were reduced by about 80 percent, saving the government thousands of dollars in child care, court costs and care for traumatized mothers.

It took only one staff member and that person made a world of difference to so many.

It was during the development of these programs that we set up some focus groups to hear from the mothers about the reality of what faced the young women of Edmonton.

One young mother told us her story. She was going to university and was supported through welfare. A social worker came to her home and actually looked in her fridge and told her she did not have enough food and apprehended her four children. There was no abuse, no evidence of neglect, no starvation, only a fridge without much food. When she tried to explain that there were three other single-mother friends living in the same apartment building and all going to university, supporting one another, and sharing food and babysitting, the social worker did not listen. The children were removed on the spot. She and the children were devastated. She had to go to court to regain each of her children at the same time as she was studying. One by one they were returned to her, but in the meantime everyone was traumatized. She graduated from university and secured a job teaching pre-school children.

Coincidentally, the same social worker had come to her place of employment and taken her out of the classroom, telling her she was not allowed to work with children because she had child welfare status.

Worse was the fact that there is no way of ever erasing it from the records. She would never be able to work with children again.

One young woman told the story of how she got pregnant and had her baby three months before her sixteenth birthday. Her parents were alcoholics and she would not bring her precious little girl into that atmosphere, so when she left the hospital she went straight to a women's shelter. She heard they would help her to get a good start. When they discovered she was only fifteen, they could not take her and referred her to a youth shelter. The youth shelter would accept her, but not her baby. A social worker came and took her baby from her. As soon as she turned sixteen she began her fight to get her baby back. With help from the youth shelter, she got herself set up in an apartment. She did get her baby back. She was so happy. Life was good. Then one day her precious baby said, "No!" and she did not know what to do. She had no idea how to cope and had no support network in place as she would not have contact with anyone from her former life. She told us how much she needed a support system. She had no idea how to handle defiance from her precious little girl. She had struggled through the best she could and her daughter was now five years old. "I do my best," she said, "but how am I supposed to know if it is good enough. I really need someone to come to my home and see if I am doing okay or not. I have no one in my life I can share with."

Her story was instrumental in the development of a support system for young mothers in Edmonton.

Another woman told us she did not have any of her children with her, but she was working on it. I asked her how many children she had.

"Seven," she replied. "They just keep taking them away from me."

I asked why she had so many children. She explained that she had her first child when she was very young and they apprehended that child. She was so heartbroken that she ended up on the streets, drinking and drugging and fooling around with men. Soon she became pregnant again. This time they took her into a shelter, took care of her and she sobered and cleaned up and thought she would be able to keep her baby. No such luck. They removed the child as soon as it was born. Her heart was broken again, she went back on the streets again, she got pregnant again, she sobered up again, and she hoped to keep her baby again, they took it away again, she was back on the streets again and the cycle went on. Now she was straight and sober and had a home for her children and had begun the fight to get them back. I have not heard from her again, so do not know the outcome.

So many stories like these were shared by the women of the Native Community with the result that most people, fearful of our systems, would not seek help.

All those involved were so proud of the program and how many people it helped. The Elders did guide everything. There was no tokenism here. Everyone had an important role.

Chapter 31

Raven's Amputation

In 1998, after we had the program up and functioning well, Raven got a blister on his big toe. He had taken a trip up north to Ft. Chipewyan and purchased new boots while there. He had worn them for too long and with his diabetes did not feel the tightness. When he returned home his big toe had already started to turn black and I knew he was in big trouble.

He refused to go and see a doctor, and he was getting sicker and sicker by the day. He lost so much weight in just two weeks, he looked like he was going to die. He did use some traditional herbs, which were stopping the rapid spread but could not reverse the damage done. Dr. Kathy Burke arrived from New Mexico. We had met her earlier at a North American Indian Physicians conference and Raven had invited her to spend the summer. Katrina and Shirley, his daughters, also came. Every day he was losing ground. I knew he would not survive for long if he did not agree to an amputation.

At one point Shirley was very upset and she told me to make him have the amputation, and that he would listen to me. "No Shirley, he will not," I told her. "Believe me, I have tried everything I can think of. If he felt he was forced, he would just become very bitter from this day forward, and I will not be responsible for that. The way I see it, he must make this decision himself, so if you want to, you make him go ahead. I will not."

Together, we finally persuaded him to go and see a specialist who told him his only option was an amputation. Raven told him he did not believe it and wanted to think about it. We went over to our apartment, and I was hoping we could stay there as we were so close to medical care, but he insisted on going back to the acreage. When I asked Kathy how much time we had if things suddenly took a turn for the worst, she just started to cry and shook her head. I turned to Raven and told him that if we went back out there we would be too far away from the hospital and he might not make it if he took a turn for the worst. "I'm not going to die, so quit worrying," he said.

We called many people together for a pipe ceremony. Danny Alexis, Raven's pupil and friend, gave him the pipe and asked him to pray for himself, to get the help he needed. Kathy sat back and watched—she had never been to a ceremony before and did not know what to do. I knew she was concerned that he could die any time. My head and heart were certainly at odds. I had worked in a hospital for twenty-five years and my head said he was dying, but my heart said no. He said over and over, "What have I done to deserve this?"

I kept reassuring him it was from the neglect of his blood sugar levels over so many years. He was seventy-four years old at the time, so his age was against him too. We had heard about Dr. Ung who was practicing in the United States. He was only amputating the affected areas, not the whole lower leg as is the practice in Canada. We contacted medical services but they would not finance anything. With the prices being so high in the States, we could not do it on our own.

The next few days I saw him losing even more ground and I knew it was too late to travel anyway. Once again we talked him into going and seeing a doctor so we could at least get some stronger antibiotics. We left for the hospital in a blinding snowstorm and I was just praying we would make it. It was May 22nd, 1998.

Coincidentally, the head of the orthopedic surgeons department, Dr Arnett, was on call. He had been in the meeting where Raven had told the doctors they knew nothing. When he came in I razzed him about that and we all had a good laugh about it. Then he got serious about what was happening to Raven. He was ever so kind as he told Raven that if he wanted to be well again the only option he had was to take the leg below the knee. He told him he could be fitted with a good prosthesis and would be able to walk normally again. Shirley was with us, and Raven asked her, "What shall I do, my girl?"

"Papa," she said, "I cannot tell you what to do. Whatever your decision, I will support you. I will be here for you."

Thank you, God, I said silently. He so needed to make this decision for himself. Then Raven told Dr. Arnett to go ahead with the amputation.

"Thank you for choosing life," said Shirley. My heart was relieved. My tears flowed. I was too grateful to say anything.

He was immediately taken upstairs to a ward and the preparation began. When they did the ECG, the heart recording, they found some abnormalities of his heart, and threatened not to operate. I told them there was nothing wrong with his heart, that it was an abnormality which had been there probably forever and had never given him one moment's grief nor had he ever had any symptoms of any kind in the past. All the staff who entered the room told him the surgery might be postponed due to his heart condition. I really became frightened then. I knew he would not survive without the amputation and I was so afraid he would discharge himself and go home and die. Every time he would hear anything about his heart he would get angry and tell them there was nothing wrong with his heart. I could see him losing the precious little strength he had. He kept saying, "Now I have told them they can have my leg, they want my heart as well. They will never stop."

I called Dr. Tom Noseworthy. I could not figure out what to do. He told me, "You have always been in the center of Raven's care and now you have stepped aside." I had not seen it that way until he said it, but realized he was right. He suggested that I go to the nursing station and let it be known that no one was to talk to Raven about his heart except Dr. Arnett who had the final say. When the top diabetes specialist came in, I stopped even him. I stood watch like an old mother hen and would stop anyone from mentioning the word heart in his presence. Then I left a message for Dr. Arnett that I was to see him before he spoke to Raven. When he arrived, he took me aside. I told him the whole story of what was happening.

"Is he not going to die without the amputation?" I asked. Dr. Arnett agreed and said he would go ahead, but he did need to talk to Raven about it as it was his right to make the final decision. "Fair enough as long as you are the *only* one he talks to about it," I said.

He did talk to him, and as every other time, Raven insisted there was nothing wrong with his heart and he wanted him to get on with it.

That afternoon they took him down to the surgery and I went with him. I was told by the porter that I could not enter the waiting area, but I told him I worked at the hospital and he could not stop me. He insisted, but I just followed anyway. As Raven and I were waiting, the anesthesiologist came and introduced himself as Dr. Hatch. I could not believe the luck. I had worked with Dr. Hatch in Whitecourt and knew he was kind and would take good care of Raven. It was so nice to know he was in good hands and I told Raven that.

The amputation went off without a hitch. When he woke up fully, he lifted his leg and looked at it long and hard. Suddenly he wiggled his stump and said, "Skippy!" and laughed. I had to turn away to hide my tears.

That evening our friends Danny and Ella came to visit. Ella told us a story about one of her friends. Ella and her friend had gone to a conference together in Toronto. There was a dance in the evening and the two ladies went. One fellow was sweet on her friend and was trying everything to impress her. Finally, after some persuasion, she agreed to dance with him. He, like Raven, had had an amputation and when he danced his foot turned backwards. Everyone cracked right up in laughter. That was the best medicine for everyone.

The next evening I told everyone to go and play Bingo as they had all been under so much stress. Raven would be fine now and I would stay with him. Kathy had never been to Bingo before and so whatever cards the girls purchased, she purchased the same. As they began to play, she, of course, being inexperienced, could not keep up at all. In order to help her, Shirley would tell her what the next number would be as soon as it appeared on the monitor. Kathy did not know that the numbers appeared on the monitor before they were called and she just kept thinking how powerful Shirley was that she could even predict the numbers before they were called.

Raven was discharged from the hospital after just four days. We were to stay at Anderson Hall and take him to physiotherapy every day.

Raven's amputation was performed on May 23rd, 1998, and on June 12th a television crew was coming to film us for a segment on the TV program, The Nature of Things, with David Suzuki. I, however, was apprehensive as to whether Raven would be able to participate.

When the crew arrived, I knew we were in trouble, because they were measuring time down to seconds and that did not fly in Indian country. We had classes that week and would not allow any filming of a session without approval by consensus of all the participants and staff. The film crew was not pleased, but I told them that the program was run that way and they were no exception. The crew had no choice but to wait and see if we got that approval. After much discussion and some persuasion about the benefit to their people the exposure would get, they agreed.

Raven did make an appearance and they did film him, but he looked so bad that I was hoping they would not use it. They did not. The program was broadcast in twenty-nine countries around the world on the Discovery Channel.

Raven kept saying that he would dance in the grand entry for the annual dance festival, the powwow at the Alexis reservation on July 1st. Everyone told him it would not be possible.

One day a young man who had lost both his legs below the knees came into the orthopedic department and I overheard him telling the staff that they had to figure out a better design for his prosthesis as he kept breaking it when he played hockey. I asked him to come and talk to Raven, which he did. That young man turned on a switch for Raven when he told him how he did everything the same as before including playing hockey. The old fight was on again.

Raven did dance with me at his side on July 1st, as he had said. It was such a big day, for it was the first time he walked in public after the amputation.

Often he would ask how I felt about him after he had lost his leg. I always gave him the same answer: "I didn't marry you for your leg. I married you for the person you are. Leg or no leg makes no difference to me."

He had to start on insulin, which he fought. He was so apprehensive as he believed that his health would deteriorate fast if he started on the insulin needles. One day I was giving him his insulin and he got so angry he picked up the needles and threw them against the wall. I stood up and told him that I would never give him another needle and he could do it himself or die. Then I walked out and did not return for four hours. I just walked and cried and walked and cried some more. Then I lay down on the grass and I asked mother earth to give me the strength to carry on. A powerful surge of energy entered my body. I felt much better and headed back, knowing I would be okay, but I had no idea what I would face when I returned.

When I entered the bedroom, Raven was lying on the bed staring at the ceiling. I became very frightened. As I looked at him he turned his head and gave me a little smile. "You came back!" he said.

"How can I not?" I said. "I love you so much." And I lay down next to him. He started to cry and so did I. There we were lying on the bed crying so hard together, holding one another until there were no more tears.

Raven always said that tears were always good. They were the washers of the soul. Our souls got a good washing that day and everything did go better. When he asked me to give him his insulin, I told him no, it was very important that he had to be independent. He just grunted and took his insulin.

After that, whenever he did the pipe for the program he always told the participants to look after themselves: he had lost his leg due to neglect of his diabetes and he did not want anyone else to go through what he had gone through.

As the value of our work became more recognized, more people came from many places. We were asked to do a presentation for the Association of American Indian Physicians in Denver, Colorado. Some doctors like Kathy Burke from New Mexico, Theresa Maresca, the president of the Indian Physicians Association and Jeff Henderson of the Lakota Sioux Nation came to Edmonton to see for themselves how the programs worked.

Even the Premier of Alberta, Ralph Klein, expressed an interest. He came for a sweat lodge at our home when he wanted guidance to help the people.

Chapter 32

Ending Our Association with Capital Health

In the fall of 1999, all the fears the wisdom committee had expressed throughout the past five years came true.

Neil Elford, the head of pastoral care, went ahead and unilaterally developed a program for emergency at the Royal Alex, which was totally research-based and had no input from anyone from our department.

I reminded him that every program was to be approved by unanimous decision of the wisdom committee. We had just had a meeting and he did not even bring his idea to them. The next meeting would be three months away and he would not wait. I volunteered to distribute his proposal to every committee member and if he could get their approval, he could proceed. When the wisdom committee turned it down, Joanne Pawlyshyn, our liaison with Capital Health, called me to her office. She asked me if I could not let this go and allow Neil to carry on.

"The Native people had let things go for 125 years and that was long enough," I said. "I have made a promise to them that it would not happen this time. You were there, you heard me say it. I cannot let it go, Joanne. I just can't." I knew by the look I got that there would be consequences for that decision, but I could not do otherwise.

After that, Neil undermined us in every way possible. Some people hinted that I was on the way out, but I did not believe it. After all we had accomplished! Joanne told me they had hired a consulting firm to review the program. As a result my position as operational coordinator was eliminated and a new position, 'regional manager of Aboriginal health,' was created. The qualifications for the new position were such that I did not qualify. All neat and legal.

I was numb. It was all so unbelievable. The fears of the wisdom committee had been confirmed. The system did take over. They did undermine the power of the Native people.

Elmer Ghostkeeper, our Métis representative who took my place, changed the logo, and the mission and vision of the Elders. Programs were cut, but at least the diabetes program and the cultural helpers programs survived, although both were now controlled by the system, not the Elders. The power of the wisdom committee was no more.

Raven stayed on for a while, but his heart was not in it. We had been such a team. He went in to the office, but no one asked for his advice. They had even stopped calling him for ceremonies.

One day Percy Potts, an old friend, called and asked if he could stay at our apartment, as we were not there anyway. We told him to go ahead. Soon he asked when we were going to move our things out as he was taking over. That was the first that we knew of that. He thought it was all arranged and out in the open.

That was the nightmare end to a beautiful career I thought I would have until retirement. Joanne wanted to have a dinner to honor Raven, but he refused, so she offered to send us on a vacation to California instead. That he did not turn down. I was in shock to think our wonderful dream could end in such a nightmare.

For the first time in my life I went into what some people call depression. I call it a natural response to something terrible that happened in my life. I loved almost everything about my life at that time. Raven and I had the opportunity to fulfill our life mission of creating harmony and understanding between our peoples in such a beautiful and effective way. I just kept thinking about how many times the Elders had predicted that once the program became effective the white people would find a way to either shut us down or take over. I had been so determined that it would not happen this time. I had been ready to fight to my death to prevent it, and it *was* a kind of death for me. Death of a dream, death of a vision, death of making a good income, death of a promise I had made to my love, my Elders and myself. I couldn't even pray any more. I had no idea what to pray for and I could not be thankful for much at that time. I just felt numb and empty. I could not even think about the future, it was too devastating to think about the past, so that left only the present.

It was through the process of living in the moment that I was able to even function from day to day and function I did. I could not bear to talk about it. I felt no one wanted to hear about it anyway and no one except Raven understood the magnitude of the personal loss I felt.

Raven kept telling me not to feel bad as I had fought as hard as anyone possibly could and I was not to blame. I did feel that too, but I also added to myself that it was not good enough. I had failed in the most important aspect of the whole project: to keep the real power in the hands of the Elders. That failure—even to this day it is hard for me to think about it.

One day in February, Danny Alexis brought tobacco and asked if we would attend a round dance which was sponsored by Capital Health. Raven could not refuse the tobacco, so we had to go. I was a little nervous about the venture as I had not seen anyone from the program since I was booted out. The round dance was held in a gymnasium on the Enoch reservation close to Edmonton. We had been requested to arrive at about six in the evening as Raven was to lead the pipe ceremony. As we entered the gymnasium, we saw there were about three hundred chairs set out on the platform lining the perimeter. It was about one and a half meters wide and raised about ten centimeters above the floor. For the first time, Raven brought a cane to help him walk. He was having some difficulty with his prosthesis as he had lost weight and he had to put on extra socks in order to keep it snug.

As we made our way to the far end where everything was set out in preparation for the pipe, we were greeted by Bob Cardinal and Danny Alexis, the cultural helpers, and Danny's wife Ella. They were the only people present. Raven immediately sat down on one of the chairs along the side of the gym, and I sat by his side. In front of us was a blanket spread on the floor. On the blanket there were about ten cartons of cigarettes which would be passed to the Elders and drummers. There were some rock eggs, eagle feathers and a tobacco can filled with a mixture of herbs which we had ground and mixed a few weeks earlier. A smudge bowl made of lava rock was placed in the center of the blanket. The bowl was filled with coals from a fire which was kept burning outside. Bob put some herbs on the coals and they created a pungent aroma. I immediately felt much more at ease. Slowly more people started filtering in, including the young men who were the helpers. All came to us and told us how happy they were to see us there. Soon the women arrived with the soups, berries, tea, cold drink, fruit, candy and various other foods for the upcoming feast. The helpers spread a tarp on the floor for the food. The young men went and got the food from the women who were waiting at the door. A blade of sweet grass was lit and placed on a little cast iron frying pan which was set on the south side of the tarp. The men smudged the food by passing it all through the smoke of the burning sweet grass. Then it was placed on the tarp in the order it was to be served. A large pillow was placed on the north side and Raven was asked to sit on it.

Bob sat facing Raven and soon took out his pipe. By this time there were about sixty people present. They too sat in a circle on the floor with the women on one side and the men on the other. When everyone was seated the prayer ceremonies began. Those I cannot describe, for reasons described earlier.

After the prayers the people put out bowls, cups, and spoons on a cloth in front of them and the men began serving the food, first to the Elders, then to all the helpers and then to everyone else. According to tradition, everything always goes in a clockwise direction and if the helpers have to turn it must always be clockwise. After more prayers over the food, everyone ate. The room was full of chatter as we all shared about family and friends and all the latest news from our area. After everyone was finished eating, there were once again more ceremonies. When they were finished everyone rose and everything was cleaned up.

Two young men brought two tables and placed them together in the middle of the floor and then placed fourteen chairs around them for the drummers to sit on. By eight o'clock they were ready to begin the dancing. The drummers brought their drums forward and they were smudged by passing them clockwise through the smoke of burning sweet grass. More people arrived. Some brought their own festival chairs which they placed on the main floor area in front of the chairs already set up.

All the drums were heated on the fire outside and brought back in and set on the table in the center. Soon the head helper took drum sticks and tobacco to one of the drummers who passed the sticks to others who joined him in the middle. They began with a song to honour the drums. Then it was time to dance. As the drummers stood and began drumming and singing, the people, holding hands, formed a circle around them. Everyone moved like a wave around the dancers, more people arrived and soon the gym was full. The drumming and dancing continued until midnight, when they stopped dancing and Tony Alexis took the microphone. He asked Raven to come forward. They were going to do an honour dance for him for all the work he had done for the people. An honour dance, as the name indicates, is done in order to recognize someone for doing something very special for their family or community.

I escorted Raven to the front and went back to my chair. Tony immediately called me back and said I had worked by his side and I was to go with him now. I shook my head as I had no desire to interfere with the community honoring Raven. Besides, I was still hurting from being fired and had no idea what the people thought. He just kept insisting, so I joined Raven. As Raven and I together started the dance in a big circle around the drummers, the staff from Capital Health filed in behind us. Everyone stood in our honour. As we finished the first round of the dance, the rest of the more than four hundred people present filed in behind us and we all danced together in a wave around the drummers.

When the dance was complete they placed a chair for Raven at the front of the stage. Bob Cardinal and Percy Potts took their places on either side of him. I went back to my chair by the wall. Soon Tony started once again to call me up. I decided to go and stand behind Raven. One by one the people, starting with the family, lined up to shake Raven's and Percy's and Bob's hand as is always done. After the family, the rest of the people in the hall moved forward. To my surprise, one by one they filed around the back of Raven's chair and honored me with a hug or a handshake and thanked me as well. With the exception of only a few they came. At that moment I realized that the Native community recognized the work I had done. Tears filled my eyes as one by one they filed by.

I had existed in the emptiness up to the time of the dance. That night I knew I had to start living again. I felt I needed to get back to having a purpose for myself in my life. By this time I was fifty-five years old, had no valid qualifications—as my license as a lab/x-ray technician had expired—and I had no idea what I could do.

I began applying for various committees and boards that paid a stipend. I did not need much, so I thought that would give my life some purpose once again and enough income to at least pay for Raven's truck.

Even though I felt I had much to offer, no one accepted me. With every application deadline that passed I was going more and more down that horrible space of nothingness that was getting harder and harder to pull myself out of. I kept hearing from one person or another how I thought I was an Elder. No self-respecting Elder would use that title for themselves and I certainly did not have the wisdom required nor would I now or ever call myself an Elder. Even Raven never called himself an Elder.

I had never paid much attention to what people said about me in the past. This time was different. Perhaps because it was stopping me from doing the work I loved. Perhaps because it was going against everything I knew and believed in, perhaps because I was just too vulnerable.

I had watched too many white people trying to be Native, and I had seen the result many times. They looked foolish. They did not have the humbleness, the understanding of spirit.

So when I heard others put me in that category it nearly broke my heart and my spirit was damaged. I never felt more Danish than I did when I was with Raven and his people. The fundamental teaching of all the Elders was to be *who* you are. I was very aware of who I was. I quit applying for anything. I could not continue. That left me with nothing again. I simply could not figure out what to do.

Chapter 33

Youngsters Back in My Home

One day, Kathy, the granddaughter who had stayed with us a few years before, called and asked if she could come back. She had been doing her wild thing and I was not sure she could handle staying with us. We had a few rules and she knew what they were. They had to go to school every day, and no drugs or alcohol even on weekends. That was it. Everything else I could work with. On those two rules there was no compromise. I reminded her of that and her reply was that *that* was the reason she wanted to come. She really wanted an education. I told her to come ahead as I really did love this young girl. She had made her way deep into my heart when she was with us before and I had been afraid for her for a long time.

My life had purpose again. She had been with us for a few days when she asked if Georgina, her cousin, could come too. I thought it was probably a good idea as she was a good kid and also struggling to get her education. That way Kathy would have company her own age and I did have some concern about if she could handle staying by herself with us two old people.

Georgina arrived a few days after. Our home had young people in it once again. I was happy. I love the energy of the young and they challenged me with everything. It kept me focused on them. Raven was so grateful that I was willing to help his grandchildren. He was a tower of strength but also had his own personal struggles with the loss of his leg, the loss of his dream and the loss of the majority of his income. It was such a low time, but now at least my life had purpose once again.

School had started the week before so the girls had to get registered. I asked them about career plans, and Kathy, to my surprise, wanted to be a police officer. When I thought about it I knew she would be good. Georgina wanted to be a lawyer or at least work within the field. Now they had a vision. I told them I would not speak for them, but coached them on what to expect. It was up to them to persuade the school to take them. Off we went to get them registered. They were so afraid of systems and nervous about the white people and if they could handle the registrations and all. I told them I would go with them, but only as a support.

When we walked into the principal's office, I made the introductions and then he asked me why we were there. I would not answer. I just looked at the girls and waited. It seemed like a long time, but finally Kathy said in a loud clear voice that they wanted an education. I was so proud. She finally spoke up loud and clear. Then he asked about their previous grades and I could see them shrink. I told him they were not great, but the situation was now different and I knew they were bright enough and had the drive to make it. He turned to each of the girls and asked why they wanted an education and what they planned to do with it. Again each answered with pride and determination.

"Okay," he said, "do you realize you both need to be in a matriculation program?" They both nodded and he just looked at them for a bit.

"Okay," he said, "I am willing to give you a chance. The regular school year has started however and so I would like you to go to outreach, a program where you can work at your own pace, taking only one topic at a time, for the first semester and then we can look at getting you into regular classes in the new year. It is a good place to start."

"Can we take the courses we need to graduate?" asked Kathy challengingly. "I do not want to go to some special education program. I have had enough of that."

He assured her the program was the same as they had at the regular school and she would be qualified.

They thanked him and off we went to outreach. The program was housed on Main Street in the middle of Stony Plain in a building which was previously a retail outlet. There were no outside facilities, no place for the students to hang out outside the school. It looked too much like a throw-away place to me. I did not say anything however, and when we met with Kelly, the head of the school, I felt much better. She explained the program was to give young people who needed an alternative to regular classrooms a chance to complete their education. Some of the students had to work and so could take their schooling in their own time. Others just wanted to finish school in a shorter time and the classroom situation was holding them back. Some just could not cope with the classroom situation and this was an alternative for them.

Again Kathy asked if they would be taking the same courses as at the high school. Would she be able to graduate with the education needed to enter university? She was assured she could and so they started school the very next day.

They were given only one course and had to finish it before moving on to the next. I knew Kathy was somewhat behind, but it was Georgina that shocked me the most. She was asked to write an essay and she asked me, "What is an essay?" She had never heard the word before. Her writing was at a grade two or three level. She did not even know to capitalize "I", even though she had a piece of paper from the Buck Lake School saying she had completed grade nine from the Buck Lake School. Oh my, I thought, how will this be possible? I told her she was to write everything herself the best she could and I would correct it and go over it with her before she handed it in. I told her about structure and content. She was so bright she caught on right away. They both worked very hard and from the start they did what was necessary to pass. I was so proud of them.

These two girls were incredibly funny. They laughed all the time while they were doing homework and I had a hard time believing they were accomplishing anything, but when I checked they were doing really well, so I said nothing.

One day we were going out to pick raspberries. Not my favorite thing to do, but we needed the berries for ceremonies. Raven told the girls to come and help, which they were happy to do. As we were picking, they were just walking along beside the berry bushes talking and laughing. I was getting more and more irritated as we did take them along to pick, not to be just talking and laughing. I did love their joy and hated to stop it, but I could not hold back any longer, so I went over and casually asked them how many berries they had, expecting there were not many. Was I surprised! Their bucket was almost full. Mine was not quite half filled. I said a silent thank you that I had not said anything before I checked. I would have made a big fool of myself.

Life went on. We had fun and laughter in our home again. These two young people found humour in everything—even when I got after them when they didn't keep things clean. I would ream them out whenever it got out of hand. They would listen politely, but I could see them holding back the laughter, so it took everything I had not to burst out in laughter as well. As soon as I was out of their space, they would just crack up. They did do as they were told however, so it was okay.

Raven did go out for meetings and as a consultant for various groups but as an Elder he could not set a price. People could pay whatever they chose and many did not know to pay very well. That was one of my biggest struggles. He was so traditional and would not deviate. The Native community knew to pay him well, the white people did not. Services not being presented with a price tag were a challenge for white people. I could not interfere.

The Provincial Museum in Edmonton, which was developing a Native display, was dealing with people from the northern communities who would clash with people from the south. Since the two areas have different cultures, they would often disagree on priorities of what should be displayed and how. Of course the meetings were run by the museum staff, who had the best of intentions, but things were not working well.

They asked Raven to come in and help them restore order, which he did, and then they were able to move forward again. They paid him only fifty dollars for a full day's work: he was not pleased. But as is the custom, he said nothing. The next time they called, he was rather cold and would not commit to work with them again. Allison from the museum called me and asked if I could possibly shed some light on what had happened. She really felt they had offended him, but had no idea how. I told them it was very difficult sometimes with the different cultures, but because she asked I decided to share with her. I asked her how much they paid white consultants to come in and help out. Why would they think the Elder's value was so much less than a consultant?

She was very embarrassed; she had understood he was volunteering his time, so she only gave him gas money. I told her it does not work that way. Elders needed to be paid as everyone else, but they could not set a price as not everyone could pay with money and the foundation of the philosophy was that he would gift them and they would gift him. That way there is balance and harmony.

Many people who came to our home for help would pay with medicines they had picked, or food they had cooked or meat they had hunted. That, too, was good payment for services. They would often bring blankets as well. These blankets would be part of a ceremony, in which they were blessed with prayers of thankfulness. The soft ones I used to always pass on to children who were struggling in their little lives. These blankets never failed to help them.

One went to my co-worker's four-year-old daughter. She had no idea of Native traditions, but she told me about how her little girl would sleep only on the floor of the doorway of their bedroom. After she got her blanket, she slept anywhere, including her own bed, but always with her blanket.

Finances were getting tight. Raven continued his work as an Elder, but it could not generate enough income to support our growing family.

There was student financing available, so we decided to apply. That was much more difficult than I had ever anticipated. The first snag we hit appeared when we contacted the reserves of which the girls were members. They had treaty status and the reserves got federal funding for education. They would not, however support them in any way.

"Are you not paid per student?" I asked.

They said they were, but they needed all the money to run their schools. There were maintenance costs, repairs and utilities and wages to be paid whether they came or not. Therefore they did not support off-reserve children. Besides, when people lived off the reserve, they paid education taxes and so were entitled to provincial student financing.

Off we went to get applications for provincial funding.

First they had to get social insurance numbers. In order to get a social insurance number, they had to have birth certificates. Those had been lost. In order to get a birth certificate they had to have identification. They had none. I was ready to give up. Then I talked to Kelly at the school. She told me they would provide school identification for them and a letter. Off we went again to get their birth certificates, then their social insurance cards and finally they were ready to apply. I was so proud of the girls for the way they took everything in stride and did all they could. After we finally had everything together and the application submitted, we got a call from the student finance office requesting a letter from the reserves stating they refused to support them. Back to the reserve we went.

They were very reluctant to give us a letter stating that they were refusing education funding to their band members—it was a political hot potato, because they were receiving the funding from Ottawa and at the same time refusing their band members. We did persuade them after promising that we would use the information only for the purpose of getting help for the girls. Just because they had treaty status, getting student financing was so much harder.

The girls also had to send a letter stating why they could not live with their parents. Neither girl was willing to say anything against her mother, so we went to work finding something the student finance staff would understand. We finally agreed to go with the fact their mothers were caring for too many other children and their home was too crowded for them to have the peace and quiet to study.

After all that, the girls finally received funding two months before the end of the school year. That was better than nothing, and there were still two more years of schooling left.

There were times when I regretted that they got that funding, for that was the end of the peace we had so enjoyed for so long. Katrina was there every payday to pick up money from her poor daughter, who felt obliged to help her. Not only were groceries not paid for, but she was never left with enough money for her own needs. When I asked her why she would give away the money she needed for school, she told me, "I have to. My mom needs it."

In the meantime I could see we were getting into trouble financially. Something had to be done. Raven could not do more than he did, so I had to figure out a way to increase our income. I could not think of a single thing that would bring in enough income and provide some flexibility, as Raven was often ill.

Chapter 34

Car Sales

One night I went to bed and prayed real hard for guidance to help the young people continue their education and still keep our home and put food on the table. First I gave thanks for my life and the opportunity to help these beautiful young people. I also asked the Creator to look after the girls' mothers and bless them for allowing me to borrow their children for a few years.

What came, after my prayers, was a big shock even to me.

"I'm going to go and sell cars," I told Raven. I had no idea how he was going to react to that: I held my breath waiting. It was new and foreign even to me, but I knew I could do it and the money was good. I would be working my own little business within the dealership and that suited me. After a long pause he said, "Why not, if that is what you want to do?"

I told him that it would be worth a try. I could not just sit there any longer when we needed the money. I got dressed up and off I went to a dealership I knew I would never work for. I wanted to glean some knowledge before going to my target place. I found out that no dealership paid a wage. Everything was on commission only. I asked what the potential earnings per year were and he said some salesmen who were very good could make up to one hundred thousand dollars. Some made very little and did not last long in the profession. In fact a great majority did not last a year. I found out about how bonuses work and the business office procedures, and what our obligation was to them and theirs to us. Just being there, observing and listening, I realized the sales staff was not treated with respect at all. I was hoping it was only there.

A little discouraged about what I had seen, I went to Zender Ford in Spruce Grove. When I came in and sat down in the boss's office I felt much better. He was a big, tough-looking guy, named Bob, but I felt a kindness under his hard exterior. When I told him I was thinking about going into car sales, he asked, "Why?"

"I like cars, I can sell and I need money," I replied.

He asked how much I wanted to make and I told him I had no plans of working for less than sixty thousand per annum. It was not worth my time if I made less. That seemed to impress him and he called in his assistant. They asked about m history, I asked about working hours and pay. I told them that if I had to lie, I would not work for them. They assured me I would not have to lie.

"Not many women last in the business," Bob said.

"Why?" I asked.

"This is a dog-eat-dog business and women are generally not as aggressive as men. Also the uncertainty of commission only, with its feast or famine cycles, is difficult for most women," he replied. "You can make fifteen thousand one month and one thousand the next."

After more questions and answers, they told me to go home and ask my husband if it was okay. I just laughed at them and said, "When do I start?" They said they would get back to me. When I asked when, they said within a day or two. "All right," I said.

On the first day I was paired up with an older man, Scott, who immediately told me he would tell me nothing. "Okay," I said "then who do I go to for orientation?" He just shrugged his shoulders and said everyone else just had to learn on their own and so should I. That made me real nervous as I knew nothing. The second day I was sent to a workshop for those beginning in the business. Great, I thought, now I will learn something.

After the presenter had introduced himself, he asked, "What is the biggest fear of the salesperson? That he will not sell, of course. No sales, no income. What is the biggest fear of managers?" was his next question. "That the sales people don't sell, of course. What is the greatest fear of the owner of the dealership?"

"Let me guess!" I said. "That the sales people don't sell."

"Right," he said, "and what is the greatest fear of the Ford Motor Company? No sales! You have to carry the load for everyone. You are the most important person here and you must expect to be put down and treated badly. That is the way until you are good. If you are not, you will be down the road in a flash."

Oh my, I thought, what am I getting myself into?

People were really surprised I was selling cars, which is at the bottom of the totem pole of prestige in Canada. "They need spirituality here too," I said, "and at least the customers would get some honesty." Of that I was determined. Native people, and women in particular, would have good service from me. Many of them were nervous about dealing in the system.

There was one other woman selling, who had been hired shortly before me. Her name was Shannon and she was one sharp cookie when it came to sales. Whatever it took to make a sale, she was not afraid to do it. She used every trick in the book and a few that were not.

When Scott refused to show me anything, Shannon was asked to help and she did, but reluctantly. It was only later that I caught on to the fact that whenever any of the sales people were tied up doing something else, they could miss a sale—and no one wanted to chance that. There were many unwritten rules of the game and no one informed the new people of anything. Sure did hear about it afterwards from the others or from the boss though! It so reminded me of when we used to put a new horse in with the herd and all the other horses would kick it and bite it until it learned its place. It was tough slogging. There was also new terminology to learn. Max, who looked like he was well past retirement age, came up to me the first day and unhappily said to me, "I only had two ups today." I tried my best not to laugh as I wondered which 'up' he was talking about. I wanted to tell him he was lucky, but thought I better not. It took a few days to learn that he was actually talking about the number of customers he had the opportunity to talk to.

I did okay at sales. I never had one month at the bottom at least. The dog-eat-dog mentality was hard. It was also a man's world and some did not fancy having to compete with women. At the first staff meeting I attended someone complained about women coming to work there as the men would have to walk on egg shells or they would be reported for harassment. I assured them that would never happen from me—I was not the reporting type. I guaranteed them that if I had an issue, they would be the first to know: I would never ever report anyone without them knowing about it first and I could not imagine not being able to deal with any issue on a one-on-one level. I told them the thought of anyone walking on egg shells around me was so terrible, that they better put that one out of their minds. I meant it and they believed me and relaxed after that. Shannon could cuss with the best of them. As a result I think they were less afraid of her.

As time went by, I did get to know my co-workers and the unwritten rules of the game. In the three years I was there, we went through a half-dozen managers. Most were not too good. The interesting part was that they would get fired from one dealership and soon they were working for another. What a world!

One manager, Jim, who was a little man, had a hatred on for women. He would take offers and questions from the men even if Shannon or I were first in line. One day I lost it. I was so angry. He told me to come into his office.

"This is not a good time," I told him. I thought I had better cool down before talking to him. He insisted and I told him it would not be nice.

As soon as he closed the door he asked me what my problem was.

"My problem is that around here you get treated like shit if you do not have a penis." His face turned red. The first time I had seen that! All of a sudden I found it so funny and I had a hard time keeping from laughing. I knew I shocked him because no one had ever heard me be anything but a woman before. They knew I hated the rough talk even if I never complained about it. After all, I was in their territory and I did not come there to change anyone. I would simply walk away.

"Whether anyone has a penis or vagina is not relevant in this place," he said.

"I do not agree," I told him, "and I suggest you change your attitude." With that I walked out of his office.

I was not optimistic about any change, and I was right, there was no change. With his attitude affecting my income as much as it did, I knew I could not stay.

I had no idea what to do next, but I knew I had to get out of there.

One day a customer came in. He wanted to make a deal on a Ford Explorer SUV which had been on the lot for a long time. I knew I could get him a good deal and I did. When we went to write up the deal, he gave me his card. His name was Jim Shortt and he was regional manager for a mortgage brokering company. When I looked at his card, a light went on in my head. I asked him about how it all worked and he told me that they found mortgages for people, that all the major banks and private lenders would pay a commission for any referrals made to them. I had bought and sold fourteen homes by that time and had made a point of learning all about mortgages. I had also helped many people with theirs, so it was something I knew how to do. He told me he liked my style of selling, which was a big part of the work, so if I was interested, I had a job.

I had to take the mortgage broker's course, but could do that via home study, which saved me from having to sit through things I knew already. I had a lot of quiet time at work and could study there as well. Jim helped me a lot. Within weeks I challenged the exam and passed.

We got paid only after the customer took possession of their home, so it would be quite a while before I would get paid for the first deal. I decided to stay on with Zender Ford until I started to get some income from the mortgages, so I was working both jobs for a while. That was too much even though the mortgage work was home-based. I soon quit my job at Zender Ford.

Chapter 35

More Youngsters

In the meantime two more youngsters had arrived. It just did not work, as they could not handle the discipline of going to school every day, or doing their share of housework, so they moved back to their parents. Kathy and Georgina stayed on and continued to do well. They decided not to go to regular classes since they were succeeding beyond their wildest dreams at outreach. I have to give so much credit to all the teachers and staff there.

One day I found Georgina in tears. When I asked her what was wrong, she said Edward, her eighteen-year-old brother, had tried to hang himself. She was devastated. I told her we could go and get him if he wanted to come. Edward loved his *mushum* and agreed to stay for a while. We went immediately to Buck Lake and picked him up. He was a rather thin lad, with a sallow complexion. He was accustomed to staying up all night drinking and playing games and sleeping all day. Not much to nourish his spirit. He was not eating properly so his body was not nourished either. I knew there were many problems at home so I was hoping he would stay. I can't really say I knew Edward, as he mostly disappeared when we came to visit. He was very quiet when he was in our presence. After about a week, I approached him and asked what he wanted to do now. Did he want to stay or leave? His reply was, "I don't know." I told him that was okay and to think about it and we could talk again in a few days.

A couple of days later I approached him again. He said he thought he would like to go to school. I asked him why. He looked at me as if I had lost it.

"Don't get me wrong," I said, "I think going to school is a great idea, but school by itself is nothing. You go to school for the purpose of getting qualified to do a particular kind of work, so what is your vision for yourself when your schooling is finished?

"I don't know," he said, hanging his head.

"If there were no barriers at all, what would be your ideal for your life in five years? If you could do anything at all, what would that be?"

Again he just hung his head and mumbled, "I don't know."

"I'm not going to let you start school until you know, so let's go to town and find you a vision." He looked at me as if I had lost it for sure, but he was respectful so came along. As we were driving I asked if he wanted to work at a trade or in an office.

"I'll never work in an office," he said.

"Good. That eliminates half the job possibilities," I replied.

When we arrived in Stony Plain we drove around and I pointed out all the things that were happening, how some men were doing road repairs, others were building houses, others driving trucks and so on. He said nothing. After much driving I was not able to tweak anything.

Finally he said. "I still don't have a vision."

"That's okay," I said. "You have a week before school starts, so you have time. Right now you must be getting hungry, so let's go and get a hamburger."

He nodded and smiled just a little. That was the first time I had seen him smile since he came to stay with us. As we were enjoying our

Wendy's burger, John, a co-worker from Zender Ford came in and we started chatting. I introduced him to Edward and told him the John was an automobile mechanic.

After he left, Edward, still looking down, murmured, "I think I have a vision."

"Great," I said. What is your vision?"

"I think I want to be an auto motor mechanic," he said quietly.

I told him to look out the window at all the cars that were going by. "You will be one of the most important people in the world. These people all have places to go, things to do and it is your work that will help them get there safely."

At that moment something happened to Edward. He straightened right up and became alive like I had never seen before.

"Okay," I said. "Now you can go to school. We will get you registered right away."

Taking him to buy his school supplies was one of the most memorable times for me. Prices on everything were very reasonable at Walmart; they had a whole wall of school bags on sale and I told him to pick the one he wanted.

"Any one?" he asked.

"Yes," I said, "any one at all." He was stunned. Then we went to find pencils, pens, paper, binder and all the rest of the things he needed. Each time I let him choose something, he would say, "Any one?"

"You can't start school without supplies," I said.

Then it was off to clothing. I told him, "New school. New clothes. Don't argue!" He could not believe it. He told me he had a good coat at home and he would ask his mom to bring it, but when it didn't arrive we went and bought one of those too. What a gift for me to see his joy!

When he got just a little grin on his face, he reminded me of his grandfather. I guess that was how Edward wound his way into my heart along with the girls.

He, like the girls, had been stuck in the special education program at Buck Lake and I was concerned if he could make it here with us or not. He had been using drugs and drinking from the time he was nine. I knew it would be very challenging for him.

He had a hard time asking me for anything. Many members of the family, especially his mother, were still bad-mouthing me so it was a struggle for both of us. He would occasionally open up and I would do anything to help him see how to do the school work. I took care to remind him how well he was doing, and that one day he would be a fine mechanic.

When he got the results of his first exam, he was not going to tell me, but that was one thing I kept on top of with the girls and they told on him. They made me promise not to tell; I told them that I would get it out of him. I did, and when I asked him about his mark, he hung his head and said 54 percent. I just started to dance and said "Celebration!! Celebration!! Do you have any idea what that means?" I said. "You are brilliant! Totally brilliant! With your previous school history, that is brilliant."

"I thought you would be disappointed," he said. "I didn't think it was very good." He was accustomed to getting good marks from the Buck Lake teachers for learning nothing.

"It is good, and you should be proud of yourself."

After going through the same routine as the girls, he too got financing. They still gave almost all their money to their mom who always arrived on payday. There was only a little left for their needs and certainly none for our household. I did not think that was fair, but Raven as usual was just happy to be able to help and was disappointed in me for thinking we could not feed our own grandchildren. We just could not see eye to eye on that one and I could not send the kids away. The only thing I could do was stop handing them cash. If they were going to give their money away, then they would be broke.

That money broke the magic of the first year Raven and I and the girls had together. It was the first time there was any real tension between the girls and me. I told the girls then to never forget the good times of past year, as it would probably be one of the happiest of their lives, and they have not.

Edward did struggle. A few times he would back-slide with his drinking and drugs. If I could, I would just pretend I did not know; it was not too bad to start with. Even if it was a hard time for him, he hung in there and finished the first year. I was so proud of him.

The next year they were not going let Georgina or Kathy return to outreach because they were supposed to move to adult education. That nearly broke Georgina's heart and she said she would quit if she could not go back. She only had one year left and she wanted to graduate with her friends. I set up a meeting with the principal of the school, told her if she wanted it bad enough she had to talk him into it. I also told her to get letters of support from her teachers.

The day came when we were to meet with him. I did not hold out much hope, but wanted her to fight for herself. She did that in spades. She was superb. For every argument he came up with, she came back with one better. Finally he allowed it on the condition she tell no one. She did not. Good for her and good for him. She did graduate. Three years it took her to go from a grade two level education to finish her high school. How great was that! Most of her family came to her graduation and everyone was so happy and proud of her.

Kathy also wanted to stay but she was willing to move to the college; as she was older than Georgina it would have been a little more difficult to keep her in outreach. Kathy did well in college, but then she got a boyfriend, and soon she was spending more time at his house. Her education started to slide. She became pregnant and gave up all together. She has had two more children. She took on the responsibility of her sisters and their children as well and for a few years carried the load for them all. I am still in touch with her on a regular basis and I still hope she will eventually fulfill her dream of becoming a cop. I keep telling her this is only a postponement.

Edward went to school for two more years, but we did finally have to send him packing due to substance abuse. He did come back, but the school needed fifteen hundred dollars for tuition and he didn't have it. No one would give him the money, so he did not get credit for his work. That discouraged him so much he quit again with only three courses to graduate. I told him to go to work and earn it. He didn't do that, so he lost out. He did get a job, and was well paid, so he decided not to go back. One day, perhaps, he will return. Edward did find meaning and value in himself. And after all, that is the most important.

These young people and all the others who have been in my life have added so much. I thank the mothers for allowing me to borrow them for a little while.

Meanwhile, I continued working with mortgages. I liked the work, but Raven was becoming more demanding of my time. He often took off his leg as he just didn't feel like having it on and would then demand that I get him everything. He was frequently ill with pneumonia and all in all life was becoming a struggle for him.

One day, when Raven was very ill and in the hospital, I received a call from Margo, my daughter. Jack, her father, was being sent back from Edmonton to his home town in the north to die. He had been diagnosed with cancer only three days before. She asked me to go with her, but I could not. I was not sure Raven would survive either. I had to be there for him. Katrina told me she'd had a vision that her father had died and was very happy as he was reunited with her deceased mother again.

I remained in constant contact with my children by phone, but could do nothing more. Three days later Jack died.

Chapter 36

Katrina's Attack

All through the years Raven and I were together, the one person who would not accept our relationship was Katrina. She always tried everything to get money out of her father and he was always generous with her. She accused me of killing her mother and stealing his money. I could never understand why she could not see the love we had for each other. We even took in her and her husband for over a year; they stayed at the acreage while we were at work in Edmonton. She always put on a good face in Raven's presence, so he never understood when I tried to point out to him that she was after his money. He would get upset with me and say, "You do not know what you are talking about. I give her money because she needs it to feed her children and grandchildren." I could say no more.

Working at home became almost impossible. Raven became not only demanding, but he would even interrupt when I was on the phone with clients.

My daughter and son-in-law wanted to start painting cars with minor paint damage to complement their windshield repair business and so I purchased the Chipmasters franchise for them, and hoped that would at least generate some income.

For the first time in my life I was having problems sleeping. I bought a bottle of Bailey's as that with hot milk was what I had used years before when I could not sleep. I kept it in the bottom drawer of my filing cabinet at the back, as I did not want the children to know that there was liquor in the house. One day I found someone had emptied the bottle. That really scared me because the filing cabinet was in my private office and not only had someone invaded that space, but had also gone into the filing cabinet which contained private information and client files. Even though I was confident that they had not bothered the files, as they would have no interest in them, I knew I had to get the client files out of there right away. I could not gamble on a breach of privacy. I thought about renting office space, but decided against it as I needed to be very flexible with hours when Raven was not always doing well.

There was no way out except to quit work altogether.

In 2004 there was a family reunion scheduled in Sønderborg, in the south of Jylland, Denmark. We were all gathering fifty years after our move to Canada. It was perfect timing for me. I really needed a break and a vacation with my family was perfect. I asked Raven to come, but he said it was too difficult for him. Therefore I asked Katrina to come and stay with her dad while I was away. She agreed. I purchased the ticket and was happily anticipating the trip and time with my family. My late brother's daughter Kerry was travelling with me and I had not had much time with her after my brother passed away. She needed to meet her father's people. Everything seemed so perfect, except for the fact that Raven was not too pleased. I assured him that it was only for thirteen days. I told him I would call every second day to make sure he was okay. And Katrina would be there to look after him.

"You always enjoy her company," I said, "so now you can have her here for two weeks."

One day, a month before I was to leave, I looked out the window and there was Katrina stepping out of her truck, followed by her oldest daughter and four grandchildren. They had brought three big suitcases and about four cardboard boxes full of clothes. It certainly appeared to me that she was moving in for the long haul, not just a few days. I could not handle that and decided to go to my sister's in Quesnel for a long weekend. I knew someone had gone through my dresser drawers as there was money stolen from my underwear drawer, and on occasion every drawer was messed up.

Before I left, I put all my clothes from the dresser in suitcases and locked them in my office. Then I wrote a message in the bottom of each drawer: "Keep out. Private. I don't snoop in your drawers, why are you snooping in mine? What are you looking for?" I got a call from another family member who was laughing so hard. I had not told anyone what I did, but Katrina had called all the family members and told them. She certainly told on herself. When I returned from my sister's, she said nothing and immediately packed up and left.

I think Katrina decided to declare all-out war on me at that time. When it was time to go to Denmark, I could not find Katrina. I heard they had scheduled a garage sale the weekend after I was to fly. My head was pounding every day. Raven didn't want me to go. I had no idea what Katrina's plans were. Raven was not strong enough to stay on his own more than a couple of days. He could cook and take care of his own basic needs but could not clean and had no transportation. I was determined to go. I could not disappoint Kerry and all my family and most of all I very much needed to spend time with my sisters and brothers as most of them never came to my place.

I had a feeling Katrina was just playing chicken with me anyway, and so I trusted she would come and take care of him. Everyone in the family knew I was going, so I knew they would not let him suffer. Off I went, with a heavy heart. The reunion was great and I was so happy on the return flight. My joy was to be short-lived however.

The moment I stepped off the plane and saw Raven at the airport, I knew something was terribly wrong. He was not the same man I had left behind. There was nothing in his actions. It was just a feeling. My head was spinning and I was dreading what was to come. He told me he had a surprise for me when we got home. There was a surprise all right. As we turned into the driveway, there it was—a brand new shiny bright navy-colored truck with red pinstripes on each side, a top of the line automatic Ford F150 4x4 super cab with every option possible. I knew list price was well over forty thousand dollars and he was always ready to pay sticker price. I had done all I could to stop him buying a truck for the past three years. He had lost his perspective about money and had gone through a bankruptcy. He had co-signed loans for his sons, had purchased a skidoo and a quad and a holiday trailer, all of which we could not afford. We were allowed to keep his 1999 F150 as he did not have much equity in it. We had managed to pay that off in the ensuing three years and we certainly did not need, nor could we afford, this new truck. I could not see how he could get permission to buy a new truck now. I thought the bankruptcy had at least stopped that. I was in shock. I couldn't believe it.

Raven went directly to the bedroom and was obviously not coming out, so I went to him. As we talked I became more at ease as the old Raven did come through. He told me he was thinking about not letting me come back, but after seeing me, decided he couldn't do that. He loved me too much. I asked him why on earth he would not allow me to come back. At first he said nothing, but with my insistence he finally said, "I have been told you went to Denmark with another man."

"Who was this man supposed to be?" I asked in shock.

"Never mind," he said, "I do not believe it anymore."

"You better not," I said, "as it is not true. How many times have I told you I would never do that to you? How could you not believe that after twenty years together?"

Jealousy had always been just below the surface. He was always fighting the green monster. Who would be so cruel as to tell him such a thing?

Then he asked me why I had packed my bags. I told him I was so tired of people invading my privacy that I had just locked them in my office until I came back. I had no intention of going anywhere and there was certainly no man in my life. He seemed satisfied, but I was feeling miserable. Why that? Why would anyone tell him I was with another man? He was insecure enough without anyone adding fuel to that fire. It was so cruel.

I said nothing about the truck the first day, but I was boiling inside. I was afraid to talk about it. I was angry and hurt that he would do such a thing when I was away. I was confused as to how he pulled it off. I was tired after twenty-three hours of travel.

On the third day I finally approached him about it. I was so determined that I would not lose my cool. I quietly asked him where he bought it. He told me a dealership in downtown Edmonton. "Not the one you have been working for," he said. "I wouldn't go there because I talk too dam' much."

He probably had a point as I had talked to them about not even attempting to sell him a truck. I asked him about the interest rate and how much he paid for it and how much the payments were. He knew nothing about interest and the price was none of my business and the payments were over $700 a month. He did not know exactly.

"How do you figure on paying for it?" I asked.

"My pension," he said.

"And how do you think we will get groceries?" I asked.

"You worry too dam' much. It will come. It always has." That was true, but he had good employment then. Now, with his deteriorating health, he did not have much at all. I was not prepared to go back to work just to pay for another truck that he could not even drive. I knew Katrina would have it before long and so my paying for it was not an option.

Then I asked him what he had done with his other truck. He told me he had given it to Chuck who happens to be Katrina's son. That was when I lost it. Up to then I was still hoping to reverse the deal and get it back. That was obviously not going to happen.

"What are you thinking of?' I shouted. "First you make a deal when I am gone, and then you give away your truck to Chuck. And to top it all off you do not even drive. What were you thinking?" I had never shouted at him like that before.

He got angry as well. "You have stopped me from buying a new truck for three years," he said. "Now I go and buy one, the least you can do is be happy for me that I could do it." He was obviously not pleased with my attitude.

I did calm down and the next day I called Waterloo Ford and questioned them as to what happened and who all was there. They told me he came in with his daughter. He told them he was making much more money than he was. I asked them why they did not check him out. They said he had always made his payments to Ford before and they approved him. When I told them they had some responsibility to check him out, they said that if he did not make that much that means he lied and if I tried to reverse the deal they would sue him for making a fraudulent statement. My head pounded as I realized there was nothing I could do.

The next time I saw Katrina I asked her why on earth she would take him in there and put us right back in debt again. "He made me take him in," she said. "He would not stop hounding me until I took him, so what was I supposed to do?"

"He's been hounding me for three years and I did not take him in," I said. "We cannot pay for the truck. It will go back. In the meantime time your son has his truck. Do you think it is fair? Raven doesn't even drive, Katrina. We need his truck back as that is the only vehicle that is paid for and we do not have money to make payments."

"It is not my business," she said, "Ask him! Keep me out of your fights about money!"

I knew there was no way out but to let the process happen.

One day Katrina came to borrow the truck. She never brought it back.

Over the next few months our relationship deteriorated by the day. Raven's anger was getting out of control. He became so demanding and wanted me there twenty-four/seven. He started going to bed at eight o'clock and demanded I go as well. I did not but he would call often until I did. His beautiful love was turning to hatred.

Every time his pension came in, he would give it to Katrina to pay for his truck. I refused to have anything to do with it. I had my car. I knew we did not have enough money and we were going into a backslide real fast. I did pay utilities and the mortgage, but the credit cards were supporting us.

Raven would not listen. He asked, "What are you worried about? They are being paid." I told him they were not, that the credit cards were carrying the load. Nothing was going right. The paint business was not yielding any substantial income. I realized then I had made a dire mistake.

Then Katrina took the money and for two months did not make the payments on the truck. That was fifteen hundred dollars. She was driving it all the time and put on some forty thousand kilometers in six months. No oil changes, no upkeep of any kind.

Raven was getting angry with me for not getting the money to pay the arrears. He did not expect me to pay out of my pocket, but thought I could figure out a way. He thought I could do anything. I had to remind him I was only human. I could not print money, so where was it going to come from? Ford Credit seized the truck. Still he blamed me, not Katrina.

As the jealousy continued and the accusations became more and more ugly, I started to lose it as well. The shouting matches became ugly and as I listened to myself I could not believe that it was me, but it was. We had had words occasionally throughout the years, but it never got ugly. Not like this. I suffered more for what I was doing than for what he was doing.

I knew it had to end one way or another, but I kept hoping he would see the light. Some members of the family told me that Katrina was promising to take care of him if he kicked me out. He began telling me to leave. I told him this was my home and if he didn't want to be with me he could go. He would not, so there we were. We both stayed. He even raised his cane a few times, threatening to hit me. I told him then that if he ever hit me with it, I would be out of there and I would never be back. He knew I meant it and always lowered it.

I tried to talk to him and assure him everything would be okay. Just as things would start to get better, Katrina would show up and Raven would slip further into his jealousy and anger. One time he accused me of being a closet drinker. I just laughed and asked him why he would say that.

"You kept a bottle hidden," he said.

"That was a bottle of Bailey's that I bought one time because I could not sleep and when I drank it with hot milk before I went to bed, it helped. Someone snooped in my filing cabinet and found it in the back of the bottom drawer and drank it up. I guess it was that person who told you," I said.

"Okay," he said, "I did not believe it anyway."

I had guessed it was Katrina's daughter Lorna. I had intended on confronting her, but one day she told me that she had caught me, that I was a closet drinker.

"So it was you." I said. "I knew someone had been in my private office, my private files and today you gave yourself away. I knew that sooner or later whoever had would get caught. You should be ashamed!" I continued, "Why on earth do you think you have a right to go through my private things? Just don't even think about doing that again."

She just hung her head and said nothing.

One day Lorna, out of the blue, told me to pack my bags and get out. I was not wanted there anymore. "*Mushum* doesn't even want you." I just stared at her. I could not believe my ears. I had done so much for this young woman through the years. I helped her through one crisis after another, put her up at my place, found her work and even drove her to it every day. Here she stood, telling me to get out!

"Don't look at me like that," she said, "or I'll hit you." I was so shocked I just sat down on the couch and shook my head.

"I suppose you're going to cry now?" she said sarcastically.

That snapped me out of the trance. "No," I told her firmly. "I am not. Nor am I leaving this house, but you are. NOW!"

"How are you going to make me?" She said with a grin on her face.

I told her that she had a choice, either leave on her own or I would call the police to remove her. "It is my home and you will go NOW!"

"I'm not afraid of the cops," she jeered.

"I really do not care whether you are or are not. I do care that you get out of my face, so take your pick. The easy way or the hard way, I don't really care."

She went and packed her bags and got her mom to pick her up. I later heard that I was so mean that I would not let her spend time with her grandfather.

Time and again different members of the family would call and warn me to be careful as Katrina and her daughter were saying they were going to get me. I really did not believe they would actually do anything, but still it was rather unnerving. Raven would not believe any of it. He had never in all those years questioned the fact that I was telling the truth. Even when we did not agree, he never questioned my integrity, except during his jealous moments, but he did now. This too was new and different and painful. One thing happened after another that left me totally broken. Time and time again I would have to pick up the pieces and put myself back together again. One day when I was praying I found myself simply asking for rest. "I am so tired now," I said. Then I remembered Raven's words. "You rest when you are dead." Was that really what I was asking for? I was not sure.

One day my friend Pauline, who publishes the Heartbeat magazine, called and told me there was a cancellation with a very good trance channeler. If I was interested she could get me in. This woman apparently channeled St. Michael among others and he helped many people when they were confused. I had never done that before, but decided to go as I so needed some direction.

The woman immediately went into a male voice with a Native North American accent. She knew nothing about me and the fact that Raven was Native. Through the channeler, a voice with a Native accent told me that I had learned much in my many journeys and one day I would share with many people. There were many other things as well. Some I remember, some I do not. The most memorable happened after the session was finished, as suddenly he said, "Take your treasures out of the house. Just in case." At that point I had not thought seriously about leaving. I thought I could still fix everything.

About a week later, I was setting up a time to meet with an Elder and suddenly, out of the blue, she said, "Take your treasures out of the house. Just in case." The exact same words! I did start to think about what my treasures were and they were not many. I moved them over to my son's place. I actually thought it was because someone was going to harm them; I still had no thought of leaving.

Raven had been pestering me about taking a trip to Vancouver, British Columbia. It was a fourteen-hour drive and I was reluctant as I knew it would be difficult. I would have to do all the driving and we did not have enough money to stay over on the road. Besides it was hard to drive, take care of Raven's every need and load and unload suitcases. He really wanted to go and I too wanted to see our friend Trish. So we went. I had thought perhaps it would be an opportunity to have a good time together and perhaps turn things around.

That was not to be. Raven went into another jealous rage and it took all the strength I had to get us back home safely. I was exhausted mentally, emotionally, physically and spiritually.

I had driven all the way home from Vancouver in one stretch. He told me to get out of his bed, so I did. For the first time since we were together, I slept on the couch. The next morning he came out of the bedroom and I knew by his walk and the sound of his cane hitting the floor hard with every step, that it was not going to be pretty, and it was not. He walked over to the couch and hit me with his cane as hard as he could on the head. I jumped out of bed and he raised it again, but as he was not steady on his feet he fell backwards. His son Chris happened to be there and he came running to see what was going on. I just told him to keep Raven away from me. He helped his father to a chair while I went to the bedroom and started packing. I could feel the bump on my head getting bigger and bigger and it was sore. Chris soon came with a cup of tea and asked me what happened. I told him. I thought he might give me a hard time, but he did not. I could see he felt really bad.

Within fifteen minutes I packed all my clothes and personal belongings in my station wagon and left.

Chapter 37

Heartbreaking Life on My Own

I went to my friend Mary's place, but realized I could not stay there. She just kept saying that Raven was trying to kill me. I did not believe that. I thought he was just so angry, he thought he would give me a thrashing. In any case I was afraid, as I knew if I did not leave the house, there would be no end to the caning, and that I could not live with. That day I went and bought a little old holiday trailer with my emergency funds and parked it in a campground by Spring Lake. As soon as it was parked, I crashed on the couch and slept all through that evening until early morning. I dragged myself into the store and picked up what I needed immediately, drove back to the trailer and crashed again. I was numb.

About a month after I had left, Raven called and said he was really sick and needed me to come up to the house. I asked him where the kids were. He said they had all left and he did not know if they were coming back. My friend Vickie was visiting at the time; as she was leaving, she said so gently, "Will you be able to sleep if you do not know that he is okay?" I told her no, and that I would go and check on him.

By this time it was getting dark. As I took the half-hour drive back to the house, my stomach started turning and my head began to hurt. That was the first time I had been back and I did not know what to expect. As I drove into the yard I saw there were no vehicles and there were no lights on in the house. I knocked on the door: no one answered. All was quiet. I opened the door, but saw no one, so I walked in. I walked back to Raven's bedroom where I found him half asleep.

"You came," he said happily.

"I could not sleep until I knew you were okay," I told him.

He said, "You better come back and take care of me." No apology, no indication that he even understood why I left, just a command to return.

I knew I could not. I cried so hard as I stood in the doorway of his bedroom. I loved him so much, and I wanted to more than anything else in the world, but I knew by the tone of his voice, the way he demanded that I return, that things would not change—I could not live that life. I could not cope with seeing him in so much pain over something I had not done. I could not cope with his jealousy. I could not cope with his beautiful love wrapped in hatred. It was too much for me to bear. I could not bear thinking about how his own family could hurt him so much.

I made sure there was food by his bed and that he had taken his insulin. When I left, I cried all the way back. I cried all night and all the next day. That was the first time I had cried and I could not stop. Finally I dozed off in a fitful sleep. The next days I spent grieving the loss of my life with Raven, and his people. The tears flowed until I was too tired to cry any longer, then I would sleep and cry some more. The pain was unbearable. My heart hurt so bad I thought it would explode.

About a week after, I had a bit of a break from the crying. I asked myself then if this pity party had gone on long enough. At that moment I saw it as such, and decided it had. I must get on with life. If I had to live it, I would not live it in pity for myself, nor in 'what could have been, should have been, but was not.'

Thank God for my friend Vickie. She too had been married to a Cree man who was tragically killed some years before. He too was very traditional, and they too loved each other deeply. She so understood the love I had for Raven and why I could not endure his abuse. She was my staunchest supporter. Some evenings she would stay until midnight, just talking and laughing and remembering all the good times we had with our men, and then sharing our tears for the losses we both suffered. Many times she would say she did not know which situation was the worse, hers or mine. It was a death either way, but hers was so final, mine was ongoing.

I knew I could not go back. I thought he would never believe I was not with another man and it would be worse than before. I could not go through living that way, and leaving him one more time was more than I could bear.

After I left my first husband, Jack, I lost every friend we had, and I was expecting the same this time with the exception of my two closest friends, Vickie and Mary.

Jeannette, a friend from Denmark, came to visit and she so wanted to go to a Native gathering. There happened to be a powwow at the Enoch reservation about ten kilometers west of Edmonton that weekend. I told her I would take her, but if there was trouble I would have to leave. She said that was all right.

When we drove into the grounds, we heard the drumming and singing in the distance. The huge parking lot was almost full and I was lucky to find a spot at the far end away from the arbour, where they danced and drummed. I looked up and right in front of us was Raven sitting in front of a camper. He waved his arm in the direction of the exit, but I was not sure if he meant the exit or to pull into the shade by the trailer. When I looked at him, I decided on the shade. We walked over to the trailer. Right away his son brought us a chair and, not long after, a cup of tea. We talked as if nothing had happened. Then I told him we were going to go and watch the dancing. He just nodded and asked me to stop in later. I told him I would.

About five hundred dancers were gathered to dance their traditional dances in their fantastic dance outfits. The band had built a big round arbour with lights so they could dance well into the night. There were four entrances into the dancing area, one for each direction where the dancers enter for the grand entry. Every session would begin with every dancer present entering the dance area one after another until all dancers were present. There were prayers and honour dances and welcoming speeches from the Chief and dignitaries. There were intertribal dances where everyone could dance before the competition began. The drums were beaten, the singers sang and the jingles and rattles marked the rhythm in unison. The traditional women with their beautifully beaded outfits lined the perimeter, all with their hands on their hips. As the caregivers of the people, they kept an eye on everyone.

Many people had come from far and wide and were camped at the grounds. Traditional hand games were being played. People were selling their handicrafts, and there were food booths selling things like Indian tacos, bannock burgers, neck bones and all kinds of soft drinks and hot drinks imaginable.

On our way to the pavilion I ran into our friends Ella and Danny. I was just not sure about how anyone would react to my leaving. Danny and Ella were Raven's friends for many years before I met them and they had become my friends too. They had both been members of the wisdom committee when we were with Capital Health.

Ella said, "I heard you and Raven split."

"Yes," I said, and started to cry again. I could not hold back the tears.

She gave me a big hug and said, "We understand. We have seen what is going on." Then she turned to Danny and said, "Give her a hug. Can't you see she needs one?" He did. One by one several people came and hugged me and told me they were sorry for what had happened. That was actually the last reaction I had expected.

We watched the dancing for quite a while. When we returned to the car, I stopped and said good-bye to Raven. How painful it was. I so wanted to stay with him, but I knew I could not.

A couple of weeks later Raven called and asked me to bring some food as he and Chris were there alone and they had no vehicle and nothing to eat. Katrina had left a few days previously, telling them that she would bring some groceries, but she never came back. I told him to get someone else. He said he had tried several people and no one could come. Reluctantly I went. I knew he was telling the truth, but I could not allow myself to be caught in a trap to return to the hell I had lived for the past year.

He was *the Raven,* and I knew he would use every trick in the book to get me back if that was what he wanted. In any case it was so painful for me to see him that I did not want to go. On the other hand I could not stay away. If they were out of groceries, I needed to look after that. I was also hoping with all my heart that he was beginning to understand why I left and perhaps we could start rebuilding what we had lost.

When I arrived with some groceries he was in the bedroom. I went in to talk to him. He then told me for the first time that he was sorry.

"Sorry for what?" I asked. I had to know if he got it or not.

"Sorry you left," he said.

"Do you even know why I left?" I asked. He just shrugged his shoulders. "I left because of your jealousy and because you took the cane to me. Don't you get it?"

"That's nothing!" was his reply. "You better come back. I need you here."

"You don't get it!" I said. "I told you several times that if you ever hit me with the cane I would leave and never come back. You hit me and I left. Have you ever known me to say I was going to do something and not do it?"

Then he got angry and told me to get out. I did. As hard as it was, I was also relieved. I thought it would be over now for sure. My heart was broken, but at least now I could grieve the relationship fully and put it behind me.

That was not to be. The family would not come and care for him, with the exception of Chris, but he had a family so he could not stay there all the time. Friends took turns. Richard Rain, his adopted son, was one that did a lot for him. or One day Richard called and said Raven had to go to the doctor and there was no one to take him. He had to work and he called everyone he knew, but no one could do it. I reluctantly told him I would pick him up. I thought I was strong enough to get through it. I knew in my heart I would never go back, but my love was not altered. How I wished it was. Then the pain would not be so excruciating. I felt he would never understand why I left or trust me again, so there was nothing to build on. If he thought he was justified, I knew it would happen again and again if I returned. I could not live that life.

The next day I did pick him up and took him to the doctor and grocery shopping. This time he never asked me to stay and I was so relieved. Maybe he had resigned himself to the fact that it was over. I felt so much better and worse. I was on a roller coaster. Later I found out the family mostly stayed away. Katrina did not keep her promise to look after him. His health was deteriorating. He refused to go to a home. I knew if I returned I would die. It was so clear. I had two choices: stay away or die—either from or stress from someone's hand. I just knew I could not survive up there again.

There was no way I could work. I was in too much emotional and spiritual pain. My only income was a pittance of a pension. I barely had enough to keep a roof over my head and food on the table. I could not even find a decent place to rent, so for the time being I knew my only option was the holiday trailer. I had to let my almost-new car go back as I could not make the payments. I bought an old station wagon, thinking that if worst came to worst I could even live in that.

Three weeks after I left the house I declared bankruptcy.

I had always been so careful with my money and budgeted for all kinds of emergencies. This was a nightmare.

Come fall I started looking for a home for the winter. The high wages and influx of people from the oil industry had pushed rent through the roof. Thousands of workers were coming in from all over the country and even from overseas. They were making good money and were able to pay high rents for the few remaining accommodations available. I knew it was bad, but until I started looking I did not realize how bad. Apartments that had rented for five hundred dollars per month were now going for eleven hundred. My pension was nine hundred dollars. For the first time in my life I was really frightened about my future. Raven was making the mortgage and fire insurance payments, so at least our home was covered and I knew one day I would get money from that. It was my immediate future I was concerned about.

My son Rocky came to the rescue. He offered to purchase a little trailer in Mobile City Estates which is a very large trailer park in downtown Spruce Grove. I found one that seemed suitable and within his budget. It was situated on an end lot and had trees in the little yard and was actually quite nice. I went and sat in front of it a few evenings and into the night as I had heard the neighbourhood was pretty wild and had a very high crime rate. I spoke to some of the residents. Some had lived there for up to twenty years. They told me they had no more problems than could be expected in any community. I was actually impressed by the fact that there were always people in the streets, doing what people do. Boys were throwing footballs, kids were riding bikes, and the teenage girls were walking the streets just as we had done. I had not seen that in any other community for many years. I spoke to the manager and he said they were very strict and had gotten rid of the trouble makers one way or the other since he had taken over a couple of years previously, so I took the plunge and Rocky purchased it.

I was still not well, but was certainly getting better. There was a Safeway store within walking distance and I decided to apply for a job there. What happened next was another nightmare for me. I had to write tests for two days and one of the tests was looking at pictures for a short time and then putting them in the same order on a blank chart. I could not do it. I simply did not have it. That had never happened to me before. The next set of questions dealt with adding prices and making the right change. They were multiple choice and the combinations were close to the same, but of course there was only one right answer. I could not do those either. The time we had was short, but at any other time I would have whizzed right through them. I failed. I failed a test to be a cashier. I could not believe it. It was humiliating beyond belief. Home I went to lick my wounds, and they hurt. My friends and family all knew I was writing the tests and of course called. Telling them I had failed was so terrible. I kept my composure while talking to them, but after I had hung up the tears would flow.

My marriage was finished, I did not feel safe from Katrina and company, I was bankrupt and I couldn't even pass an exam for a cashier. I was living in the poorest part of town in a tiny trailer. How low can you go? I thought. My pity party for one was getting to be a long one this time. I knew I had to continue to work my way through the darkness until I saw the light of day again and somewhere, deep in my soul, I knew it would eventually come. Either the light of day or my death. At that time I do not think I cared. I occasionally got calls from family that Katrina was still out to get me. I tried to keep the thought out of my mind as it served no good purpose and I did not want to allow fear to consume me. I would not allow the negative to take over my life.

That was when I went into living totally in the moment and wrote the following poem:

LIFE IN THE MOMENT

Life in the moment is a clear blue sky,
The sun the color of gold.
Life in the moment doesn't wonder why
It helps to keep a hold.

Life in the moment is grass so green,
The bugs that call it home.
Life in the moment is being seen,
Is having the courage to roam.

Life in the moment is a gentle rain
That cleanses the beautiful land.
Life in the moment is relief from pain,
Relief that gives us a hand.

Life in the moment is the sky at night,
The stars that twinkle so.
Life in the moment is rays of light
Allowing our spirits to grow.

Life in the moment is snow on the trees,
The frost you see with the cold.
Life in the moment allows you to be
Just who you are, young or old.

Life in the moment is the powerful sea,
The waves that come and go.
Life in the moment is being me,
Allowing myself to grow.

Life in the moment is all that is real,
So make it all it can be.
Life in the moment is what you feel
So look at yourself and see.

That is what got me through. I continued to look for the beauty in the moment. There were birds living in the trees in the yard. It was as if they knew I needed cheering up and they would perform and play games. Chicklet, my little dog, was a life saver. She forced me to get up and let her out to pee. She had to be fed and she wanted attention. I so struggled to even do that, but it was that struggle that kept me going. She left me little choice.

I even stopped answering the phone, with the exception of my children and one friend, Mary, who was also going through her own pity party. Misery likes company they say, and we were good company for each other. I thought I was helping her and she thought she was helping me and I think we were actually helping each other, which kept us both feeling a little useful in all the mess we were in. Sometimes we would spend two hours on the phone. We discussed, raged, cried and laughed together. Thank God for Mary. She was a friend when I needed one the most.

I thought I was at the bottom, but no. I had to go down even further. One morning I got out of bed and found I could not stand on my feet. It felt like I was stepping on needles. I went to see the doctor, who prescribed some insoles I could not afford. I tried foot baths, rubbing, raising my feet, every kind of cream anyone had that might help. I could barely walk. It was incredibly painful.

I knew I had to get to a medicine man, but did not know who I could trust. I did not know how the people felt about me after I left. Some knew about black or 'bad' medicine as they called it. I felt that was the cause of my pain anyway and I could not take a chance of something worse happening. I was in bad enough shape as it was.

A few years before, when visiting in Denmark, I had met a very nice young Native fellow from New Mexico. I decided to try to contact him for a referral down there. I got it.

When I called Tyrone, a Native Dene from Albuquerque, he told me that I was welcome to come down and he would help if he could. I told him that I was not familiar with his ways and asked if there was something particular I could bring. He said if I could find a home-tanned deer hide he would appreciate it. I told him they were hard to come by, but I would do my best.

I called Trish, one of my best friends, and asked her. She was working for Indian Affairs in Vancouver, so I thought she might know of someone. She told me she had one and would be happy to send it to me. She also picked cedar and mailed me a big box of it. She is one kind person! Raven had actually introduced me to her shortly after we met, and we had been best friends ever since. She too had been married to a Native man.

My sister Lis had just left her husband too, and so I called her and asked if she wanted to make the journey with me.

I had to sell poor Chicklet. I found her a good home, so now I had money to go.

Lis had never been in the Native community before and she wanted to be respectful to them and their ways, but was uncertain about what she was getting herself into. Lis asked what she was supposed to do when we arrived at the medicine man's home. I told her to not ask questions and be herself. "That is all. They will probably have a great sense of humour and tell jokes. I feel we will have a good time, so just relax, and remember not to ask questions."

"Can I at least ask you?" she said.

"Only after we get back to our hotel," I said.

"You won't let me make a fool of myself, will you?" she asked with apprehension.

I promised her I would not and if she did anything wrong I would let her know right away. That was not her world and she felt it. Then I remembered how apprehensive I was myself at the beginning and I told her again, "Do not worry. It will be okay. Just be yourself."

It took us four days to drive there. Tyrone and Sophie met us at a service station by the highway and led us to their place. They had a lovely Spanish-style home on an acreage just outside Albuquerque, New Mexico.

Tyrone reminded me a lot of Raven. He had that same aura about him as the Elders of the north. He was short in stature, but filled a large space with the energy that surrounded him. I told him I had some gifts for him and asked if I was to bring them in now or present them during the ceremony. He told me to bring them now. While I went to the van to get them, Sophie made tea.

I brought cedar, tobacco, various roots and sage from the north. Sage differs much from one area to another. As he opened each one he was delighted. "Now I am rich!" he said.

That brought tears to my eyes, as Raven had said that so many times when someone brought him medicine.

Tyrone was most delighted with the hide. "This is the best!" he said. "I have tried for a long time to find a home-tanned hide. It is so much work—the young people have stopped making them. The factory-tanned hides do not have the same sound and they do not last like the home-tanned. Thank you, thank you so much." I told him to thank my friend Trish and say a special prayer for her as she was going through a difficult time with her son.

Tyrone immediately called his nephew to come and drum. That evening the two of them drummed and sang. We all sat on the floor. I said a prayer of thanks to the Creator for guiding us to these people, to this place. I was so grateful. Afterwards we just sat and visited. We learned that Sophie was a practicing lawyer, and then she shared how she was actually Jewish.

"How did a young Jewish lawyer end up in Indian country?" I asked.

"Love, I guess," was her reply.

"I know that one," I said.

Then she went on to share how she felt and saw so many things, and when she met Tyrone he helped her find the answers she was seeking. Her story was my story. It was amazing—as I looked at the two of them I saw Raven and myself in them. I knew I had come to the right place.

That evening Tyrone, with prayer, gently massaged my legs and feet and then he blew smoke on them from a special healing wood fire which Sophie had lit. He told me he wanted me there in the morning again. We checked into a Super 8 hotel that was close to Tyrone and Sophie's house. That night we slept very well.

The next morning we went back and he once again did a treatment on my feet. They were much better but not back to normal. He then told me I had to put up a meeting the next Saturday. This was Wednesday. I asked what a meeting was. I had no idea. He said, "That's okay. You can do your cooking here. We will guide you." This was exactly the same situation that I had encountered so many times in the past, when I first started my journey with Raven's people. The difference was that this time I had the knowledge and the confidence that it *would* be okay.

When Sophie was off by herself, I caught her and asked her for guidance. She said many people would come and I had to provide food for them all. I also had to give Tyrone money for the wood and an honorarium for the fire keeper and helpers.

"And Tyrone, of course," I said.

"That I cannot tell you," was her reply. "He is my husband and I cannot ask for anything for him. It is up to you." How familiar was that!

She did give us a grocery list and told us what we had to do to prepare. I was getting really low in money and I had not expected Lis to contribute—after all, this was for *my* healing. She insisted on paying for half. I told her that something good would happen to her because she did that. Every evening someone came and they drummed and sang. It was ever so good to hear that again. How I had missed that. It had been such a long time.

Saturday came and we cooked all day. That evening many people showed up. They erected a big teepee in the yard. Everyone was chatting and telling stories. It was so cozy. Then it was time to go to the teepee. I was told it would last all night. I was exhausted and wondered if I could make it. I was asked to sit next to Sophie who sat next to Tyrone. My sister Lis was on the other side of me. Sophie was terrific. She guided us in whatever we had to do. Tyrone asked me to tell the people about the purpose of the meeting.

"I have been married to a beautiful Cree man for twenty years," I said. "He had diabetes and his health was beginning to fail. Someone told him many lies and he became insanely jealous and angry with me for something I did not do. I could not live with his sorrow and his anger so was forced to leave the house. He is with his family now. I ask that you include them in your prayers.

"I do not know your ways," I continued. "This is new to me, so I want to apologize in advance if I offend anyone. It is not my intention. I also want to thank you all for coming here this evening. I am so touched that so many people came to pray for this stranger, someone who is from so far away that you have never even met. My heart is touched," I said as I held my hand over my heart. "I also want to thank my sister for taking time out to come with me. It means so much to me to have her here. Thank you."

Then the drumming and singing began in earnest. As the evening progressed into night, the fire keeper used the coals and made different formations. Everyone was passed medicine and Lis and I watched intently so we would not do anything wrong.

Sophie whispered to me, "When Tyrone comes and gives you medicine, you must swallow it all. It may want to come back up and if it does come it is okay. Just let it come out in front of you. The helpers will come and take care of it. Do not be embarrassed. It is the way it is."

Medicine was passed to everyone and as I partook I was okay. Then Tyrone gave me some medicine which he had prepared. I took that too, and I was still okay. I felt I would make it. I did not want to throw up in front of everyone. After I took the medicine I felt what I could best describe as little round heads travelling all through my body and chomping up all the bad things they could find. Then they headed back to my stomach. Suddenly I became violently ill. How embarrassing! I threw up in front of all those people. It was awful. Sophie just said it was good and a young man came with a shovel and took it away. I was embarrassed, but had seen a similar result before, so knew it was good to get rid of whatever had invaded my body. The drumming and singing just carried on. Then Tyrone gave me more medicine and the same thing happened again. At about four in the morning, I guess, they stopped drumming and whoever wished to speak could do so. I said nothing; I was so weak and tired. Stories of their trials and how they were struggling or had overcome them were shared.

One gentleman, who was very dark, was sitting a quarter of the way around the teepee to our left. He told my sister and me how he admired us for coming all that way to get help. He told Lis she was such a good sister for coming and supporting me. Suddenly out of the blue he said in perfect Danish, "Jeg har cyklet i Århus." My ears perked up and I asked him to repeat it. He did. That I could not believe, and I said, "Here I drive four thousand kilometers to this place in the desert of New Mexico, sit in a teepee in the middle of the night with all you people, and I hear my own language."

We all had a good laugh over that one. After the break, the ceremonies continued throughout the night and into the early morning. There are no words that fully describe the feeling in that teepee that night. We were all one, one in spirit.

When the ceremonies were finished, everyone came out of the tepee, greeted the morning and said good morning to each other. Lis and I went to finish preparing the food, but the other ladies made us sit and they took over. We all ate together, talked and laughed. It was fantastic. The pain in my feet was completely gone. I felt many pounds lighter and knew I would be okay.

Lis and Sophie wanted to go swimming, but I just wanted to rest. We all did as we pleased. That evening we said our good-byes and headed home. I was happy again. I could once again walk without the excruciating pain. Not only that, but all the negativity I was carrying was gone, and whatever evil that was sent my way had left. I had a new lease on life.

On the way home we got an extra bonus. We happened upon a place called Thermopolis in Montana. There are hot mineral springs and we treated ourselves to a night at the Holiday Inn, which had the hot springs right in the hotel. It was like dessert.

A year later I asked my sister what she had told people about the ceremonies. "Nothing," she said with emotion. "I could not find any words."

Chapter 38

House Burnt

I was once again well enough to consider working. There were plenty of stores where I could get jobs, but the wages were so low it was hard for me to even consider working there. Besides I was apprehensive about having to write another test. At least I was not going to tell anyone this time.

I decided that a part-time job in a business office at a car dealership would be much better. Although they, like the salesman, worked on commission, there was always some money coming in. I knew it was a lucrative business. I delivered a résumé to every dealership in Spruce Grove and Edmonton. With a perfect combination of car sales and financing experience, I thought I would be snapped up right away. Not so!! I had one interview and they wanted full time. I knew I could not handle working that many hours.

One day I went over to Zender Ford to see my old colleagues. They told me the owner's oldest son Chad had come back and it was so much better to work there. Shayne, the youngest, had been the used car manager for some time. I knew him from before and he was a good guy. One of the sales people had just quit and they all asked me to come back. I told them I would think about it. The thought of going back to that world was hard. After sleeping on it overnight, I laid out my options and decided that was the best one. At least there were no tests. I knew my job, and I knew most of my co-workers. I could walk to work which was certainly a plus, so back I went to car sales.

One day every tenant in Mobile City got a letter that they were redoing all the sewers in the trailer park and we were all to move our trailers out until the work was complete. That was not possible. The majority of trailers had sat on the lot for many years and had decks and additions built on. They were very old. They would not tolerate a move. Besides there were zoning laws prohibiting trailers from parking in most areas of the county, so there was nowhere to move them to.

That letter really took the wind out of my sails one more time. I realized the owner knew nothing about trailer living and had no feel for the people. It was rescinded after about a week, but it shook me. I was afraid he might get fed up and close the park. I felt fragile once again. On the lot the trailer was worth almost fifty thousand dollars. Off the lot it was worth about four. I could not take the gamble and started looking into selling. I was shocked to discover how much prices had increased in just a few months. I realized that selling was my best bet as I could pull seventeen thousand dollars out. That would at least give me some badly needed cash.

Raven, in the meantime, was thinking about moving to Buck Lake with Katrina. I told him that if he moved out, I was going to move in. That would give me a roof over my head and mortgage payments I could handle.

On October 12th, 2005, I went out to check on our home as I had been told he was staying at Katrina's place. As I rounded the corner and drove into the driveway, I went into shock. The house was burnt to the ground. Nothing left but the east end where our bedroom was. I got out of the car. Chris, one of Raven's sons, was there. I stood there and heard myself saying over and over, "After twenty years and this is all that is left. After twenty years and this is all that is left." Then I started to cry. It was just too hard to hold it in. Chris came over and put his arms around me.

"Chris," I asked, "how could this happen?"

He said he did not know, but he had received a call from Katrina that it had burned.

"How did she know?" I asked.

"I don't know," he said.

I had to hurry in to Spruce Grove to report it to the insurance company before they closed.

The next day I contacted the fire department and was shocked to find out they would not give me a copy of the investigation. It went to the insurance company only and if I wanted a copy I would have to go to them. I told them it was my house, I paid their wages and I had a right to the report. No luck. Another home had burned in the area some six months before and I contacted that owner and he too had tried to get an investigative report from the fire department, to no avail. Another time I would have pursued it further, but I was tired.

Two days later I got a phone call that Katrina had reported me to the police. She told them I had burned the place down and not only the house, but also a car—that had been stolen from me and burned three years before! Fortunately I had a friend who was an ex-RCMP and I drove to Fort Saskatchewan to ask for his advice. He told me that she might have done me a favour.

"How?" I asked.

"You are automatically first suspect anyway because of the insurance money. If anyone comes forward with an accusation before there is even proof of arson, they become the prime suspect as the suspicion is that they are trying to steer the investigation away from them." He suggested I do nothing as I might not even be contacted. If I was, I should seek legal counsel right away. I felt much better.

The next few weeks were spent filling out forms, listing belongings and meeting with the insurance adjuster. In the meantime Raven and

Katrina were busy shopping for new appliances, furniture and clothes. All supplied by the Erminskin Band. It was bizarre.

A woman I knew offered me her basement. I knew it was not great, but decided to take it for the winter at least. By spring I was hoping to have the insurance money and maybe I could buy a small place. I liked the plan. It felt solid to me.

Chapter 39

Healing at Old Fort Saskatchewan

When Raven and I split, I had no idea about my future in the Native world and so thought I had better try to integrate back into the non-Native world. My friend Mary was connected to a group who called themselves the "Free Spiritual Thinkers." They were lovely people who met once a week and discussed every topic of spiritual connection.

In that group there were people with their own ability to see spirits. There were people with scientific instruments that would detect orbs and spirits. There were people who could not detect anything at all. They were all good people who were always open to learn new things.

On November 10th, one month after the house burnt down, the group made arrangements to go to the old Fort Saskatchewan. It was an old trading post erected when the settlers first arrived in the area. In its heyday many people lived and visited there. There was a school, a church, a courthouse, a store, a doctor's office and several private homes. All were built of logs, since the post was situated in what was a wooded area in pioneer times. People would come from all the surrounding area to trade, mostly furs, for supplies. It had been a hub of activity.

We all met at the courthouse, one of the buildings where many people had encountered spirits. It housed not only the judges' chambers but also the jail. That was where anyone awaiting execution would be housed. The organizer, Stuart McGowan, told the spirits that we were not there to intrude, only to visit and we would be respectful. For that I was grateful as I do struggle with abuse of any kind and had wondered ahead of time what the attitude would be. I did not know these people well.

As we moved from one building to the next I just stayed in the background and listened. I had never seen any scientific instruments used to detect spirits before.

One woman could see things that happened in the past and she gave us a very vivid description of much activity in the main square—what everyone was wearing and the comings and goings of the people.

The most powerful for me was when we went to the doctor's office. As everyone was moving about the building, I found the old waiting room. It was in semi-darkness as the only light came from an adjacent room. As I sat there by myself it suddenly came to me to ask the doctor for help. I told him with telepathy that I had been ill for a long time and asked if he could help me now. What happened next was something else! There was a swirling of energy all around me. It moved up and down and around my head. Suddenly I felt the fog that had surrounded me lift. Everything around me became much brighter. Colours became more intense. Even my mind was clear. It was a wonderful feeling and I needed to thank the doctor for the help. The only way I knew how was the Native way. I did not want to do anything in the people's presence as it was my own private ceremony I needed to do. I stayed back until everyone left except Stuart, who was locking up.

Whenever Native people connect with the Creator and the spirit world, tobacco is the key to that connection. That is their protocol. Therefore I carried tobacco in the cubby hole of my car wherever I went, just in case the need arose, as it had this evening. I needed to do a little ceremony of thanks for the healing I had received. As I turned to give Stuart a farewell hug, I felt totally alive. It was so good to be back. To be *me*.

Chapter 40

Raven Dying

Raven and I continued to keep in touch via telephone and he so wanted me to come to Buck Lake. I knew my life was in danger if I went. He did not believe it and it drove us both almost insane. I could not get to him and he thought I *would* not.

One day I got a phone call from the youngest daughter, Joanne. She told me Raven was in the Wetaskiwin hospital and would probably not live until morning. "He is asking for you. Will you come down?"

"Of course," I told her. "I'm on my way."

I called my daughter Margo and we headed down together. I knew I would be sworn at for sure. In fact we talked about it on the way down and I planned on totally ignoring his family and just walk in to be with him.

When we arrived at the intensive care unit at the hospital I was met by Katrina and two of

Raven's other children. They stood in front of the doorway, blocking me from going in to see Raven when he was dying and asking for me.

Katrina said, "You are not going in."

"I *am* going in. He is asking for me," I said quietly as I moved closer to the door. Katrina started yelling and grabbed me by my coat. My spitfire half-pint daughter stood right up to her and told her to let go of my coat. Margo was much smaller, but fearless. Katrina clenched her fist and brought it back to hit her. Margo told her defiantly, "Go ahead! Please do!"

That was when security showed up. They got us separated and told me to go and cool off. Half the family was saying I had no right to be there. The other half told them I was his wife and they had no business keeping me out. They listened only to the ones who were trying to keep me out.

I was escorted by security downstairs and they told me to leave the premises. I refused. I told them I would not cause trouble, but I would not leave the premises as long as my husband was lying up there in intensive care dying and asking for me. The family members that supported me also came down and tried to explain who I was, and told security that he was asking for me. Margo went over to the police station to get help from them. They told her it was a domestic matter and they could not come.

Over and over I asked: "Why is no one listening to Raven? What difference does it make who I am? This is not about the children and not about me. It is about him. Why won't they listen to him?" I could see the light go on for the security guard, and she told me if I promised to not make any trouble she would go and enquire at the nursing station.

I laughed. It just struck me funny. I told her I had but one purpose and that was to see

Raven, and if she could help in any way I would appreciate it. She did go and check with the nursing staff and they told her that he was not fully aware and they did not trust that he knew what he was talking about. Then I really got frightened again. "What if he dies while you are holding me here? I don't get it. I have to see him! Figure it out. I have to see him!"

Fortunately, a police officer came by at that moment. We thought he had been sent to take care of our situation, but as it turned out, he just happened to be there. I told him my husband was dying and he was asking for me, but his children would not allow me to see him. He told me he would go and talk to them.

About twenty minutes later he came down and said he had negotiated five minutes with Raven, and he and a family member had to be present.

"That is bull-shit. My husband is dying and asking for me and you are negotiating with them? What right do they have to keep me away? Under what law can step-children keep the wife away when the husband wants to see her?" I was pissed right off, good and proper.

"Look," said the officer "you did leave him and I had a heck of a time getting that five minutes, so take it or leave it."

"Okay," I said "I will take it."

We went upstairs and I pulled the curtains right back. I did not care who saw us. I knew there would just be the two of us anyway, so if anyone wanted to watch—go for it! As soon as I saw him, I knew he was not going anywhere that night. He was totally with it. We just hugged and held each other and he kept saying, "You came! You came!"

"Of course I came," I said, "You asked for me, didn't you?"

He was smiling and so happy. I told him everyone was here to be with him. I could not bear for him to know what they were doing under the circumstances. We were alone, just he and I, together. How we loved each other!

Too soon I heard the officer's voice: "Your five minutes are up." I just ignored him. Then in a few minutes he said it again. I still ignored him. Raven just kept looking at him trying to figure out who he was. His eyesight was very poor, but he had worked with the RCMP for so many years and he probably thought it was one of the officers he knew. Finally, the officer said, "Ma'am, you really do have to go."

"Okay," I said and I kissed Raven goodbye. I did not want to cry in front of him, but it was so hard to hold it back. Raven asked me if I would be back. I told him I would try.

"Don't try," he said. "Just be here."

"Okay," I said, "I will find a way." When I turned to leave, the police officer had tears streaming down his face. "It's going to be okay," I told him and kind of laughed inside at the craziness of that statement.

When we got out, I told the police officer I needed to talk to Shirley, who had always been a good support. He did go and ask her, but she refused to talk to me. She told him it was too hard just then. Then I asked to talk to the head nurse. She did come in and told me that I could not see him because my name was not on their file. I told her that of course it was not on there. Because of family interference we were no longer living together, but I was still his legal wife and he was still my love.

"What I do not understand is that the hospital staff is not listening to Raven? This was his journey. Why is he not free to see who he wished?"

"You do have a point," she said.

"Legally I am still his wife and you have no legal grounds for keeping me away." She asked me to go back downstairs as she did not want trouble on the ward. She would call in the head of the hospital to straighten it all out. I reluctantly went back downstairs as I did not want to aggravate the situation any more. "I will do whatever it takes to see Raven again."

In about a half hour a woman came to the waiting room, and told me that she was the head nurse at the hospital; she had talked to the family and told them they could not stop me from seeing him. Everyone was relieved and Margo said, "Can we just go home now?"

"In a bit," I said. Then I turned to the woman and told her I needed that on the chart so all the other staff knew about it. I also needed security and the front desk to know. I could not go through that nightmare again. She agreed. Then I went back upstairs to make sure there would be no trouble. Still one member of the family was right next to me. I did find that a little funny as I wondered what they thought I would do to him. It was bizarre.

The nurses asked me to leave as they were ready to prepare him for the night. He made me promise to return the next day. I told him I would.

The next day I returned with Richard and Margaret Rain. They were the couple Raven had adopted many years before. He always referred to Richard as his son. The rest of the family had also accepted him and called him their brother. I thought they would be a good choice to accompany me. I did not dare go alone.

When we arrived Raven had been moved out of ICU and into a regular ward. There was no one around as we entered his room. He recognized us immediately and was ecstatic to see us. It was so nice to have a little time together without the tension. Just to have a few moments of normalcy. I asked how he was really doing and he said he was okay. He was looking forward to going home.

"Are you going back to Katrina's?" I asked. He said yes.

I always knew that one day he would return to his family, but I did not know that they would keep me away from him. I thought with her children staying with us and getting their lives together, it would ease Katrina's pain and aggression. Unfortunately it went in the opposite direction.

Just then the family returned and they were not happy to see me there. Immediately Lorna, Katrina's daughter, came and sat on the other side of the bed. I started chatting just as we had always done, asking some general questions about where she was living and how her boyfriend was. I just wanted everything back to where we could co-exist, especially now. She asked me if she could talk to me.

"Of course, Lorna," I said. "You know you can talk to me at any time." She motioned that she did not want to talk in front of Raven. "Lorna," I said, "This is all about love. We all love him and he loves his family and he loves his wife. It is only about love."

"It is not that simple," she said.

"It *is* that simple," was my reply. "Unless someone makes it complicated, it *is* that simple."

Then I overheard Richard in the hallway talking to the family. Shirley was really angry and said loudly, "See, she is getting everyone on her side with that kind of talk!"

It saddened me so much to think they couldn't get that simple concept of love. Some of the people who turned on me now, I had complete trust in before. The hatred they felt was there and it was not going anywhere. A hatred based on the belief that their mother died because we got together.

I knew then that I would probably never see Raven again. I did not think he was near death, but if he was discharged, it would be unlikely he would ever go back to the hospital as he would sooner die. I said my good-byes then. All the way home I just cried.

All those years Raven would say that good would conquer evil. At that moment I questioned that. He also used to say that when you do something wrong, you will pay later if not sooner. I wondered if this was about him not making peace with his family for things that happened during his drinking days. Had they all been given one last chance to do that? I knew how protected and guided he was, there had to be a bigger plan. That night I really prayed about that.

Suddenly it all made sense. The only way he could have had a chance to make peace with his family was if I was out of the way. The only way I would get out of the way was exactly what happened. It made sense, and I knew it was true.

As hard as it was, I could now accept what happened because it was what had to happen. Raven was a good man. What he did was so out of character for him. Chaos could reign supreme all around us, but we always had a place of peace and harmony together, a place where true love lived. We had many times just lain together on the bed, saying nothing, and our spirits would come together as one. The whole world would be out there somewhere, but we would be in a bubble, just the two of us in our own little world. Suddenly I was overcome with gratitude for what we'd had. I knew at that moment that I needed to celebrate what we had instead of mourn what we did not. A thousand pounds were lifted from my heart. Everything was as it should be after all.

Chapter 41

Leaving Canada

Raven was to remain in the hospital for another week, but I could not get anyone to take me down to see him and I did not dare go alone. I phoned almost every day. Sometimes I would get an update and sometimes I would get a snotty nurse who would tell me not to call. One day when I called, he was discharged, so I tried to call him at Katrina's. Whoever answered the phone would not put him on. That became the result every time I called and I finally gave up.

The 20th of December, 2006, I got a call from the insurance company adjuster: the company had a cheque ready for me and as soon as he got our signatures he would release it. When I told him Raven was too ill to come in, he told me that if I could find a commissioner for oaths to certify his signature that would do. My head was pounding again. How I was going to get to him was beyond me. I called Vicki, "I'm a commissioner of oaths," she said. I knew she had told me that, but I had forgotten. She told me to arrange the meeting and she would be there.

I decided to call and try to get something arranged. I disguised my voice the best I could. Tried to sound as Native as I could. I was told he was back in the Wetaskiwin hospital. That was not good for him, but a stroke of luck as far as getting to him anyway.

Vicki and I drove down to Wetaskiwin the next day. I prayed for a clear path, that nothing would get in the way. As I went to the front desk to find out where he was, my heart was pounding. I was so worried that either the information staff would not tell me or I would meet up with the family. Neither happened. We got to his room and he was alone. I thanked the Creator and spirits for clearing the path for us. We talked for a few minutes, then I told him about the forms which needed to be signed in order to pick up the money. At first he was reluctant. They really did get to him, I thought. Then I reminded him that I had never gone against him before, so why would I do it now? "You have to trust me," I said. "If you do not sign, we will get nothing."

He did sign and Vickie signed and got ID from him so it would be totally legal. I then told him I would bring him some money the next day, if he wanted it. He told me no, that he had just got his pension, so he was okay. I asked him what he wanted to do with his share and he told me to just hang onto it, that he knew he could trust me. He might purchase another trailer to put on the lot. "I will take care of it," I told him. "But if you ever need anything, then let me know and I will get the money to you right away."

The money was released, but because it was in both names, I had to deposit it to the joint account which we kept open so I could help him with his bills. The rest I transferred into my account to keep it safe. Then I heard from all the members of his family who were keeping in touch that I was being accused by Katrina of stealing his money. They all asked me to hang onto it as she just wanted it.

On December 23rd, 2006, I went for breakfast with a friend. As I entered the restaurant I was pulled aside by an RCMP officer, whom I happened to know. He asked me where I was living and I told him I did not have a home. "I just need to ask a few questions about your car that was stolen from you three years ago."

"Dennis," I said, "it was parked at my daughter's place and the next thing I knew, I got a call from you. That's all I can tell you!"

That night I went to bed and prayed for guidance. I had no idea what to do with my life any more. It was just too much. The next morning I woke up and said out loud, "Goin' to Denmark!" That was a surprise to me—why would I be sent to Denmark? When I actually considered the idea, I thought, "Why not?" I had the money. There was nothing for me here. I was living my life looking over my shoulder and I hated it. I did not think Raven would die any time soon. I thought I had time to go and have a rest.

I informed my children. They protested that it was too far away. I told them, "When I am here, we are on the phone a few times a week and we see each other once in a while. If I live in Denmark, we will still be on the phone a few times a week and we will still see each other once in a while. I will be only twenty-four hours away and on the other end of a phone any time." Both families were so busy they had no time for me anyway.

Margo said, "At least you are safe over there!"

I made arrangements to leave, but first I went and talked to a lawyer. I told him the whole story, and that I wanted to go to Denmark, but I did not want it to backfire on me. He told me as long as there were no charges, I could just go. "I do not think you have anything to worry about, so go and get on with your life. If you do get charged, let me know and we will deal with it."

I booked a flight to Europe via New Mexico for early January. I wanted to visit my friend Kathy Burke and go to a ceremony with Sophie and Tyrone before leaving the continent. The next couple of weeks I spent putting my belongings in storage and then going around and saying good-byes to every place I had lived and frequented. I said good-bye to every street, to every restaurant, to everything. I had learned from Raven to make sure I took all of me with me if I travelled anywhere—it was too easy to leave parts of yourself here and there and all over; if you did, then it would never go well wherever you went. I did not know if I would stay for a long time or a short time. I just knew I needed to go to the land of my ancestors.

I was very fortunate to get a seat on the plane by myself. As we crossed the border to the United States, the sorrow was almost too much. I decided to go through the sorrow to the very core of my heart and there I realized there was no pain. I knew then that I would get through this. I would be okay.

The only hiccup happened at the airport when I was boarding for the last leg of my journey to Europe. The woman at security pulled me aside and told me I had been chosen for a complete security check. My heart fell. I did not know if I was actually being searched or if I had been charged back in Canada and was being pulled out. I also had my pipe and sweet grass, a sacred smudge, with me. I was so nervous about them removing either item. As it turned out it was just a search. The woman who actually performed it knew what these things were and was very respectful. I wanted to give her a big hug, but thought perhaps it would not be a good idea, so I just thanked her and got on board.

Chapter 42

Raven's Death

I arrived at my cousin's house in Denmark on January 15th, 2007. What a sad day it was for me—it was Raven's eighty-second birthday and I could not be with him! I tried to call him but I was told he was in the hospital in Wetaskiwin again. I called the hospital hoping at least to be able to wish him a happy birthday. Once again the family had put a restriction on any communication with me. I asked the nurse to at least tell him I had called and that I had not forgotten his birthday. It was always important to him.

I rented a little studio on a farm just outside Fredericia. It was a good place as it was ever so peaceful and I could walk to the forest and the water.

On the 6th of February I got a call from Margo that Raven had died. I had seen the number 6 many times recently when I thought of him and figured he would leave in June. I thought that would give me time to perhaps try and be with him one more time. I just walked the floor and kept saying over and over, "He wasn't supposed to be dead. He wasn't supposed to be dead." I had so wanted to be with him when he left, but that was not possible. It was not fair. Not fair at all. I was devastated. I did not know whether I should go back or not, but then I got a call from Bonnie, one of his granddaughters, that I was very close to. She told me to come, that it would be all right. "We need you here!" she said. "We need you here!"

I so wanted to be there as well, so decided to jump on the first plane out. I was so hoping she was right, that it would be okay. There was delay after delay and after twenty-four hours I finally arrived in Toronto. From there I decided to call a few people about details for the funeral. The first person I got in touch with was my daughter, Margo. "Thank God you called," she said." You cannot come! They will kill you if you go near their place!"

I thought she was just exaggerating, so I called a few more people. They verified that there was going to be big trouble if I came. I was stunned. How could this be? We were together for twenty years and I had travelled all the way from Denmark—and I would not get the opportunity to say goodbye? I went numb. It was too much.

That morning my son picked me up at the airport. It was minus thirty, but felt more like minus forty. I called a few more people and they too confirmed that I should just stay away. I contacted Trish, our dear friend who had come up from Vancouver. I felt she was my stand-in through everything. She was a very good friend to both of us and we both loved her very much. She understood people's mentality very well. She too told me not to come. She said there would just be a lot of trouble. Some of the young men were ready for me if I showed up. Like I said, I was numb and so it did not affect me anymore.

She did suggest that I should think about giving the kids the money that was Raven's share of the fire settlement. She said it would go a long way to ease tensions and he had told everyone toward the end, including her, that I had stolen his money. That brought me out of the numbness and back into excruciating sorrow. She said to think about it anyway and do it if it felt okay.

As soon as she hung up, I knew I had to give it to them. It would bother me for the rest of my life to think I had kept his money which he considered stolen. So I immediately called my friend Randal, who I knew was going to the funeral, and asked if he could come over to my son Rocky's place and take something to the funeral for me. Then I wrote them all a long letter telling them how much he used to brag about them and how much he really loved them, even if he did not always express it to them. He bragged about how one had the best horses, one was the best cook and could bake a cake without a recipe, how one could set a teepee so tight it would sound like a drum if you hit it. About each one he would brag about something. I also told them that he had left the money with me for safe keeping and although it was legally my money, I felt that he would want them to have it. I wrote a cheque to each of his children and sent it with Randal. How odd that was! As I sat there writing these cheques, I realized that I was giving away money I could have kept to people who had various degrees of feelings for me, ranging from love to pure hatred.

For each one I said a little prayer. I knew they really needed it in their time of sorrow for their father. In my heart I knew I was doing the right thing. It was rightfully his money and his children should have it.

I am ever so grateful to those family members who supported me. I know it was not always easy. I have to admit I was very naïve about the effects, on others, of our union. I am so sorry for the pain anyone suffered. I tried my best to help, but I could not. They did not want my help.

As soon as the cheques were written and picked up, I drove out to our acreage. There I sat by myself and grieved. I was very quiet. I was taking care of business. How I loved that place! How I loved my life there! At that time, I did not want to think about the nightmare of the last year. I just wanted to pay respect for the good things we had, and there were many. In this place was laughter, joy, tears and sorrow, but most of all there was love. I wanted to remember that more than anything—and I did.

For the rest of the day I drove around alone to all the places we had shared together and remembered the good times. Many times I felt Raven's presence. We had a good day together.

The next day, when I knew the feast was on and everyone would be there, I drove down to Hobbema and visited his grave. As I stepped out of the car, I stopped dead. On the cross was written: Lawrence Raven Mackinaw—the names he had long ago left behind were first and last.

How could they have put the name he so hated on his grave? How could they? As I stood there it was as if I were gone. Nobody home. I felt nothing, I knew nothing. I was in a trance. An emptiness that was total. I knew I was standing there. I knew I could not or would not move. I did not care. My body just stood there frozen. Suddenly I heard a far-away voice saying, over and over and over, "It's okay. It's okay. It's okay." The same words from far away. Finally I broke out of the trance. I did my own ceremony for him. Then I grieved. I cried the tears that needed to be cried. I let them flow until they would flow no more, and then I returned to Rocky's.

I could handle neither the small talk nor the big talk. I needed my own bed. I needed my own space; I needed peace—so I changed my flight and headed back to Denmark the next day. Coincidentally my friend Carina was on the same flight. That was good, as I *had* to stay somewhat focused. I knew I was not far away from leaving, and I did not want to do that, as I did not know if I would be able to return. She helped me hang on for the moment.

My cousin Steen picked me up at the airport and invited me to stay at their place. I told him I needed my bed. I needed to be alone for now. He respected my wishes. As I walked up the stairs to my little home I thought it was so strange. Everything had changed and yet everything was the same. I was standing in the middle of the floor looking from one thing to the next. Then I decided to go to bed and think some more tomorrow.

I slept almost all the next day. I left just long enough to get groceries and return. Then I ate a little and slept again. The next few weeks I spent just wandering, mostly down to the woods close to where I was living. Thank God for the woods! There I found peace. There I found harmony in all the chaos. It was good.

Torkild and Charlotte, my new friends in Denmark, opened their home and their hearts for me as did Walther and Bjarne. I also had my cousins Birgitte and Steen close by. I always knew I could go and be with good people when I needed them. Many other people came into my life and soon I had a network of friends and family.

One piece at a time, I slowly put my broken self back together.

But I also began to grieve the fact that I had no opportunity to do any of the things I should have done for Raven when he died. I knew I had to do something. One day I went to see Jerry, the Native man living in Denmark, whom I had met previously. I brought him tobacco and asked him if he knew the directions of the pipe for the deceased. Thank the Creator one more time! He did know. I made arrangements to put up a little feast for Raven. Charlotte and Torkild so generously offered to host it at Tanggård and Charlotte invited me to plant a tree in Raven's memory.

I did.

Chapter 43

Return to the Reservation

Life in Denmark was certainly different from anything I had ever lived before. For the first time ever I was on my own. I did not have to take care of anyone. Not even an animal or plant. I was totally free. I decided to go back to living life in the moment. I would do what I wanted when I wanted. Some very interesting things came out of that. I slept for only three to five hours a night and I was not sleepy during the day. I ate four meals a day instead of three. I became acutely aware of my every need. They were what came naturally.

I would spend most of my time in the woods or at the beach. How I loved the smell of the salt water! It brought memories of my childhood. The changes from day to day were amazing. I had never before visited the same beach more than once, as we lived fourteen hundred kilometers from the nearest beach. I had no idea how different it looked from day to day. The water would create different patterns in the sand as there was a shift in the water level with the tide and wind.

The rocks were fantastic as well. I found a log which was just the right height to sit on. It was ever such a good log. It too shifted with every storm, so I never knew where it would be for sure. I knew it too would leave one day, but it stayed around for a year. Miss that log? You betcha! I often wonder where it wandered to.

I began writing and that was good. I did a few personal power workshops which were ever so satisfying. The papers and magazines learned of my story and I was invited to do presentations. People also came for one-on-ones for life strategies and spiritual coaching. That kept me going financially. I had really thought my life was finished and had resigned myself to that fact. I thought I would do nothing but put in time the best way I could. I guess there were other plans in the works.

It was then that I made the decision to make Denmark my home. I applied for a residency and work permit. I filled out a very simple form and I got it for one year.

That summer I went back to Canada and gave away all my belongings, except my art work, and wrapped up business there. I knew I would be back and forth as my children were there and Canada would always be my home as well.

Dan Alexis, who was Raven's apprentice, was putting up the sun dance that summer. Raven was his teacher for more years than I had known him. I wanted to bring offerings as Raven had always done, but was not sure about my reception among the people who were going to be there. Besides, I kept hearing that it was still not safe for me. I went to give Dan the offerings and tobacco on the Wednesday; the ceremonies were starting on Thursday. He told me he would be happy to do it, but that I should do it myself. I told him some members of Raven's family were still angry and there could be trouble. I could not bring that to the sun dance.

"You have been with my people for so many years and you belong to our reserve. No one will hurt you here and you can camp with us."

I told him I would think about it.

I then went to see his sister who was doing the pipe for the women. She said the same thing. I went off and prayed about it and then I knew I had to go. I had no idea how I would be received, but this had been my life for twenty years and I missed it and I missed the people.

The next evening when the first ceremonies were to happen, I entered the ceremonial grounds with a very heavy heart and some apprehension as to the reception I would receive. When the singing began, they started with Raven's song; I could not hold back the tears. How I missed him! How I missed him! It was so hard.

After Dan was done singing, he returned to sit and take the offerings from the people. One by one, as the people returned from their prayer requests, almost all came and thanked me for coming back to their people. All those years Raven was the one out front. I was a support to him and until that night I had not realized how much the people appreciated what I had done for their community. I had felt rather anonymous up to that point and that was okay by me. That night, I was so touched.

I decided to make the second pail of soup for Raven. I needed to make four all together, as that was the custom, and this was the perfect place for it. I would bring it to the lodge on Saturday. Saturday morning they had the dance for the sick. Everyone with physical, mental, spiritual challenges and those in mourning were invited to dance for healing. I danced.

In the afternoon I was ready to bring in the soup. My friends Tony and Ella came with me for support and to help. As I stood outside the lodge waiting for the signal to enter, I got a message so strong from Raven: "You have cried long enough. It is time to stop. This is to be a happy thing you are doing. You know that." At that moment a huge weight was lifted from me. All of a sudden I felt so light. The sorrow in my heart was physically lifted. I could feel it go like a cloud lifting. I could not see it, but I could feel it. When I finally entered and did the dance, it was with joy. Joy for the life I had with Raven and joy for the life I had with these people. It was a great moment. I knew I would never again go back to the black hole of my unhappiness.

While I was eating the soup, I noticed two of Raven's cousins had arrived and there was no way out except to walk right past them. I had no idea how they felt and I decided to walk straight by so I would not create a scene. As I did, I saw out of the corner of my eye, one of them give me a little wave. I then went over and shook her hand and she said, "Thank you for doing that for my brother."

"You have no idea how much that means to me," I said holding my hand to my heart.

"Oh, I think so," she said. I do think she knew. I was so grateful.

My old friend Jim stopped me on my way back to camp and asked me where I was now. I told him I had returned to Denmark. "I am now with my people," I told him.

"Interesting," he said. "All you people who have been with us for many years are now being sent home."

Epilogue

I returned to Denmark after the sun dance where I continued to put my broken self together by spending much time in the forest and by the water, drumming and praying and just being in the space and time that was.

Every day I thanked the Creator for the journey of my life and asked for the strength to keep going.

The poem on page 295, "Life in the Moment" best describes how I was able to cope and move on.

In Denmark there is much interest in the Native culture and in particular the Native philosophy of life. Soon I was asked to share my life experiences with various groups of people. I facilitated workshops in personal power and energy healing, and one step at a time my life became full and whole again.

When I turned 65 I returned to Canada to be nearer my children and grandchildren. With the insurance money from our burnt house, I have been able to purchase a new home and am settling in fairly well. I do struggle with owning again, after being so free for last five years. I have divided my home in two. With a tenant in residence, I have help with the expenses and it leaves me free to travel.

Since Raven's death five of his grandchildren joined him, the last being Sherry, who died of cancer. I loved this girl very much and needed to go and say goodbye to her. Another granddaughter Bonnie travelled with me to Mameo Beach where the awake and funeral were happening. I had no idea how I would be received, but knew I would be welcomed by Sherry's father, mother and siblings. As I walked in the door, filled with apprehension, I was greeted with heartfelt welcome from almost everyone. Even Katrina came and gave me a hug and told me she was happy to see me there. Tears were close to the surface the whole day. Tears for the loss of a beautiful young woman and tears of gratefulness to be back with the people who were my family for so many years.

I have since then went to ceremonies with the family and put up offerings for all to stop hurting because of what happened in the past. After much talk and many tears we have been able to mend our hearts.

I am still in contact with Karen and Kathy and we have a very strong bond which cannot be broken. Karen has had many problems coping with life. She moved back on the reservation where she has had various jobs off and on. She ended up in the child welfare cycle I wrote about in chapter 30. She lives in an abusive relationship and has to date given birth to 11 children. They have all been taken away by child welfare due to the violence and substance abuse in her home. I pray the system will one day see how broken it is. Karen is the perfect example of one person who should be apprehended with her children and given the intense help she needs in order to provide a good home. She loves all her children and if child welfare continues their pattern of removal of her babies, she will likely continue hers of having more.

Kathy now lives in the city of Calgary with her husband. For a few years she took care of Karen's children, but it became too much for such a young person on her own. She has had now five children all in a row, but has not given up her dreams of becoming a police officer. "It is just on hold", she says. I do see she has picked up many of my teachings around parenting so think her children will have a much better chance. Time will tell.

Georgina has worked at various jobs here and there and is currently off on maternity leave from her job in the store on the Sunchild reservation where her father lives. This is her first child.

Edward has a wife and one child. He did finish high school and has been working regularly. He currently lives in the city of Edmonton.

I do see hope for these people, but also remember the Elder's teachings about what you do today will have the most effect in the seventh generation. At least it has been a start.

My motto is 'Life is Good' and even though I could not always see it when I was too far down, there came a day when a new understanding immersed from the misery and I did find purpose in the lows as well as the highs.

Today I do not know what new adventures lie ahead, but I do have the confidence that I will be guided by the Creator and the spirits who look after me. Perhaps I will be led far afield—or remain close to the nest, I have built for myself in my autumn years.

Life is good.